SILK AND RELIGION

SILK AND RELIGION

An Exploration of Material Life and the Thought of People, AD 600–1200

XINRU LIU

DELHI
OXFORD UNIVERSITY PRESS
CALCUTTA CHENNAI MUMBAI
1998

Oxford University Press, Great Clarendon Street, Oxford OX2 6DP

Oxford New York
Athens Auckland Bangkok Calcutta
Cape Town Chennai Dar es Salaam Delhi
Florence Hong Kong Istanbul Karachi
Kuala Lumpur Madrid Melbourne Mexico City
Mumbai Nairobi Paris Singapore
Taipei Tokyo Toronto

and associates in

Berlin Ibadan

ISBN 0 19 564452 2

Typeset by Rastrixi, New Delhi 110070
Printed in India at Wadhwa International, New Delhi 110020
and published by Manzar Khan, Oxford University Press
YMCA Library Building, Jai Singh Road, New Delhi 110 001

For All My Mentors and Teachers

Acknowledgements

Several years ago Professor Romila Thapar suggested that I further pursue the study of trade and religion. I chose silk trade as my topic and soon found myself outside the borders of my field. The silk samples I had to deal with were not necessarily related to China or India. The religious forces involved were not only Buddhist. But the role of silk trade in the ancient and early medieval world was too interesting and too important a topic to give up. Encouraged by Romila, I tentatively stepped out of the world I had been familiar with and started to explore areas so far unknown to me, including the early Christian and Islamic theologies and institutions.

After delivering a lecture based on primary research to an audience in the History Department, University of Texas, Austin, in 1988, arranged by Professor Edward Rhoads and the Center of Asian Studies, I felt confident that the topic would interest a wide audience and thus be worth pursuing in greater detail.

I extend my thanks to the Woodrow Wilson Center for International Scholars, Washington, D.C. for its fellowship and wonderful research facilities, and the warm help of the staff which made this book possible. Dr Mary Bullock, Director of the Asian Programme, and her assistants went out of their way to help me make acquaintance with scholars and locate research resources in Washington area. My assistant, Mr Michael Taylor, also had to extend his field of study to search for materials in languages he was not familiar with and did a wonderful job. Many of the research fellows that year contributed their knowledge and insight which made my research work easier and more rounded. Among them, Aryeh Kosman, Professor of Philosophy, Haverford College, introduced me to Christian theology.

The many museums and libraries in Washington area provided resources for a project that covered a wide area of research.

Dr Carol Bier, Curator of the Textile Museum in Washington, D.C., offered expert knowledge of early medieval textiles; Mary Elizabeth Samms, Librarian of the museum, helped me with literary information. The authorities at the Byzantine Library in Dumbarton Oaks graciously gave permission to an outsider to use their collection. In the library, Annemarie Weyl Carr shared her knowledge of the Byzantine silk industry and Christian religion with me.

I spent the Fall Semester of 1991 at the University of Texas in Austin, where scholars from both the History Department and the Centre for Asian Studies shared with me their knowledge of their specific fields. Professors Richard Lariviere and Gregory Schopen discussed relevant information pertaining to Dharma literature and Buddhist traditions with me. Professor Martha Newman helped me answer certain questions on Christian theology. Professor Denise Spellberg not only introduced me to Islam, but read an early draft of my book with critical comments.

Back in Beijing, my colleagues, Professors Yang Haocheng, Liao Xuesheng and Guo Fang, at the Institute of World History, Chinese Academy of Social Sciences, were kind enough to read my drafts and provide information and criticism.

It is impossible to list the names of all the teachers, friends and colleagues who encouraged and helped me deal with this topic. Special mention should be made of Valerie Hansen, Professor of History, Yale University, and Professor David Ludden, University of Pennsylvania, both of whom read an early draft and made suggestions for changes. Christina Gilmartin, Professor of History in Northeastern University, Mass., read a later draft and improved the writing.

The result of research at an earlier stage has been published in an article in volume 6, number 1 of the *Journal of World History* (March 1995).

All my efforts as well as those of my friends are contained in this book. I hope it will prove useful in improving our understanding of the past.

Contents

Contents

Abbreviations

CHI	The Cambridge History of Iran
CHL	Chang Hsing-lang
CII	Corpus Inscriptionum Indicarum
CS	Chou-shu
CTS	Chiu-T'ang-shu
CTW	Ch'üan T'ang Wen
FYCL	Fa-yüan Chu-lin
HHS	Hou-Han Shu
HS	Han-shu
HTS	Hsin-T'ang-shu
HT	Hsüan-tsang
HKSC	Hsu Kao-seng-chuan
KHMC	Kuang-hung-ming-chi
SS	Sui-shu
SKSC	Sung Kao-seng-chuan
TFYK	Ts'e-fu-yüan-kui
THY	T'ang Hui-yao
Tripitaka	Taisho shinsho Daizokyo
TTCLC	T'ang-ta-chao-lin-chi
Turfan	T'u-lu-fan Ch'u-t'u-wen-shu
WPW	Ta-T'ang Hsi-yü-ch'iu-fa-kao-seng-chuan
YHC	Yang, Hsüan-chih

Introduction

This is a story of silk, and of much more than silk. It is an attempt, using silk as a thread, to examine a series of historical events which took place in several cultural regions of Eurasia from the seventh to the twelfth centuries. Following the traces left by transactions in silk, this book tries to reveal the possible economic and cultural interaction between these events and regions on the one hand, and certain changes caused by interactions within various societies which traded in silk. During the sixth and seventh centuries a significant cultural pattern emerged across Eurasia. Certain political and cultural events heralded a period of frequent communication and interaction between the few existing cultural regions—East Asia, South Asia, West and Central Asia, the Mediterranean and West Europe. China was reunified under the Sui Dynasty in AD 581, after almost four hundred years of political fragmentation. Unified China reached cultural brilliance under the T'ang Dynasty (618–907). In the relatively dark period of post-Gupta India—as compared to the splendid cultural achievements under the Kuṣāṇas and Guptas—the sparkling short-lived empire of King Harṣa (AD 606–47) entertained and patronized the first and most prestigious Buddhist pilgrim from T'ang China, Hsüan-tsang, thus ensuring a stream of cultural or religious exchanges between the two civilizations over the following centuries. Around the Mediterranean, Justinian's reconquest of the former Roman territory was not consolidated after his death (AD 565), but the Byzantine empire firmly retained its cultural supremacy over the western part of the former Roman empire, while Western Europe sank into its dark age. Christianity, as the only common link between the two different cultural domains, was the main thread between the two parts of the former Roman empire. Between East and West the rise of Islam as well as an Islamic empire enfolded Mesopotamia,

Egypt and Persia, all ancient civilizations, into a new political domain by the mid-seventh century, and this subsequently gave rise to a new religious and cultural domain.

Among these major cultural domains there were many links. Material transactions persisted, as is evident from ubiquitous coins and artifacts, and from sporadic literary records. Silk, textiles and fibre were the most widely exchanged, and the largest in terms of quantity. Among the cultural exchanges, religious undertakings—pilgrimage and missionary—had the most profound impact on these different cultural domains.

These material and cultural links from the late-sixth century, to the time of the Mongols' conquest in the thirteenth century, were interrelated and often inseparable. It was a time when people in various parts of Eurasia were concerned with the problem of life and death and the world after death. Theological discussions and ritual practices addressed this concern. Among Buddhists and Christians, this was often expressed in the form of relic-worship and translations. The eschatological concern so dominated philosophical thinking and deciding perspectives in life that it often guided people in earning, accumulating, spending and exchanging their material wealth. All these material links could be represented by silk transactions, because silk textiles have been found in various parts of the continent, and this textile seems to have prevailed as the most desired luxury. The desire for silk was shared by rulers, the elite, priests and even commoners.

Though the movement of silk persisted through the centuries, the form and nature of silk transactions changed fundamentally. In the seventh century, exquisite silk textiles were strictly restricted items in both Byzantium and China, the two major producers of silk. The government monopolized the production and consumption of silk. By the ninth or the tenth century, fancy silks were available in many parts of Eurasia, though they were used mostly for religious purposes; subsequently there was a total collapse of all sumptuary regulations on silk in China and later in Europe.

Expensive silk textiles have always been considered a luxury item. According to Arjun Appadurai, luxuries are 'goods whose principle use is rhetorical and social, goods are simply incarnation signs, the necessity to which they respond is fundamentally political' (Appadurai 1986, 38). He ascribed five attributes to luxuries: 1) Restriction, either by price or by law, to the elite; 2) complexity of acquisition, which may or may not be a function of real 'scarcity'; 3) semiotic virtuosity, that is, the capacity to signal fairly complex social messages (as do pepper in cuisine, silk in dress, jewels in adornment and relics in worship); 4) specialized knowledge as a prerequisite for their 'appropriate' consumption, that is, regulation by fashion; and 5) a conspicuous connection between their consumption and the body, person and personality of the user.

When examining shifts in the status of silk as a luxury item in the period under study, with the five traits attributed to luxuries by Appadurai, one obvious change is that prices replaced the law as the main way to restrict the use of silk. This change had a long-term effect on many later historical developments. The shift meant that silk became a real commodity in the market. The increasing demand for luxury goods, including silk, was the main reason for the expansion of trade, industry and financial capital in Europe from the fourteenth to the eighteenth century (Appadurai 1986, 36–7). With the revival of trade in Europe, textiles, particularly silk, were a major commodity of exchange. The industrial revolution also began with textiles. Ancient silk textiles which had mostly been preserved in church treasuries were brought out by research institutions attached to textile industries for the purpose of study. All these developments were possible because the consumption of silk, from being 'restricted by law' became 'restricted by price'.

When T'ang China and the Byzantine empire effectively monopolized and regulated the production and transaction of silk, restrictions on exquisite silks were implemented through the law. The purpose was essentially political—both China and Byzantium enacted a set of code for clothing to distinguish their bureaucratic echelons and ecclesiastical hierarchy, and thus consolidated the political order in their countries. For purposes of diplomacy China and Byzantium had to negotiate with encroachers into their territories—the barbarians, nomads and hostile states—with silk textile and clothing, thus rendering the textile an effective diplomatic weapon.

For both domestic and diplomatic purposes, rulers in various parts of the world tried to impress their subjects and neighbours with rare goods. As William McNeill has pointed out, the rulers of civilized societies from early antiquity learned that to trade rare goods at their command with the scarce resources they desired was more sensible than to make military expeditions (McNeill 1982, 6). 'For many centuries, trade was largely confined to the exchange of scarce commodities between the rulers and administrators of civilized lands and the local potentates of distant parts. Civilized rulers and officials were the only people who had access to luxury products made on command by specially skilled artisans' (ibid., 7). For political purposes, rulers who regulated and monopolized the manufacture and use of silk made every effort to retain this privilege. However, after the twelfth century, though political forces were still effective in controlling the demand and supply of luxuries, including silk, they no longer used legal restrictions like capital punishment. By the beginning of the nineteenth century, this demand in Europe 'was freed from political regulation and left to the "free" play of the market places and of fashion. From this point of view, fashion and sumptuary regulations are opposite poles in the social regulation of demand, particularly for goods with high discriminatory value' (Appadurai 1986, 38). However, before expensive silk textiles became real commodities regulated by fashion and the market, forces other than political and economic had to release them from the firm legal control of rulers. In this transitional period religious institutions and practices in various parts of Eurasia played a vital role in de-regulating the transaction of luxuries, including silk. Indeed, they probably constituted the major force that brought about the transition of silk from being a luxury good to one used for religious purposes.

In the period under examination, religious houses were the most powerful social institutions in both Europe and Asia. Religious activities—pilgrimage, missionary, worship—were the most prestigious and the best documented apart from political events. All the major religions of that time—Buddhism, Christianity, Islam, Zoroastrianism, Judaism, Manichaeism and various heresies—offered different explanations of basic issues such as cosmology, life and death, etc. They all, nevertheless, provided the eschatology, a clear picture of the world after death. Their explanations regarding this matter shaped the pattern of behaviour of their followers when dealing with problems of birth and death, and in their purpose and method of accumulating and spending wealth. In the period under study, textiles notably silk textiles, were a major form of wealth in many societies. Religious activities, if concerned with the accumulation, consumption and display of wealth, inevitably involved silk transactions.

Research on the mutual influence and interactions as a consequence of silk transactions and religious activities between peoples who spread all over Eurasia involves a study of world history. However, most works in the field of world history have concentrated on the period after the discovery of the new world, when the influence of one culture on another is most evident: on the impact of New World food crops (Alfred Crosby, *The Columbian Exchanges, Biological Consequences of 1492*, New York, 1972); on the role of epidemics (William McNeill, *Plagues and Peoples*, Garden City, N.J., 1976); technology (Daniel Headrick, *Tools of Empire*, Oxford, 1981); the widening of the trade network (Philip Curtin, *Cross-Cultural Trade in World History*, Cambridge, 1984); and weaponry and dominance (William McNeill, *Pursuit of Power*, Chicago, 1982). In dealing with one theme on a global scale, authors of world history have sought to establish links between nations, peoples and civilizations. This literature, as rightly pointed out by Patrick Manning (1993, 6), tends to treat nations or civilizations as independent acting units. Meanwhile, the theory of the World System offers a paradigm for the study of world history after AD 1500. In an attempt to incorporate various nations and peoples into a global pattern, Immanuel Wallerstein's *The Modern World System* (1974, 1980, 1989) projects the construction of a single economy that links many states, with an unequal relationship between the highly developed centre and the less developed periphery. An alternative to the world-economy model is the model of a world-empire, with political dominance as the link between various nations.

Though this model of the World System has invited strong criticism from both those who study Europe, the core regions of Wallerstein's world economy, and those who study third world regions, the periphery of the system (Manning 1993, 41–2), it nevertheless raises an old question for historians whose study extends beyond the limits of one nation or one civilization. Is it possible to find a rule, a pattern, a common rhythm of historical development among different regions with seemingly totally different cultures? This question is also relevant for scholars of pre-capitalist histories, as increasing archaeological discoveries and other historical evidence show links and even causal relationships between events that took place in regions remote from each other, which cannot be explained under the assumption of the model of separated and isolated civilizations.

The model of the World System had been applied to the period before AD1500 with modifications. Janet Abu-Lughod postulates that in medieval times, the prosperity of various regions was related to the world trading system in which Europe was not the only core region (*Before European Hegemony: The World System AD 1250–1350*). This World System model needs even more revision when applied to the Roman empire. While the political boundaries of the Roman empire did not encompass the entirety of Eurasia, its commercial relationship with Asia was definitely not based on unequal exchanges between the core and peripheral states. In many cases it was virtually a relationship of centre to centre exchanges with the Romans running at a deficit (Thapar 1992, 5–6). Other researchers tried another approach to identify a world historical pattern by relating the momentum of various historical events in Eurasia with those in Central Asia (Andre Gunder Frank, *The Centrality of Central Asia*, Amsterdam, 1992). Frank convincingly refuted the false equation between nomadism and barbarism, and advocated that more attention be paid to Central Asia. However, the entire history of Central Asia still evades our knowledge and even an outline of the history of this region is yet to be reconstructed. Much has to be gleaned before an accurate evaluation is made of the significant role of this region in shaping world history.

The question nevertheless remains irrespective of whether or not a global pattern and a World System provides a satisfactory explanation. When a historian examines an ancient culture, a region, or a people, he cannot escape the many, often unexpected, similarities and instances of interactions between peoples stationed geographically far apart. This story of silk and religions, which encounters the similarities and interactions existing among the peoples of China, Central Asia, India, Persia, the Arabian Peninsula, the Mediterranean and West Europe, is not an attempt to build any model or pattern. I have tried, by gathering sporadic facts and tracing clues regarding the extent of communication between peoples of remote regions, to find an explanation for the similarity in certain basic concepts and common behaviour patterns; and the contribution of interaction between these peoples in creating the similarities as well as the contribution of certain major human concerns shared by all races and cultures. Whether or not a picture or a puzzle emerges out of these facts and analyses, I do hope this work helps us to answer, or at least understand, the old quest to search for the common rhythm in the history of the human race.

Before going into the long story of the transition of silk from being a restricted item to becoming a commodity, and the role of religious activities in the process, I will briefly survey previous studies regarding the silk trade, particularly those inspired by the romantic Silk Route. A summary of the development of silk production and trade before the period under study is also given to show the general pattern of silk transactions prior to the period dealt with here.

The Romance of Silk Trade

The Silk Route has captured the romantic fantasy of adventurers, scholars, artists and tourists since the nineteenth century. Travellers braved some of the most inhospitable terrains on earth to unveil the mystery of past civilizations. In more recent years UNESCO sponsored and organized large-scale expeditions to explore the cultural and material transactions that took place on the ancient routes. While scholars involved in a study of the Silk Route share a basic curiosity regarding the history of the deserts and mountains, their perspectives on specific subjects often vary greatly. Chinese, European and Islamic scholars view the silk trade (the most important trading activity carried on along the ancient routes) from different angles and thus present diverse pictures.

It is common knowledge that silk was China's contribution to the world. Most Chinese, including many scholars, regarded the Silk Route as a conduit for silk textiles and yarn that flowed out from the northwest borders of the ancient empires—the Han Dynasty (206 BC–AD 220) to the T'ang Dynasty (AD 618–907)—to the West, i.e. Persia, India and the Mediterranean. This picture was probably true at the time of the Roman empire, as is evident by the abundant literature on the fantasy of Chinese silks in Rome and from archaeological evidence found in sites close to the Mediterranean, such as Palmyra. However, most of the silk samples that survived in Europe dated to a later period and were of a different kind. Western experts in ancient and medieval textiles, therefore, mostly dealt with Byzantine silk samples preserved in Christian churches and sanctuaries. Occasionally they encountered an exotic oriental textile—Persian, Coptic or Islamic. When referring to the Silk Route, places such as Samarkand, Bukhara or Merv appear more often in their analyses of provenance and catalogue than does T'ang China.

Textiles have constituted a major field of study for Islamic art historians. Museums and libraries keep comprehensive and detailed catalogues of kaftans, carpets, rugs, tapestries and *ṭirāz*, i.e. textiles with borders inscribed with silk thread. Art historians in the field of Islamic textiles discovered to their excitement that silk textiles woven in Islamic countries had penetrated into European markets in the early medieval period. Though pre-Islamic Persia and India actively participated in the silk trade, studies on the textile history of the two countries suffer from the lack of preservation of silk samples of this period. Sparce documentation allows for speculation on the question of how much the exports from Persia and India to the ancient Mediterranean world were their own products and how much were re-exports of Chinese products. Central Asia was at the crossroads of many cultures and was a storehouse for many varieties of ancient and medieval silks. Chinese literature and documents found in the tombs of this region refer to Roman silks, Persian silks, Kucha silks and Indian silks (*deva* silks). In short, the ancient silk trade involved a more complex transaction than just a one-way flow of the commodity along the Silk Route, which appears on many maps as a simple line, though curved and twisted, across the entire Eurasian continent. In a recent study on all the silk samples (more than one thousand) preserved in Western churches dated from the seventh to the twelfth centuries, Anna Maria Muthesius found only one noticeable sample from China (Muthesius 1990, 129). Surely this finding does not negate the fact that plain and simple woven silk textiles and silk yarn reached the West during this period, when many camels loaded with silks headed west from the T'ang empire along the Silk Routes. To study this complicated system of the production and transaction of silk in the late antique and early medieval world, and to find some pattern guiding the circulation of silks as luxuries, as currency, as religious items, one needs to adopt a wider historical perspective, instead of viewing the problem only from the perspective of a single culture; one needs to link this material transaction with other historical processes such as religious movements, instead of treating it purely as an economic phenomenon.

Early Silk Trade along the Silk Route

China started to export silk as early as the second century BC and remained the major silk producer for centuries. By the fourth and fifth centuries AD, silk markets and the problems of supplying them had become more complex. Sassanid Persia, Byzantium and India all had their own silk industries. This development ushered in a new era in silk trade, for both the old and the new silk producers exported and imported silk fabrics. High quality polychrome silk flowed between different countries to satisfy the demand for foreign exotic goods. Silk was not inherently a rare material. Silk, unlike diamonds for example, did not have an intrinsic value. Its value derived from the intensive labour and technology involved in its production. Therefore, its demand and price mostly fluctuated in a different historical context.

Silk was a common material for clothing, though not as popular as hemp, in Han China. Simple tabby silks were produced in peasant households and often used for paying taxes to the government. However, the government always tried to control the weaving and sale of certain kinds of silks, such as polychrome patterned silk, fine fabric with complicated weaving and embroidered cloths. These silk fabrics were reserved for the exclusive use of the royal family and officials. High quality silk required more intensive labour, higher technology and a greater division of labour than individual peasant households or even professional weavers could afford. Because poor people could not afford to wear these silk products, rich merchants were the most likely to break the sumptuary rules. Thus the Han government forbade merchants from wearing *chin* (polychrome patterned silk), embroidered silk and other fine textiles, or to wield weapons and to ride on horses or horse carriages (HS, 1/65). Still, because these silks symbolized a high status, rich city dwellers continued to covet them for their prestige value.

In addition to reserving high quality silk for their own use, the Han rulers also bestowed them on foreigners for diplomatic purposes. From the second century BC, China engaged in a protracted warfare with a nomadic group, the Hsiung-nu, along the north-west border. The Hsiung-nu was a loose confederacy of nomadic tribes. The shan-yü, head of the Hsiung-nu confederacy, relied on luxury goods from a sedentary society to retain the loyalty of the tribal chiefs and on constant warfare to maintain the solidarity of the whole confederacy (Barfield 1981, 530). In the period before the Han military forces were strong enough to attack the Hsiung-nu (133 BC), the government often tried to stop them from harassing border towns by bribing them with thousands of bolts of silk, including both fine silk and commoner weaves. Nevertheless, according to Barfield, the silks and provisions which the Hsiung-nu demanded from the Han government were just enough to allow the shan-yü and his court to live in style. Nothing was for the common tribesmen.

Once the Han imperial government under Emperor Wu (140–86 BC) felt confident enough to fight with the Hsiung-nu, its policy was to send gifts, mainly silks, to Central Asian states and other nomadic groups in order to form alliances against the Hsiung-nu. The first envoy to Central Asia was Chang Chien who went to the Yueh-chih. Regardless of whether or not China gained actual allies against the Hsiung-nu, much silk flowed out of China as a result. In exchange for the silk products, China received horses, furs, precious stones, woolen and cotton textiles, and other products in the form of gifts and tribute, and purchased commodities from Central Asia and further west. The Chinese elite soon acquired a taste for these goods, especially horses, which were both necessary for developing an effective cavalry in the battles against the nomads and also ritually essential for the rulers. Some Central Asian horses gained the status of a 'dragon horse', with only the royal family members entitled to mount them. By the first and second centuries AD the Hsiung-nu had retreated to the north steppe and were no longer a threat to the Han empire. However, the Han troops still fought with the Hsiung-nu over control of the trade routes to Central Asia. Silk became more than just a medium of diplomacy, for the Chinese exported it in exchange for exotic foreign goods. The elite from Central Asia to the Mediterranean also acquired a taste for silk.

At the other end of the silk trade, during the first century AD, the Romans were quite familiar with silk fabric. Pliny includes the 'seric tissue' in his list of the most costly products (Pliny xxxvii, 67). Pliny thought that silk grew on a tree. He probably confused silk with cotton (vi, 20). His description of 'tree wool' shows that the Romans were still ignorant about the process of silk production. Its mysterious origin added more glamour to the beautiful textile from afar. Demand for silk continued to increase in. the second and third centuries. However, conflict with Persia hindered the flow of silk via overland routes. At the same time sailors of the eastern Roman empire acquired a knowledge of the trade based on the monsoon winds of the Arabian sea. Silk was transported via Central Asia to Barbaricon, a port on the mouth of the Indus, and to Barygaza, a port on the gulf of Cambay, where Roman ships carried it across the Red Sea to the Roman Orient. Silk fragments found in the tombs of Palmyra in Syria are the first material evidence of Han China's silk trade with the Roman empire (Maenchen-Helfen 1943).

This westward flow of silk certainly stimulated the flow of commodities from the Mediterranean region to East Asia. Roman gold and silver coins, silver wares, and goods from the Mediterranean or places along the route, such as coral, wine, sweet clover, perfume, glass, clothing, styrax, chrysolites, dates, antimony, orpiment, frankincense, slaves, etc. reached western Indian ports (Warmington 1928, 261–72; Schoff 1912, 167; Periplus 28, 39, 49; Pliny xxxii, 11). Indian traders, under the Kuṣāṇas, who ruled north India and partially Central Asia, and the Western Kṣatrapas, who ruled west India, profited from the exchange between the Mediterranean and East Asia. They procured Chinese silk which was sold to the Romans along with imported goods, such as coral, styrax and frankincense, and indigenous goods, such as cotton textiles, crystal, lapis lazuli and glassware. The rich collection of Chinese goods from the east, Roman goods from the west and indigenous goods from the south which are buried in Begram in Afghanistan, the site of the summer palace of the Kuṣāṇa king, Kapisa, shows that the Kuṣāṇa rulers collected toll from this trade (Wheeler 1954, 163). Cities and towns in the Kuṣāṇa territory prospered with a rise in Eurasian trade. An increase in economic activities in north India took place when Buddhist theology and institutions underwent dramatic transformations, and Buddhist proselytizers made great inroads into Central Asia and China.

Early Buddhist Proselytizing and Silk Trade

During the first few centuries AD, Mahayana Buddhism developed in northwest India. This new school of Buddhism introduced a totally new cosmology to Buddhist devotees. Unlike the earlier Hinayana school, in which Sakyamuni Buddha was the only major saint, Mahayana Buddhism introduced an entire pantheon of Buddhas, bodhisattvas and other deities. Many of the deities carved out a piece of heaven for themselves in the new Buddhist cosmos. The best known is the western pure land of Amitabha (*sukhāvatīvyūha*). Some of the bodhisattvas, such as Avalokitésvara came down to this world to offer help to devotees (*Saddharma-pundarika* XXIV). With this new cosmos in sight, the goal of Buddhist devotion lay less in achieving the abstract, remote state of nirvana, and more in improving one's material conditions and status in the next or even present life-cycles.

This new cosmology developed in the commercial environment of urban centers. Cities prospered from the domestic and inter-cultural trade under the rule of the Kuṣāṇas. The values of traders were inevitably involved in the theological developments of Bud-dhism. Buddhist Sanskrit texts composed in this period emphasize worship and donation in return for tangible benefits instead of individual efforts to gain merit through meditation or self-sacri-fice. In short, religious merit could be obtained in exchange for material goods, just like other commodities. Numerous votive inscriptions dated to the Kuṣāṇa period contain statements that benefactors expected their donations to win them merit which would bring welfare to themselves and to their loved ones.

The rise of these commercial values among Buddhists paralleled the institutionalization of Buddhist monasteries. Urban prosperity brought great wealth into Buddhist monasteries. Traders, artisans and other urban dwellers, as always, donated handsomely to mon-asteries and thus facilitated the expansion of Buddhist institutions. As a group whose status was not very high in Brahmanical hierar-chy, the urbanites sought prestige from Buddhist society. The new commercial ethos in Buddhist theology gave more impetus to donate. With more wealth in the form of money and valuables flowing into monasteries, monks no longer went out individually with their begging bowls for daily food. They relied on donations made to their monasteries for provisions. A giant stone symbolic of a begging bowl was placed in front of monasteries to testify to the transformation of financial transactions between lay devotees and Buddhist institutions. Surplus from the maintenance of monasteries went to monumental buildings such as stupas and resulted in the splendid Buddhist art of the Kuṣāṇa period, i.e. the first few centuries AD. Here the devotees, either monks or laymen, were encouraged to worship these stupas with many valuable items, which were easily available from long distance trade. The most important goods were silks, often in the form of banners draped on the stupas, and the Seven Treasures.[1]

Buddhist sanskrit texts openly advocated the offering of silk by devotees. In the Mahāvastu, one of the major Buddhist texts extant from the early centuries AD, it is stated that 'he who has placed a festoon of fine silk on a monument of the saviour of the world prospers in all his aims, both among gods and among men, avoids base families and is not reborn among them; he becomes wealthy and affluent, a sovereign in this world' (II, 365, p. 332). Without a stable silk trade traffic which made silk banners available to devotees, this kind of statement could not have been made. It, in turn, encouraged greater silk purchases for donation.

Buddhist devotees in that period probably followed the scriptural prescription to use silk for worship. But the first definitive evidence of this practice dates to a later period. In the early fifth century AD when the Chinese pilgrim Fa-hsien visited India, he noticed that silk banners were widely used in Buddhist rituals. For example, silk banners were hung in the Buddha's garden near Sravasti (860b) and were used in a parade of the Buddha's image in Pataliputra (862b). A century later, the pilgrims Sung-Yün and Hui-sheng saw 'several tens of thousands of silk banners hung over' a stupa in Uzuntati, Central Asia (YHC v, 266). Certainly in the seventh century, when Hsüan-tsang visited India, this practice was still in vogue (HT, 382). Large quantities of silk banners found in Tunhuang and other places in Central Asia show that silk banners for Buddhist worship continued to be popular even in later periods.

Sanskrit literature of the Gupta period shows that silk banners

[1] *Sapta-ratna* consisted of gold, silver, crystal, lapis lazuli, coral, pearls, etc. I have discussed the evolution of the concept of the Seven Treasures in Buddhist theology at length in my book, *Ancient India and Ancient China: Trade and Religious Exchanges* AD *1–600*, Oxford University Press, Delhi, 1988.

were also used in non-Buddhist rituals and on secular occasions in India. The practice of using banners and flags made of Chinese silk for ceremonial purposes first started either among the Indian or Central Asian elite and then spread to the religious sphere, or was initiated by Buddhist rituals. No matter which, the wide-spread practice of decorating stupas with silk banners indicates that more than a few high-ranking people were involved in the practice. Because silk fabrics served as a token of Buddhist devotion, commoners were endowed with the right of purchasing the finest weaves for religious purpose. The popularity of silk strengthened their desire to obtain fine silks, and they thus legitimately released silks to a large market outside the small circle of upper social groups.

From the fourth century onwards, trade among these countries entered a phase of decline. This was a time when the Guptas retreated to the middle Ganges, the Roman empire fell apart, China was tormented by warfare between divided states and routes in Central Asia were quite dangerous. Yet this chaotic political and economic situation provided a fertile breeding ground for religion. Buddhist institutions gained unprecedented prosperity in China. Pilgrims and preachers went back and forth between India and China in spite of difficult conditions on the road. Just as Chinese rulers continued to look to the west for exotic goods, Buddhist devotees continued to pay high prices for the Seven Treasures prescribed by their belief. These factors stimulated the export of Chinese silk. Thus Buddhism sustained the silk trade by contributing to the demand in India and Central Asia for Chinese weaves. However, by this time China was no longer the sole producer of silk textiles. Many countries were involved in the silk market and supply system, and cultural factors other than Buddhism affected silk production and marketing. The rise of new centers of silk weaving created a new pattern of silk transaction. Christian and later Islamic religious activities also wrought adjustments on the pattern of transactions. Before looking into the fundamental changes, I will give a brief survey of the new centers of silk weaving.

Silk Market and Supply in Eurasia

Outside China, silk weaving began in the early centuries AD in

West Asia, but was dependent on China for the supply of silk yarn. The technology of breeding silk worms and unrolling silk cocoons was introduced a few centuries later. Indians had made silk yarn from species other than the mulberry silk worm at an early date. From the fourth century AD, many countries began to produce polychrome patterned silk, although the Chinese retained their monopoly on translucent, thin fabric. While Chinese-patterned silks remained desired commodities in various countries, products from the Central Asian states, Sassanid Persia, India and Byzantium also reached foreign markets. The patterned silk textile products were traded among these countries as luxury goods because they differed in weaving technology and artistic design. These differences, stemming from the different cultural backgrounds of the producers, made them exotic in foreign countries and added to their appeal as luxury goods. Again, because of the high labour and transport costs, transactions in silk often took the form of diplomatic gestures. Certain kinds of silk were reserved exclusively for very powerful and wealthy people. We will now look at these complicated markets country by country.

CHINA As mentioned above, the Han government tried to bar merchants from wearing embroidered and polychrome silk, and later Chinese rulers certainly perpetuated this tradition of controlling the use and sale of luxury goods. The Northern Wei (AD 386–534) rulers tried to register all goldsmiths and other artisans; they ruled that whoever—whether a prince or a commoner—hired these artisans at his home exposed his whole family to a death sentence. A special category of artisans under government control was referred to as the 'silk weaving households' (ling-lo-hu) (Wang Chung-lo 1979, II, 536). During the T'ang Dynasty (AD 618–907) the royal manufacturers monopolized the production of certain kinds of polychrome silk, such as those patterned with sacred animals (jui-chin), which often appeared within or outside of large pearl roundels, and those patterned with confronting pheasants, confronting rams, flying phoenix, Chinese unicorns (ch'i-lin), etc. (Liu Man-ch'un 1982, 87). Since various Chinese governments used a large quantity of silk as gifts to foreigners for political reasons or in exchange for desirable foreign goods, they also tried to control its export. An edict of 714 forbade the sale to foreigners of the most exquisite silk products: polychrome patterned silks, damasks, gauzes, crepes, embroideries and other fine silk (Schafer 1963, 24; THY, 86, 1581).

These efforts were not always successful. Though the rulers tried to reserve certain luxury goods exclusively for themselves, the commoners, especially the wealthy among them, continued to imitate the style of the elite. As long as the technology for producing the luxury silk was available, those enticed by the possibility of high profits risked their necks to make and sell fine silks. In the era of Shen-kui (AD 519–20), towards the end of the reign of the Northern Wei, the government tried to revive the sumptuary law that forbade merchants and artisans to wear gold and silver ornaments, as well as embroidery and polychrome patterned silk, but it could not enforce the law at all (YHC, 205). During the rule of the T'ang dynasty, there were so many silk-weaving centres that the government could not possibly control the production and export of silk. A study of the silk samples found in Central Asia shows they came from various parts of China (Liu Man-ch'un 1982, 88).

At the time that domestic silks lost their glamour because of their popularity, imported ones gained in value. It is not yet known when exactly foreign made silk entered China. As early as the fourth century AD, there is a record of women in the west frontier region, Ho-hsi, wearing a five-coloured silk fabric made in foreign countries (Hsi-ho-chi, 1). This information is not specific enough to determine the nature of the silk. Later records show that the foreign produced silks that entered China were from the Central Asian countries, Persia and Byzantium. A few debentures and contracts found in Turfan mention the polychrome patterned silk of Kucha, and one of the documents mentions 'Kucha polychrome patterned silk made in Kao-ch'ang (Turfan)' (Turfan I, 181, 187). These Chinese documents are dated mid-fifth century, when Turfan was under the rule of the Northern Liang, one of the sixteen states in north China in this period. It seems that 'Kucha polychrome patterned silk' referred to a specific kind of silk fabric, probably originating in Kucha. This silk entered a region under a Chinese ruler and was even copied there because of its popular appeal. Another kind of Central Asian silk fabric, zandaniji, woven in a place near Bukhara around the seventh century, was also found in Tunhuang (Shepherd and Henning 1959, 22–4, 35).

The best foreign silk products, as well as any other luxury goods from far away, were supposed to be presented to the emperor by either envoys or traders. From the sixth century, Sassanian polychrome silk became very famous, so that visitors from Central Asia and South Asia brought Persian silk as gifts or tribute to the Chinese court. The Hua state (an unidentified state in Central Asia) sent Persian silk along with a yellow lion and white sable fur in 520 (CHL, iv, 71). Envoys from Khuttal and Kapisa offered Persian polychrome silk to a T'ang emperor (Schafer 1963, 202; TFYK, 971/7b, 14b). Official records concern only exchanges between governments. The favoured Persian silk probably also entered China through unofficial channels, as testified to by the Persian silk samples from Turfan (Ast. i. 6.01, Ast. vii. 1.01, Hsia Nai 1963, 71).

Polychrome silk from the Roman empire has been mentioned in the biography of the late fourth century Buddhist preacher, Kumarajiva. It is said that the king of Kucha honoured Kumarajiva with silk from Ta-ch'in, i.e. the Roman empire (KSC, ii, 331a). Although it is hard to accept the early date of the fourth century for Roman or Byzantine silk appearing in Central Asia, we can conclude that silk from the Byzantine empire was known in China by the sixth century, because the author of the biography was a Chinese monk living at that time. In his famous book, *The Golden Peaches of Samarkand*, Edward Schafer identifies a sample from Astana, Turfan, with its octagonal design (Ast. vii. 1.06, National Museum, New Delhi) as representing a Byzantium Greek style (Schafer 1963, 202).

The import of silk fabric from other countries introduced some changes in Chinese silk weaving, both in technology and design. From Han to T'ang, the weaving technology of patterned silk first underwent a transition from warp-faced compound tabby to warp-faced compound twill. While the warp threads were still the carriers of patterned colours in compound twill weaving, the more complicated technology produced a more aesthetic effect than the simpler tabby weaving. The more fundamental transition in weaving technology was the change to weft-faced compound twill. Weft-faced technology was traditionally used for wool weaving in the west. When these countries developed silk weaving they naturally adopted this technology. Using weft-faced technology meant that weft threads were carriers of colours for designed patterns. The coloured weft threads were operated by hand and were thus more flexible in forming patterns than were the warp threads which were fixed on the loom. This flexibility gave high-T'ang silk a wider breadth, with larger and more elaborate patterns than that of previous periods (Meister 1970).

More apparent still were the changes in pattern. Whereas auspicious animals such as the tiger, horse, deer and phoenix, and other traditional Chinese sacred symbols dominated the designs on Han silk, foreign influence on designs made itself felt from the fifth century. When Buddhism flourished in China, auspicious objects in India, such as the peacock, lion, elephant and bodhi tree joined in the menagerie of Chinese animals on textile design (e.g. Sinkiang Uighur Autonomous Region, Museum of, 1972, pl. 23, 26, 27). Central and Western Asian influence resulted in some designs showing stiff animals and plant motifs in contrast to the lively floating Han motifs. One beautiful example is a fifth or sixth century piece found in Astana with rows of birds and sheep facing each other, separated by rows of trees (Sinkiang Uighur Autonomous Region, Museum of, 1975, pl. 79). A more obvious Iranian influence appears in the design of animal motifs in pearl roundels, where small circles form a larger circle with an animal motif inside (Meister 1970, 261–2, fig. 26). By the late seventh and the eighth century, weft-faced compound twill with typical Persian animal motifs and roundels had become very popular in China.

These Chinese polychrome silks with foreign designs were produced for both foreign and domestic markets. Those with Indian motifs may have had a religious meaning, and were thus suitable for Buddhist pilgrims or Buddhist traders who carried them as donations westward to the land of the Buddha. From the seventh century, Yang-chou in south China specialized in making 'polychrome silk for the robes of foreigners' (Liu Man-ch'un 1982, 88). Traditional warp-faced technology was still adequate for export purposes. Meanwhile, the Chinese elite built up their taste for imported silk. When genuine imported silks could not meet the Chinese demand, domestic copies were also sold. Here western technology enabled T'ang artisans to not only make quite authentic foreign style silk, but to also absorb foreign traditions in weaving domestic style silks, thus producing silk with a high aesthetical value.

CENTRAL ASIA   From the second century BC when silk trade started along the Central Asian routes, people there both benefited and suffered from the trade. Since they occupied a unique position, the people of Central Asian were inevitably the earliest agents who both transported silk products and transferred the technology of silk weaving and sericulture. However, these people were by no means a homogeneous or a stable population. While the sedentary communities which resided in oases along the trade routes were relatively stable, nomadic tribes and states were constantly on the move. After the Hsiung-nu retreated to the north steppe, Scythians, Hephthalites, various Turkic tribes and Arabs all controlled different parts of Central Asia in different periods. Both the sedentary communities and the nomadic tribes were involved in silk trading, but in different ways.

In addition to dealing with silk products, the oasis people began sericulture at an early date. Some painted bricks excavated from the tombs of Chia-yü Gate, a border region between the interior of China and Central Asia, depict scenes of people cultivating mulberry trees and taking care of cocoons (Museum of Chinese History, Beijing). These tombs date to the third or fourth centuries AD. About a century later, literary sources referred to sericulture in the oasis states of Turfan and Argi (CS, 50/916).

Being constantly on the move, nomadic people could not engage in sericulture or silk weaving, but nonetheless were interested in silk. I have mentioned that for the Hsiung-nu, acquiring silk from Chinese rulers was a way to strengthen the leadership and to consolidate the otherwise loose confederacy. Both sedentary communities and nomadic tribes desired silk, either locally made or imported from the east or the west. They kept silk fabrics bought from outside for their own use, and so it is possible for us to examine excavated samples of silk originating from various places. But these Central Asian kingdoms used certain means of obtaining silk that did not endear them to their silk purchasing neighbours: capturing traders and commodities was not beneficial for long distance trade. One reason for the T'ang government's annexation of Turfan in 639 was that the kings there always stopped traders (Han 1979, 223). However, sending gifts for diplomatic reasons did facilitate the exchange of silk between distant lands.

Another factor which increased the flow of silk fabric into

Central Asia was the special role of silk in this region, i.e. its function as a medium of exchange. Politically unstable as Central Asia was, no currency of just one government could prevail in this region over a long period, especially the Chinese currency, which mainly consisted of copper coins. The flourishing trade along the trade routes required a common currency, and because silk was the most popular commodity, and it was actually a currency parallel to copper coins in China, it naturally remained the medium of exchange in Central Asia for centuries. Kharoṣṭhi documents dated to the late third or the early fourth century AD from Central Asia mention that silk fabric and garments were used as payment in transactions. The price of a woman was forty-one bolts of silk (Burrow 1940, 1, no. 3). A Buddhist monastery listed fines in bolts of silk for monks who broke its rules (ibid., 95, no. 485). As a monastery was a station for pilgrims and traders, it is not surprising that the monastery and monks preserved silk as their property. Chinese documents from Turfan also record the practice of using bolts of silk as money. A female slave cost only three and half bolts of Kucha silk in the fifth century (Turfan I, 187). Some letters even mention 'coins worth a hundred bolts of silk' or 'things worth a hundred bolts of silk' (Sinkiang Museum 1972, 13).

INDIA The silk industry, from sericulture to weaving, was well established in India during the Gupta era. The wealth of the well-known Mandasor silk weaving guild (AD 436, CII, 1981, vol. III, 322 ff.) testifies to the prosperity of the trade. In the early seventh century when Hsüan-tsang visited India, he listed silk as one of the most popular materials for clothing in the country (HT, 176). But he used the word *kauśeya* for the commonly worn silk fabric because it was from a species of wild silk worm (ibid.). Throughout his travel records and his biography, Hsüan-tsang clearly distinguished between the two kinds of silk. Obviously the difference between kauśeya and Chinese silk was quite clear.

Indians imported both fine silk textiles and silk yarn from China, as India controlled part of the silk trade between China and Byzantium. Before the Byzantine acquired the knowledge of sericulture, their silk industry was heavily dependent on Chinese yarn, which they obtained through the Persians. The Persians in turn bought silk yarn from the Central Asians and Indians

(Procopius xx, 9–12; Maity 1957, 178). If Persia had to buy silk from India, the Indians were obviously dealing in *seric*, i.e. Chinese silk yarn. Some of the so-called Chinese silk in India, *cīnāṁśuka*, used by the Indian elite, was probably silk woven from Chinese yarn in India.

PERSIA   Some legends suggest that the Persians began to weave polychrome silk in the fourth century AD, but reliable literary records and material evidence come only later in the Sassanian period (CHI, III, 1108). By then, Persian polychrome silk fabrics, especially those woven with golden thread, were famous in both the east and west. Golden brocade trimmed with precious stones was the material of royal robes (Ackerman 1981, II, 691–2). The fame of Sassanid textiles reached as far as Gaul in the fifth century (ibid.). A Chinese source, the *History of the Sui*, states that Persia produced polychrome silk, silk cloth (*yüeh-no-pu*, probably from Persian *baru vala*) and brocade with gold threads (CHL, iii, 102). Hsüan-tsang, whilst in India, also heard that Persia was famous for its polychrome silk (HT, 938).

Since no silk textile fragments dating to the Sassanian period have been found in Persia, the study of Sassanian silk is based on motifs from other art forms, such as stone carvings, frescos and silver ware. The most representative motifs are said to be those of the reliefs at Taq-i-Bustan (CHI, III, 1108). The motifs mostly show rather stiff animals within a roundel. Silk samples which have been identified as Sassanian are often found in European churches and Egyptian tombs, in addition to a few pieces from Central Asia (ibid., 1109). Sassanian silk clearly reached the territory of Byzantium and beyond. Thus Christian devotees have enabled modern scholars to examine Sassanian silks which were lost in their native land.

Even though Sassanian silk fabrics were so popular that both westerners and easterners tried to copy them, the Persians probably had to import some of the silk yarn for their looms from China. Business with China via the land routes began in the second century BC, mainly through trading posts in Sogdiana (ibid., III, 739). As the Sassanians bought whole cargoes of Chinese silk from the Indians, they had an upper hand over Byzantium until the latter developed its own sericulture.

BYZANTIUM   Silk weaving with Chinese yarn started in the Syrian cities of Antioch, Berytos, Tyre and possibly Gaza in the Roman

period (Day 1950, 108). Later, Greece and Egypt, as part of the
Byzantine empire, also acquired the silk industry. However, even
by the time of Justinian's reign (483–565), Byzantium still depended on imported silk yarn. Competition with Persia for access
to silk yarn was so stiff that Justinian tried to work with the
Ethiopians. He proposed to the Ethiopian king, Hellestheaeus, that
the Ethiopians purchase silk from the Indians and sell it to the
Romans, so that both the Romans and Ethiopians could profit.
But even this effort did not work (Procopius I, xx, 9–12).[2] It is said
that finally Byzantium obtained the eggs of silk worms through
some Nestorian monks from Serinda, probably Central Asia or
China, which enabled Byzantium to start its own sericulture (ibid.,
VIII, xvii, 1–14).

Byzantium and T'ang China—Two Centres of Silk Culture

By the seventh century, silk production in the Eurasian continent entered a new stage. Quantity, variety, technology and
artistic achievement reached an unprecedented level. Among the
various silk producing areas, Byzantium and T'ang China emerged
as the two major centres of silk culture. Persia succumbed to Arab
conquest and therefore Persian silk designs developed along the
lines of Islamic silks. Indian cotton textiles were more famous than
its silk fabric. Byzantium and T'ang China produced the greatest
quantity and the best silks in the world. Large-scale royal workshops
were established where silk production and distribution were tightly
controlled. Both governments enacted and tried to enforce
sumptuary laws regarding silk consumption. In the process of
establishing a bureaucratic and an ecclesiastical hierarchy to wash
off the remains of republican traditions, Byzantium used silk textiles
to establish differences in status. Similarly, when T'ang China built
a bureaucratic system on the ruins of a disintegrated polity and the
remains of a decadent aristocracy, it reorganized the old custom of
regulating the clothes worn by different social groups into a system
which helped to distinguish the new bureaucratic echelon.

While the royal courts of China and Byzantium encouraged
costume parades of silk fabric which contained a variety of colours
and patterns with golden and silver decorations, other forces were

2 For the validity of this legend, see p. 74, note 1.

at work trying to break the government monopoly and regulations on expensive textiles. In Asia, Buddhist proselytizing and
pilgrimages continued to boost silk transactions. In Europe, churches accumulated a host of silk samples, many of which, dating
from the seventh to the twelfth centuries, are available even today.
Meanwhile, conquest by the Arabs amalgamated a large area of
Central Asia, south Asia and west Mediterranean into an Islamic
empire. In the tent culture of the Arabs, textiles constituted their
major items of furniture and decorations. The caliphate inherited
the silk industries along with the other rich material cultures of
the conquered lands. Silk production and trade prospered, and
new styles and technologies evolved. This was due to the new
converts to Islam who moved up in Islamic society through the
military and civil services. Under the banner of the equality of
all Muslims, Islamic society perhaps tolerated social mobility
more than any other medieval society. Enterprising traders, particularly those dealing in all kinds of silks, enjoyed the highest
status in Islamic countries. Unrestricted trade in silk occurred at
a time when Chinese and Byzantine emperors no longer enjoyed
a monopoly in silk manufacture and trade. Perhaps Arab dominance of the silk trade hastened the collapse of the monopoly
in silk enjoyed by the Byzantine and Chinese emperors. Islam,
combined with a powerful polity, brought a new dimension to
silk trade. Not only did their geographic scale and location make
Muslim traders a link between the West and the East, the com-
merce-oriented peoples who joined Islam introduced new ways
of expressing religious piety. Silk production and transaction
reached new heights with the stimulation of new values.

Religious and commercial movements since the sixth and the
seventh centuries made silk trade a complex business. The picture
of Chinese silks being carried by Central Asian camels all the way
to the eastern Mediterranean, to reach Italian, Arabian and Persian
ports by ship, is romantic and beautiful, but not comprehensive.
Featured silks, the expensive luxury items, which involved much
labour, technology, artistic creativity and more important, cultural
patterns, under the guidance of certain forces, followed tested
routes to specific destinations. Religious movements, the most
active and powerful social forces in late antiquity and the early
medieval periods, inevitably invited researchers of silk trade to
trace the routes of this commodity in the sphere of religions.

According to the distribution of surviving samples of silk and literary records in different languages, trade in exquisite silk textiles in this period can be roughly divided into three major circles. The first one was between China and India, with the main flow being of Chinese silk into India. Though there is no surviving sample of T'ang silk in India due to the climate and the custom of cremation, this pattern is well documented in Chinese, Sanskrit and Tamil literature. The second circle encompasses trade between the Byzantine empire and western Europe. This is evident from the many Byzantine silk samples preserved in church treasuries in western Europe. The third circle encompasses the Islamic world, stretching from the west Mediterranean region to Central Asia. The three circles happen to coincide with the three religious domains, namely the Buddhist domain in Asia, the Christian domain in Europe and West Asia, and the Islamic domain which included many areas of ancient civilizations in Eurasia.

The circulation of silk within the three circles flowed in spite of the monopoly imposed by the Chinese and Byzantine empires. In fact, transactions were actually encouraged by the rulers of the two empires because both were deeply involved in religious activities. As Buddhist eschatology shaped the concept of after life in the minds of Chinese rulers, their support for pilgrimages to India was natural. As Byzantine emperors aspired to become the spiritual leaders of the Christian world, they were obliged to patronize churches.

Besides transactions in luxury silks, ordinary silk textiles were also traded. This kind of trade established greater links between the three circles, and between the East and the West. Outside of the three major religious domains, there were many followers of other religions—Nestorians, Zoroastrians, Manichaeans, Jews—who travelled between the three domain-circles and acted as intermedia of cultural influences and carriers of silks. The religious activities of such traders were less documented or their documentation was not as well preserved as those of the followers of the three major living religions, and thus we may not be able to discern a clear·pattern of their participation in the Eurasian silk transactions. However, this does not lessen the importance of the links they provided between the three religious domains and trade circles.

Chapter I

Rise of Buddhist Folk Religion and Relic Transactions

S ilk trade between China and India started on a large scale in the early centuries of the Christian era. This trade developed with the spread of Buddhism from India to China. By the sixth century, when Buddhism was already established in China, the silk trade exemplified the various theological and institutional changes that had occurred in Buddhism in both countries. Along the ancient Central Asian routes and the recently developed sea routes, Chinese silk products continued to flow westwards, partially to India. Although other countries, including India, started to produce silk, China still exported silk in large quantities. As payment for Chinese silks India sent precious stones and other jewels as well as incense and spices to China from the early centuries AD. A combination of these luxuries gained a sacred status in Buddhist rituals and eventually crystallized in the Buddhist concept, the sapta-ratna (Seven Treasures). A few centuries later the Seven Treasures, though still highly esteemed among Buddhist devotees, became more or less common commodities in the trade. In the seventh century, a new and more eagerly sought after commodity entered long-distance trade—Buddhist relics. As Buddhist activities in both T'ang China and post-Gupta India evolved around relic-worship and translations, and as pilgrimages were undertaken for commercial purposes, the silk trade and the pilgrimage trade in Buddhist relics intertwined and formed the core of Sino-Indian cultural exchanges.

Buddhism in India suffered a general decline during the post-Gupta era, in spite of the patronage of a few staunch royal supporters such as King Harṣa (AD 606–47). This decline was marked by the emergence of Tantrism as a predominant phenomenon in Mahayana Buddhism, as well as in other Indian religious schools.

Tantrism was a religious phenomenon which encompassed a variety of religious theories and practices, ranging from certain esoteric theories which appeared earlier in Mahayanism, to some extremely vulgar practices derived from folk religions. Tantrism was not necessarily the cause of the decline of Buddhism as an institution, but it certainly signified another major transition where Buddhism deviated further from the original religion of the Buddha, and where the concerns of Buddhist theologians and mass devotees were even more similar to those of other religions. While the different religious groups shared certain esoteric traits, hostility between these sects became vehement due to fierce competition for royal patronage and followers. In this background, some Indian monks, Tantric teachers among them, went to China to preach and to make their careers.

In contrast, Buddhism in China was on the ascent, and reached its apex under the T'ang Dynasty (AD 617–907). Buddhist concepts, such as the causality between karma or the behaviour of individuals, and their welfare in the cycles of rebirth, were rooted in the minds of the Chinese populace. The Buddhist cosmos was woven into the large Chinese cosmology. Chinese Buddhists, however, also faced difficulties. Royal patronage was never stable. While the open minded T'ang emperors respected both Buddhism and Taoism, they were also open to other foreign religions—Christianity, Manichaeism, Islam—whose influence had just reached China. Puzzled by the new mysterious trends in Indian Buddhism and the new foreign teachings, Chinese Buddhist monks eagerly sought the real meaning of the religion to which they had devoted themselves. Some pilgrims like I-ching went to India to learn the disciplines which, he hoped, would strengthen Buddhist institutions in China. Others, like Hsüan-tsang, went there in search of new knowledge which could be imparted to Chinese Buddhists.

While Buddhist monks increased intellectual communication and the spread of knowledge between India and China, commercial transactions between the two civilizations also grew. As always, merchants, accompanied by pilgrims and preachers, travelled in caravans along the dangerous Central Asian routes or navigated the perilous seas. Pilgrims and preachers themselves also functioned as agents of transactions by carrying goods—silks, Buddhist texts, icons, relics—to pay for their travel costs, to win patronage and to receive hospitality. The complex of transactions in ideas and goods reveals some interesting phenomena in the pre-modern commercial world. If it seems amazing that a commodity like silk, useful and beautiful, but highly priced, prevailed across national borders and cultural boundaries for a long historical period, the emergence of some body residue from cremation as a sacred object and precious commodity in trade would be equally puzzling to a modern viewer. However, the transactions of these two kinds of goods, one secular and useful, the other sacred but of no use value, were interrelated, and modified the nature of each other. Silk became sacred when used for religious purposes, especially for relic worship. The relics of the Buddha gained in commercial value when there was a market demand for them. Buddhist relics played a special role in the silk trade, and the silk trade played a special role in the development of Buddhism. In the following pages, I examine the developments that took place in Buddhism in India and China, and then proceed to analyze the silk trade in the background of Buddhist pilgrimage movements.

Buddhism in India

The decline of Buddhism in many parts of India became obvious in the sixth century AD. The many deserted monasteries near desolate urban sites must have saddened the hearts of pilgrims from China, Korea and Sri Lanka. A pessimistic attitude also prevailed among Indian Buddhists, who read in this phenomenon the message that Buddhism was declining in the cycle of time. In India, it was rumoured that when the statue of the bodhisattva Avalokiteśvara in Bodha Gaya sank into the earth, the Buddhist dharma would no longer prevail in this world for this time cycle. When Hsüan-tsang visited the Mahabodhi monastery in Bodha Gaya, he noticed that the statue was buried upto its chest (Hui-li, 65). To the consolation of the pilgrims, the liberation of Buddhists was still feasible, even though they could not help the whole world cross the ocean of suffering as the Mahayanists wished to do. When Hsüan-tsang saw some empty monasteries in southwest India along the deserted trade routes, he believed that the monks there had ascended to heaven by achieving arhatship, a stage in the progress of reaching the Buddhist form of highest bliss, the nirvāṇa (Hui-li, 85).

Although Buddhist institutions still maintained a strong presence, a fundamental deterioration occurred in Buddhist theology. Tantrism emerged from being an obscure school to becoming an influential sect and even gained a foothold in the most respected Buddhist university of Nalanda. In the realm of theology, Tantrism is considered as the last stage of Indian Buddhism and is associated with its decline. It is hard to say whether Tantrism was the cause or effect or just a parallel phenomenon associated with the decline of Buddhism, as Tantrism appeared in both Buddhism and Hinduism at the time and Hinduism was reviving. But its appearance did indicate that Buddhism and Hinduism were drawing closer and there was a new development of religious emotion and practices among the Indian populace.

Though Tantrism was a general phenomenon among Indian religions of this period, Buddhist Tantrism had its own track of development and was based on Mahayana thought and practices. Mahayana bloomed into a popular school during the period that urban economy and commerce flourished in the Kuṣāṇa and Śaka states. While Nāgārjuna and other Mahayanist teachers advocated the philosophy of śūnyatā, the emptiness and meaningless of everything, monastic wealth increased rapidly. Surely this contradictory attitude towards material wealth was inherent from the very inception of Buddhism. While the Buddha preached eternal liberation by admonishing his disciples to ignore material wealth because worldly possessions were ephemeral, he had to appreciate and praise the lay patrons whose donations made the very material existence of the sangha possible. However, this inherent contradiction was certainly pushed to extremes in Mahayana thought and practices. Lay devotees and some monks traded their donations for religious merits for future and present benefits. Just like traders who wanted to make immediate profits from material transactions, Buddhist teachers also resorted to positive actions to gain immediate effects. They invoked magic *mantras* and *dhāraṇīs*, practiced meditation, even with physical aids (*haṭhayoga*), for reaching nirvāṇa in a short time, namely in one life, for protection in perilous situations, or for other tangible benefits. These magic invocations and physical practices became formalized and ritualized, and formed the essence of late Tantrism.

The difference between Mahayana and Tantrism was not in their doctrine, but in the means and speed of reaching nirvāṇa.

Tantrism almost totally depended on esoteric yogic exercises and incantations to shorten the process of achieving enlightenment within sixteen lives in the Lower Tantra and one life in the Higher Tantra (Basham 1975, 94–5). Between the two major Mahayana schools—Mādhyamika founded by Nāgārjuna and Yogācārin by Asanga—the latter placed more emphasis on yoga or meditation and was therefore more similar to the Tantric schools. A few yogācārin texts, such as *Yogācāryabhūmi Sastra*, were considered Tantric texts by some Buddhists and scholars. According to Tantric tradition, Asanga who lived in the third century AD received Tantra texts from the Maitreya. Here the link between Mahayana and Tantrism is obvious.

A set of Mahayana texts called *Prajñā-pāramitā* (perfection of wisdom) may provide an illustration of this transition. These texts were mainly Mahayana in nature. But two short versions of this group, i.e. *Vajracchedikā Prajñāpāramitā Sūtra* (*Vajra Sūtra* or *Diamond Sutra* in short) and *Prajñāpāramitā Haridaya Sūtra* (*Haridaya Sūtra* or *Heart Sūtra* in short), were well know Tantric texts for invocations at rituals and on perilous occasions. The very term *Prajñāpāramitā* came to be synonymous with the Buddhist goddess Tāra, who was the mother of all the Buddhas and a companion of Avalokiteśvara (Majumdar 1964, IV, 263).

The earliest text with the Sakti cult, namely *Guhyasamāja Tantra*, was probably composed as early as in the third century AD (Bhattacharyya 1931, xxix). It may have been secretly circulated within a small group for a long time. Some archaeological evidence of female consorts of Buddhist deities has been dated to the fifth century AD (Banerjea 1987, 53–4). Irrespective of when Buddhist Tantrism originated, it became popular only when all major religions in India accepted Tantrism. It was now that the Buddhas, bodhisattvas and Hindu deities all began to have female consorts. Therefore, one must cross the borders of religious schools to examine this phenomenon. This was a period when agricultural expansion from the Gupta period brought more and more tribes into the pale of civilization. As Brahmanism was inclusive in the religious practices of these tribes, the animal cults and female deities of tribal societies, especially the matriarchal ones, were assimilated into the Brahmanical pantheon (Sharma 1987). As for Buddhism, the development of Mahayanism, i.e. the combination of an extremely negative philosophy regarding

worldly affairs and an urgent searching for immediate physical
or material benefit through action, opened the door for various
cults in folk religions.

Buddhism was now so different from its earlier form, not only
from its primitive state but even from early Mahayana Buddhism,
that it presented a great challenge to Chinese Buddhists who had
always looked to their Indian teachers for guidance. The Buddhist
pilgrims who tried to discover the real meaning of their religion
noticed that when magic invocations and rituals became popular
among different religious groups, the teachers who were versed
with the most sophisticated knowledge of religion did not give up
their disputes. They studied the theories of other sects in order to
engage in debates. Competition for royal patronage through theological debates became sharp. When recording his experiences in
India, Hsüan-tsang often gave an exaggerated account of his triumph over other religious teachers. In fact he owed his victory in
a debate at Kanauj to the support of his patron, King Harsa, who
even threatened those who challenged Hsüan-tsang with harsh
punishment: 'Whoever dares to hurt the Dharma teacher (Hsüan-
tsang) will have his head cut off, and whoever dares to curse the
Dharma teacher will have his tongue cut out. Those who want to
discuss words and meaning (of the religion) are not subject to the
punishment.' The followers of the other sects were so scared that
no one voiced any opinion during the entire eighteen days of the
debate (Hui-li 109).

While Buddhist monks and other religious teachers, backed
by the security of landed property contributed by various feudal
lords, vehemently debated the most subtle differences between
their doctrines, the commoner devotees in India, along with
many other devotees of the period, sensed the similarities contained in different religions and adopted a more practical approach to devotion. These practices also provided pilgrims with
special experiences. Hsüan-tsang should have been grateful when
the temples of other religious sects provided hospitality to him
(Hui-li 45). Once, when he was robbed of all his belongings,
three hundred important residents who belonged to other religious sects in Takka city went to pay their respects to him and
each one donated a piece of cotton cloth to him (Hui-li). Though
he was convinced that he had converted these residents to Buddhism, it is more likely that they respected him from a feeling

of general religious piety. On another occasion, when Hsüan-tsang was almost killed by worshippers of Durga for sacrifice, he was once again released when the people found out his religious character, though he believed he had been saved by the Maitreya Buddha (Hui-li 55). A less self-centered monk, Hui-ch'ao from Sila (Korea), rightly observed that the piety of the Indian people existed throughout the 'five parts of India'.[1] Thus, religious travellers did not carry food with them as they could easily beg for, and receive, food everywhere (Tripitaka v. 51, 976c).[2]

Though the lay followers of Buddhism were not necessarily sensitive to the subtle differences in theology among the different sects, they had a long-standing special practice which made them different from the followers of other religions. The Buddhists paid great attention to funeral rites and commemorated the dead with stupas from early times. *Śarīr pūjā* (funeral ceremony) was performed for both the Buddha and other monks (Schopen 1991).[3] The cult of the stupa and the related cult surrounding the corporeal remains of the Buddha were essential for early monastic life (Schopen 1989).[4] However, one should remember that for Buddhists, the funeral ceremony was not an occasion to mourn the end of life, but to send loved ones to the other state of being, which ranged from the worst state of being tortured in hell or wandering as a ghost, to the less terrible possibility of being born as an animal or a human, to the better outcome of enjoying heaven as a deity, to the best choice of reaching nirvāṇa. Buddhist artists often depicted life after death on the sculptures of stupas, especially scenes in various Buddhist heavens, which often appealed more

---

[1] 'Five parts of India' was an ancient Indian geographical concept which divides the known world of Indian civilization into five parts—middle, north, south, east and west. Chinese pilgrims since Hsüan-tsang adopted this appellation for India.

[2] Hui-ch'ao did not specify the kind of travellers who begged for food. But he excluded kings and chiefs, and traders as people who would not be likely to beg; this left religious figures as those who travelled and begged.

[3] In his article, Schopen convincingly argues that *śarīr pūjā* did not mean relic worship during the early stage of Buddhism, but meant a funeral ceremony, and that only later did this word indicate relic worship; p. 203.

[4] In his article, Schopen argues that though the extant Pali *vinaya* does not include clear rules about the stupa cult, these rules very likely did exist but were eliminated later on, judging by other evidence.

to devotees than the carefree but bland state of nirvāṇa. They used their vivid imaginations derived from experiences in the living world. After Mahayanism introduced the many heavens and Buddha's lands into the Buddhist cosmos, the sculptures on stupas looked even more like an effusion of life.

Concerning the wide diffusion of the remains of the Buddha, one popular belief is that the relics of the Buddha taken from the funeral pyre at Kusinagara were divided among eight kings. In the third century, the Mauryan king Aśoka (c. 273–236 BC) opened seven of them and redistributed the relics to build numerous stupas. Archaeological evidence from some Central Indian sites, namely Sanchi, Andher, Satdhara and Sonari, proves that stupas enshrined the supposed relics of the Buddha and his disciples from the second to the first century BC (A. Ghosh 1989, vol. I, 270a). The stupa cult and relic worship were the distinguishing religious practices of Buddhism, and these stupas with famous relics were established as centres of pilgrimage. From the sixth century AD, those relics attracted many Indian and foreign pilgrims. The quantity of relics was exceedingly large in every important stupa, and they were distributed over the entire subcontinent.

One can hardly attribute the wide distribution of relics totally to the efforts of Aśoka, because the distribution of relics or sacred Buddhist sites and pilgrimage routes obviously changed in each period. It is well known that Śakyamuni spent his whole life in the middle and lower Ganges region. The earliest Buddhist sites associated with his life stories were all located there. During the early centuries AD when Buddhism flourished under Kuṣāṇa patronage, and northwest India became the centre of an urban economy, many sacred sites appeared in this region. Trapuṣa and Bhallika were places near Bactra which had two stupas where the hair and nails of the Buddha were stored (Hui-li 32). These two place names were the same as the names of the two earliest devotees who offered food to the Buddha just when he attained enlightenment. The name Bhallika suggests a link with Bactra. Whether these merchants originally came from this region or whether people later used this name to create a local legend is neither clear nor important. What is important is that whatever locations could be linked with the Buddha became pilgrimage sites. Using the legend that the Kuṣāṇa king Kaniṣka fought with a middle Indian king for a famous bowl of the Buddha, Kuwayama made a historic-geographic analysis of the rise of Buddhist cults in north-west India. According to him, this legend was deliberately created to make the bowl a symbol of Buddhism in the heart of the Kuṣāṇa state (Kuwayama 1990, 49). In the early fifth century, it attracted many Chinese pilgrims, namely Chih-meng, Fa-yung, Hui-lan, Tao-yin and their fellow travellers, to Purushapura (ibid. 49–53). Actually, this legend reflects the connection between Buddhist shrines and trade routes during the Kuṣāṇa period.

In the T'ang period, some of the pilgrims from China still followed the northwest routes in spite of the many inconveniences encountered due to the de-urbanization of that area. By then, the Buddha's begging bowl had somehow disappeared from the scene, but his bones and other body relics had become even more important. Hsüan-tsang passed through Bactra, Bamiyana, Nagara-hara and Kapisa. He was disappointed with the empty altar which used to hold the sacred bowl at Gandhara, and so he proceeded to Kashmira before descending to the north Indian plain. Compared to the route that Fa-hsien followed about two hundred years earlier, Hsüan-tsang made a great detour. The obvious reason was that there were more places containing relics for him to worship in his time, a result of Buddhist missions which spread the ritual of relic worship. In Bactra, there was a tooth and a broom of the Buddha, in addition to the hair and nails buried inside a stupa in the nearby city of Bhallika (Hui-li 32). In Bamiyana, there was Buddha's tooth, about 15 × 12cm (5 × 4 ts'un) in size, plus a tooth (9 × 6cm, or 3 × 2 ts'un) of the king of the Golden Dharma Wheel, a legendary figure in Buddhist myths (Hui-li 34). At Nagarahara, he worshiped the same parietal bone of the Buddha that was worshiped by Fa-hsien, in different circumstances. When Fa-hsien was there, the worship ceremony was a state affair headed by the king. Hsüan-tsang attended as a pilgrim by paying one gold coin. In the same manner as other pilgrims, Hsüan-tsang bound a piece of silk around the bone to make a silk rubbing by paying five gold coins, because he was told the rubbing print could predict one's future. Many people were willing to practise this in spite of the high cost (HT 229). Hsüan-tsang was luckier than Fa-hsien and was able to see the skull of the Buddha which looked like a lotus leaf and the Buddha's eye which was as big as a small apple (HT 228). He also saw a smaller piece of parietal bone and other remains of the Buddha in Kapisa (HT 154, Kuwayama

1990, 280). In Gandhara, a stupa stored as much as a hundred litres (one hu) of relics (Hui-li, 39) while more than one litre of relics was stored in Kashmira (ibid., 43).

In east India, another litre of relics was in a stupa near the city ruins of Pataliputra (ibid., 64). There were some relics near the Venuvana Garden near Nalanda. It was said that the Magadha king, Ajātaśatru, built a stupa there to store the relics of the Buddha, and King Aśoka obtained these relics to distribute them all over India (ibid., 71). The Mahabodhi monastery in Bodha Gaya not only held relics but also exhibited them at an annual ceremony held in the first month of a year. There were two kinds of relic worship activities—of bones and flesh. The former were small balls, reddish-white in colour. The latter were fresh red balls, the size of peas (ibid., 97). The relics in east India were transported by the new route of pilgrimage and trade—the sea route. The Mahabodhi monastery in Bodh Gaya was donated by a king in Sri Lanka during the reign of the Indian king, Samudra Gupta (FYCL v. 29, Tripitaka v. 53, 502c). On the island of Sri Lanka, an extremely auspicious and efficacious tooth of the Buddha was worshiped with all kinds of jewels and was strictly guarded. It was believed that if the tooth was lost, the whole island would be swallowed by a rākṣasa (HT 880, WPW 68). There must have been other relic sites which Hsüan-tsang neither visited nor heard of. It is surprising that this widely travelled pilgrim neither visited nor heard of such important Buddhist relic sites as Sanchi and Nagarjunakonda. Hui-ch'ao mentioned a big tooth and some bone relics of a pratyeka Buddha in north India, but he did not give the exact location (Tripitaka v. 51, 976c). By the eighth century, when I-ching undertook his travels in South and South-east Asia, worship of the tooth in Sri Lanka was the first priority for the sea route pilgrims. Judging from his records of about sixty pilgrims from China interior, Korea, Central Asia and Tibet, the above sites, in addition to a few others, such as the stairs to commemorate the descending of the Buddha from the heavens to the north Indian area of Samkisa, constituted the commonest itinerary followed by pilgrims (WPW). To bind a piece of silk cloth on the parietal bone to get a rubbing print from the relic of the Buddha was routine, but the precious bone was somehow shifted from Nagarahara to Kapisa (WPW 11, 32). An increase in the number of sites containing relics indicates that relic worship among the Buddhists had gained popularity in the preceding centuries. This development was rooted in the particular eschatological concern of Buddhism about the world after death and the emphasis on rituals for the dead. The growing popularity of relic worship was probably due to the spread of Buddhist eschatology and the Buddhist absorption of the religious practices of folk religions; the emphasis shifted from meditation and philosophical thinking to rituals and invocations, and the relics, which represented the person of the Buddha, provided the best objects for worship and were considered instruments for invocations.

The frequent visits of pilgrims to the sites of relics throughout the subcontinent resembled a booming tourist business. In the seventh century, the many stupas recorded the historical or quasi-historical sites, and the sites of relics along the trade routes were made ready for accepting donations from worshippers. Though tradition has attributed all of them to Aśoka (Hui-li 94), they surely represented the efforts of many generations of kings, Buddhist institutions and lay devotees. If inventing historical sites was a common means of creating a pilgrimage centre, fighting for relics became more common in the seventh and later centuries. King Harṣa took the tooth of the Buddha, 4 cm in size (1.5 ts'un), from Kashmira by force and guarded it in a monastery near Kanauj as his personal object of worship (Hui-li 109–10).

In addition to the attraction of relics, some travel facilities were established for the tourist business. I have mentioned that the Mahabodhi monastery was a donation by a king of Sri Lanka during the Gupta era. Tradition has it that a Gupta king built a monastery for Chinese monks to the east of the Nalanda (WPW 103). The Chinese monastery had been abandoned by the time of I-ching's visit, but the Gandharachanda monastery, probably built by the Kuṣāṇas, offered hospitality to monks from the northern countries such as Central Asia, China and Korea and accepted them as formal members (WPW 101). A monastery built by the Kapisa state to the east of the Mahabodhi also accepted people from the north. Another monastery built by a southern sovereign hosted monks from the south (WPW 102). I-ching felt that there were not enough monasteries to host Chinese pilgrims, and so he pleaded with the T'ang emperor to build monasteries in India even before he returned home (Wang Pang-wei 1993, 39). About two centuries later, when Chi-ye went to India in 964 along with three hundred Chinese monks, he stayed in a Chinese monastery, supported by eight villages, in Magadha, where (Chinese) monks came and went as if it was their home (Tripitaka v. 51, 982a). There seem to have been more Chinese monasteries around that region. An *araṇya* near New Rajgraha was attached to this Chinese monastery (ibid.). There was a Kashmir Chinese monastery and a West Chinese monastery or the Old Chinese monastery near Nalanda (ibid., 982b). Wang Pang-wei suggests that the conditions for Chinese pilgrims improved considerably after I-ching's visit, as there were several more monasteries to host them (Wang Pang-wei 1993, 39).

We do not know who built those Chinese monasteries, but we know Chinese pilgrims and sovereigns did try to commemorate their presence in these sacred places. The inscriptions on stelae made by the monk, Tao-hsi, and the T'ang envoy, Wang Hsüan-ts'e, in the Mahabodhi monastery are no longer extant. But a stele made by Chinese monks in the late tenth century and another by an envoy in the eleventh century for a Sung emperor have survived (Cunningham 1961, 72–2; Chou Ta-fu 1957). These stelae with foreign scripts must have been spectacular objects in an age when pilgrimages were popular.

Popular Buddhism and Relics in T'ang China

The trend of absorbing folk religious practices and Tantrism within Indian Buddhism also influenced Chinese Buddhism, for Chinese devotees had constantly looked for inspiration to their Indian teachers. In a strict sense, several Tantric Buddhist teachers from India and Central Asia—Subhakara (Shan-wu-wei), Vajrabodhi (Chin-kang-chih) and Amoghavajra (Pu-k'ung-chin-kang)—started a new school in China by introducing Tantric rituals into the T'ang court (Chou I-liang 1945, 246). These Tantric practices prevailed in China for only about two hundred and fifty years, if one does not count its revival a few centuries later. Its impact on Chinese thought was as limited as its duration (ibid., 246). However, if one considers Buddhist Tantrism in a more general sense, i.e. as a part of popular beliefs among Indian and Chinese Buddhists and other religious schools, its influence on China was earlier and greater.

As I have mentioned earlier, early Tantric texts were a part of

Mahayana texts. However, differences in content and style widened when Tantrism became involved with extreme religious practices. Buddhist Sanskrit in early Mahayana texts was a sophisticated literary genre, but 'Sanskrit in which the Tantras are written, is as rule, just as barbarous as their contents' (Winternitz 1971, v. 2, 401). Nevertheless, Chinese Buddhist scholars, who were as learned and sincere as Hsüan-tsang, could not tell or did not care about such differences. Actually, one of the major purposes of Hsüan-tsang's trip to India was to learn *Yogācārya-bhūmi Śastra* (simplified as *Yoga Śastra*), a yogācārin text with Tantric elements. During Hsüan-tsang's stop in Kucha in Central Asia, the local teacher, Mu-ch'a-chu-to, tried to persuade him to stay there instead of going farther into India, as 'all Buddhist texts are available here'. Hsüan-tsang then questioned: 'Is *Yoga Śastra* available here?' The teacher admonished him: 'Why do you ask about this heretic text? True followers of the Buddha should not learn this text.' Hsüan-tsang simply took this advice as a sign of his ignorance and lost respect for the teacher (Hui-li 26). During the entire period of his stay in India, the *Yoga Śastra* was his major course of study while he also explored other fields of knowledge, including Brahmanical literature, linguistics, philosophy and sciences (Hui-li 67, 74, 75). For him, understanding the *Yoga Śastra* was the very standard of learning. On hearing that some teachers from Sri Lanka were extremely learned, Hsüan-tsang tested them with the *Yoga Śastra*. He was relieved when he found that their knowledge of this particular text did not exceed that of his own teacher in Nalanda, and thus not his own (ibid., 87). He was discerning enough to realize the differences among various Buddhist texts, but he argued that when emphasizing one aspect of learning, the sages did not mean to oppose each other in their teachings. Only those who were puzzled by the differences thought they were contradictory doctrines (ibid., 97).

Actually, Hsüan-tsang's own religious practices were much closer to the practices of folk religions than many people realized. Once he learned the *Heart Sūtra*, one of the short versions of the *Prajñāpāramitā* group, from a sick beggar in Sichuan in southwest China. This sutra became the most efficacious mantra for him when travelling in the Central Asian desert. It helped him even when the invocation of Avalokiteśvara failed (Hui-li 16). The *Heart Sūtra* became quite popular in T'ang China. A T'ang legend has it that a man came back to life after death because he recited Buddhist texts, including the *Heart Sūtra* (Chang Chuo 68). On returning to China, Hsüan-tsang offered a more accurate translation of the *Vajra Sūtra*, another short version of the *Prajñā-pāramitā* texts, at the request of the emperor, because the text was well respected in India (ibid., 153) and its recitation generated much merit. Of the vast literature that Hsüan-tsang brought back from India, this text probably had the most far-reaching influence. A book entitled *Yu-yang Tsa-tsu* by Tuan Ch'eng-shih (*c.* 803–63) contained anecdotes about Ch'angan, the capital of the T'ang, including a whole chapter on the miracles wrought by reciting the *Vajra Sūtra* (v. II, ch. 7). The *Vajra Sūtra* could save one from hell when all Buddhist merits from other deeds failed. A story goes that when a man who loved eating meat but who also used to recite the *Vajra Sūtra*, faced trial in hell, there was a high pile of dead animals and a pile of text rolls of the *Vajra Sūtra* placed in front of the judge. The texts, as evidence of his merit, automatically wiped out the pile of dead animals, evidence of his sin, thus freeing the man from hell (Tuan 267).

When Tantric teachers from India competed with Chinese sorcerers for royal patronage by praying for rain or stopping floods and other plagues (see Chou I-liang 1945), ideas and legends of Tantric Buddhism and folklore were woven into Chinese mythology. Buddhist cosmology with its many heavens, Buddhas' lands, human worlds and hells was well known to all Buddhist believers or even non-believers in T'ang China (Tuan 31). Taoists, unwilling to accepted the cosmology, produced a parallel one with the same kind of hierarchy (ibid., 12 ff). Later these two parallel cosmological systems became interwoven and eventually formed the specific Chinese mythology with different sets of deities occupying various corners of the cosmos. In the *Hsi-yu-chi*, a fiction on Hsüan-tsang's pilgrimage written in the Ming Dynasty, the Jade Emperor of Taoism occupied the highest throne in heaven, most Buddhist deities were clustered in the western heaven and the Avalokiteśvara stayed in the southern sea.

Below the level of theology, Buddhist monks, both Indian and Chinese, practised all kinds of sorceries in T'ang society. It is not surprising that so many stories abound of monks chasing away evil spirits by using invocations and mysterious rituals and symbols (e.g. Tuan 10, 19, 212) because the means of Tantrism, the *mantra* (invocation), *mudrā* (hand gesture) and *maṇḍala* (ritual circle), were very similar to the witchcraft of all cultures. But in a specific area of religious practice, i.e. funeral rites, Buddhism had an advantage over other popular beliefs or even orthodox Confucianism. Confucius never commented on the world after death. Confucian rationalism was too cruel for most people who constantly faced the pain of death and separation from loved ones. The Taoist salvation of immortality was not easy to achieve. Though the Chinese had placed various burial goods in tombs since the dawn of civilization in the belief that death was a continuation of life, there had not been a systematic and logical explanation of how these items served those who passed away, until the advent of Buddhism. Even among Indian religions, the teachings of the Buddha were the first that explicitly depicted the life-death cycles via continuous rebirths. The early monastic sites of Buddhism in South Asia were often associated with cremation or burial grounds, suggesting that monasteries were engaged in funeral rites in early times.[5] As Buddhism provided the most vivid pictures of what happened after death, and Buddhist monasteries did not mind taking care of the dead, this part of Buddhist theology became the most deep-rooted concept in Chinese popular belief, and Buddhist rituals became essential at the funerals of emperors, royal family members and commoners. Soon after Emperor T'ai-tsung consolidated his hold on the throne, he sponsored Buddhist services in 628 for those who had died while establishing the T'ang Dynasty, and for the deceased rulers of the preceding Sui Dynasty (Weinstein 1987, 12). Whether T'ai-tsung believed in Buddhism or not, he trusted that Buddhist services would console the souls of his dead friends and followers and pacify the souls of dead enemies. Family monasteries and cloisters were built to take care of the souls of the dead and nunneries were built to accept widows. Buddhist rituals were so powerful that they could either expel or absorb all the evil elements of death. Hsüan-tsang had the famous

[5] With his unique graceful humour, Gregory Schopen convinced his audience at the Center of Asian Studies, University of Texas at Austin, that quite a few early monasteries in Central India were actually built on cremation grounds or graveyards. This association means that when Buddhism spread to that region, monasteries started their religious practice with funeral rites. The lecture entitled 'Immigrant Monks and the Protohistorical Dead—the Buddhist Occupation of Early Burial Sites in India' was given on 24 Oct. 1991.

stupa in his Ts'u-en monastery built at the expense of the numerous women who passed away in the emperors' harem—the
emperor gave the order to donate all the clothes of these women
to build the stupa (Hui-li 160).

In its ability to satisfy people's imaginations about future lives,
Buddhism had the most appeal for the masses. However, during
the T'ang Dynasty (AD 618–907) many religions and beliefs prospered, and many legends circulated among the people. In addition
to the preachings of Christianity, Manichaeism and Zoroastrianism, legends from India gained easy entrance into T'ang China.
Yakṣasa, benign and lovely spirits in Indian myth, became ugly
and evil creatures in China, but hurt only those who ate beef
(Tuan 135).

In the confusion of religious ideas and legends, serious Buddhist teachers were concerned with explaining the differences that
existed among various beliefs to their lay followers. When he
met the Turkic chief, Yagub Khan, Hsüan-tsang observed that
the Turkic people worshipped fire and thus did not use wooden
beds or seats. Probably sensitive enough to realize that the Khan
would not understand much Buddhist philosophy, he preached
to the nomad about good behaviour that avoided killing, and
tried to convince him that *Prajñāpāramitā* could save him from
the cycles of sin (Hui-li 28). The Khan seemed to accept his
teachings, probably out of general piety for all religions. With
this kind of experience, Buddhist teachers understood that the
worship of objects that embodied Buddhism was necessary for
their lay followers. During his stay in India, having witnessed
how Indian Buddhists treasured the relics, Hsüan-tsang must
have recognized the symbolic and practical significance of bringing back some relics in addition to the texts and images of
Buddha, especially after he heard the story of King Harṣa obtaining a tooth of the Buddha from Kashmira by force, and after
he observed the vigilant manner in which another tooth of the
Buddha was guarded in Sri Lanka. He did not record how he
obtained the relics, but an inventory of the things he brought
from India lists a hundred and fifty pieces of flesh relics (Hui-li
126). In summarizing Hsüan-tsang's life achievements, Yen-tsung
again listed the 'more than six hundred kinds of Buddhist texts
in both Mahayana and Hinayana, seven images of the Buddha,
and more than a hundred pieces of relics' (Hui-li 229). All the

items, of course, were received with great enthusiasm by the emperor and the people of T'ang China.

The worship of relics did not begin at the time of the T'ang Dynasty, even though Hsüan-tsang may have believed that he was the first one to have brought authentic relics from India. Starting in India, Buddhists liked to commemorate the relics and activities of Śakyamuni or other Buddhas. King Aśoka had the stupa for the Buddha 'Konākamana' enlarged, and had stone monuments built at the birth place of the Śakyamuni Buddha (Durt 1987, 4/1226). The appearance of many Buddhist sites in the northwest region of the South Asian subcontinent in the first few centuries AD, as discussed in the earlier part of this chapter, also resulted from archaeological efforts to locate the relics and miracles of the Buddha. Since the fourth century, Buddhist *archaeologia sacra* became popular in many parts of the religious domain of Buddhism, including China and Korea (Durt 1987). Chinese Buddhists made archaeological surveys and excavations to discover the relics of the Buddha under the so-called Aśoka stupas, which were supposed to have been built in China during the reign of the virtuous Indian Buddhist king (Zürcher 1972, 277). By the sixth century, these efforts were obviously supported by the rulers. In 538, Kao-tsu of the Liang Dynasty declared amnesty twice due to the discovery of 'real relics'. On the first occasion, the relics were found while repairing a so-called 'Aśoka stupa'. Another time a relic was found by a peasant when cultivating his land (KHMC v. 15; Tripitaka v. 52, 203c–204a). In the second year of the Sui Dynasty (AD 582) the emperor issued an edict announcing the distribution of the relics he had received from an Indian monk before he gained power. Because the relics had brought good fortune to the emperor, he decided that they should be worshipped all over the country in thirty prefectures. Thirty monks who were good at preaching led thirty missions which carried the relics. Two attendants and one officer were part of every mission. A procession of five horses carried 120 catties of frankincense. After a ceremony, the emperor personally divided the relics from a container made of the Seven Treasures into thirty bottles made of red glass, which were in turn put into golden bottles. After sealing the bottles with glue made of frankincense, the thirty missions carried the relics to the thirty stipulated places. Meanwhile, all the thirty prefectures had built a stupa and were ready to receive the relics with all the attendant rituals. Later, every prefecture reported the good omens that occurred when the relics were received (KHMC v. 17; Tripitaka v. 52, 213a–221a).

In spite of all the elaborate preparations, these relics did not have authentic Indian origins. Furthermore, as the Sui emperors had used these relics to claim their legitimacy, the T'ang emperors certainly did not want to inherit them. Perhaps Hsüan-tsang's coming back with relics inspired Kao-tsung of the T'ang Dynasty. His envoy, Wang Hsüan-ts'e, brought back the precious parietal bone from Kapisa in 661, to be worshipped at the imperial palace (FYCL v. 29; Tripitaka v. 53, 497c–498a).[6] A few years later, in 664–665, a teacher of Vinaya Hui-ning went to Kalinga, where he translated a section of an early Buddhist text, *Agāma*, along with an Indian teacher, Jnanabhadra. He sent a disciple with this translation which dealt exclusively with the Buddha's instructions for his own cremation and the merit to be derived from worshipping his relics, back to China in order to get the attention of the emperor. I-ching noticed that this text differed very much from the nirvāna texts of the Mahayana school (WPW 77–9). Hui-ning noticed the detailed explanation given in this text to the merit incurred by worshipping relics. According to this text, the worship of a portion, no matter how small, of the real relics would give the same amount of merit as the worship of all the body relics of the Buddha (Tripitaka v. 12, 900–906).

However, as relics were well guarded treasures in India, not all pilgrims were able to acquire them. The fortunate ones, such as Wu-k'ung, who went to India in the late eighth century, received a tooth of the Buddha from his instructor (Tripitaka v. 51, 980b). But the Dharma teacher, Ming-yüan, was less fortunate. He tried to steal the famous tooth of the Buddha in Sri Lanka but was caught. He suffering greatly from the resultant insults and died while still on his pilgrimage (WPW 68). Thus, most pilgrims who went to India were satisfied with bringing back new texts and authentic images. For example, the monk Ling-yün, scrupulously copied the image of Maitreya and the image of the Buddha under the bodhi tree with the exact measurement in every detail (WPW 168) and these images were probably well regarded in China for

---

[6] This was not the parietal bone worshipped by both Fa-hsien and Hsüan-tsang, which was in Nagarahara, but the smaller one in Kapisa.

the purpose of preaching Buddhism. Among the many images brought back by the envoy Wang Hsüan-ts'e, the one from Bodha Gaya became a model for making statues of the Maitreya under the bodhi tree (Chang Yen-yüan v. 3, 135).

In spite of the other sacred items available, the body relics of the Buddha were the most desirable objects of worship, because they were explicitly considered objects of worship from the earliest stage of Buddhism, and because they were the simplest, most direct personal link between the Buddha and his followers. With the spread of Buddhism over a large geographical area, the demand for such personal links increased. But an increase in the supply of relics would mean a reduction in their authenticity. In the event the gap between the increased demand for and the rigid supply of relics was bridged in a practical way. Some Buddhist texts recommended the use of substitutes made of gold, silver, lapis lazuli, crystal, agate or glass, i.e. one of the sacred Seven Treasures (P'ang 1989, 35). Though the concept of the Seven Treasures that appeared in Buddhist literature dates to the early centuries AD, till that time the precious items were used only as donations and decorations for relics and stupas. But now, as objects of worship, they gained in value. For those who could not afford these luxuries, clean sands and materials such as bamboo and wood were moulded into the shape of relics (P'ang 35). Another kind of substitute was 'Dharma relics'. These were copied sutras stored in micro-stupas made of ash from the burning of incense (Hsiang Ta 1957, 120–1). The relics found in Lin-t'ung in Shensi province, under the stupa of the Ch'ing-shan monastery, dated to the T'ang period, were of crystal in the shape of rice grains. They were stored in two green glass bottles, which were set in a golden coffin within a silver outer coffin under a precious canopy (P'ang 35). Of the four finger bones found in a cell under the stupa of the Fa-men monastery, dated to the T'ang period, in Fu-feng county, Shensi province, only one of them was a kind of bone. The other three were circular cylinders, probably also made of crystal.[7] A report on the discovery of the four finger bones gives the impression that the 'bone' most treasured by T'ang worshippers was the one made of crystal, 40.3 × 17.55 × 20.11mm in size. It was covered with eight layers of containers made of various precious materials. The

7 I saw the relics at an exhibition held in the History Museum, Beijing, 1988.

real bone was also covered with four layers of containers, in addition to one layer of silk textile with golden threads (*People's Daily*, 2 June 1987, p. 3). Apparently, whether of bone or crystal, the fingers received respect.

As Buddhism was the predominant religion in T'ang China, with stupas spread all over the country, the quantity and variety of relics worshipped must have been phenomenal. Perhaps inspired either by stories of obtaining relics at the death of Buddhist sacred characters, such as the king of the Golden Wheel, or by the Indian example of treasuring relics of the Buddha's disciples, the relics of some divinized monks gained the status in China of objects of worship. For instance, a boy who was supposedly born in the posture of the Buddha and who started to recite the sutra *Saddharmapundarika* at the age of seven produced some granule relics after his cremation (Tuan 259).

Though the popularity of Buddhism made substitutions necessary, and though the Buddhist texts made these substitutions worthy of devotion, the issue of the difference between authentic relics and domestic imitations had to be solved on a practical plane. The authenticity of certain relics did not derive from the materials of the object, i.e. whether they were human or animal bones, or something totally non-biological, but depended instead on their Indian origin. Genuine relics were those from India with an authentic history or pedigree, which implied that they had been fought for by kings, or had been worshipped for generations by renowned pilgrims. These genuine relics from India were virtually state property, as no commoner could afford to keep a major object for worship and pilgrimage. The parietal bone obtained by Wang Hsüan-ts'e from Kapisa no doubt belonged to the emperor. Relics brought by Hsüan-tsang and the tooth by the monk Wu-k'ung were duly given as tributes to the court (Tripitaka v. 51, 981a). This tradition continued till the Sung Dynasty (960–1279). Monk Chi-ye, who travelled to India in 964, presented the relics he obtained to the emperor Kao-tsu (Tripitaka v. 51, 982b).

Since the relics were state property, their worship was also a state affair. The relics kept in the imperial palace were worshipped on a daily basis, probably by designated personnel. Those kept in the important monasteries were frequently taken out for display and worship by imperial order. The finger bones in the Fa-men monastery are the most well-known example. In the year 819 the bones were taken to Ch'ang-an under an imperial order. After being worshipped in the imperial palace for three days, they were taken to every monastery in Ch'ang-an for display. 'Princes, dukes, scholars, and commoners competed with each other to make donations, everyone was afraid to be left behind.' The whole process was so extravagant that a famous scholar, Han Yü, also a minister of law, wrote a severe criticism to the emperor (CTS v. 15, 460). He warned the emperor:

For a mind so enlightened as your majesty's could never believe such nonsense. The minds of the common people however are as easy to becloud as they are difficult to enlighten. If they see your majesty acting in this way, they will think that you are wholeheartedly worshipping the Buddha, and will say: 'His majesty is a great sage, and even he worships the Buddha with all his heart. Who are we that we should any of us grudge our lives in his service?' They will cauterize the crowns of their heads, burn off their fingers, and in bands of tens or hundreds cast off their clothing and scatter their money and from daylight to darkness follow one another in the cold fear of being too late. Young and old in one mad rush will forsake their trades and callings and, unless you issue some prohibition, will flock round the temples, hacking their arms and mutilating their bodies to do him homage. And the laughter that such unseemly and degenerate behaviour will everywhere provoke will be no light matter (Birch 1965, 252).

His appeal to rationality did not change the attitude of the T'ang emperors. On another occasion, in the year 873, the ceremony was even more grandiose. The procession consisted of ten thousand people carrying silk banners and other ritual decorations. The sound of worshipping the Buddha shook the earth; the emperor went to the monastery personally to worship while distributing silver bowls, brocade and silks to the elders of the city. It was such an important event that all the residents crowded the streets to watch. One cut his arm and another burnt his head to show his devotion (Su Er. 2/13b ff).

The significance of relics in T'ang China motivated worshippers to undertake pilgrimages to obtain them. Information about relics in India was widely circulated in T'ang society. While Tuan Ch'eng-shih collected information about there being a tooth in Bamiyana (ibid., 97) and relics in Kapisa (ibid., 98) the T'ang emperors had the sacred sites, including the sites with relics, duly recorded (FYCL; Tripitaka v. 53, 496c). This record mentions all the sites with relics and their miracles. It notes that Buddhist sites in India at that time, involved with stories of Buddha's former births and his achievements during his lifetime, were all commemorated with stupas and inscriptions. Even though the city of Kapilavastu had been in ruins for centuries, the sites related to the Buddha's life, such as the gate through which Śakyamuni left home to become a recluse, were labelled. At the location where the Buddha saw the old, sick and dead people and where he saw *śramaṇa* (recluses), there were statues of these characters to commemorate the scenes. An image of *mahānirvāṇa*, i.e. a statue of Buddha in a lying position, was located near the site of Kushinagara city where the Buddha passed away. In short, 'every step and stay of the Buddha was commemorated with stupas' (FYCL v. 29; Tripitaka v. 53, 504b). While Indian Buddhists built these stupas and statues, Chinese authorities had them recorded and compiled into a guide book. It seemed to be a joint effort from both the Indian and Chinese sides to encourage pilgrimages.

Thanks to the efforts of many pilgrims, and occasionally foreign rulers,[8] many important monasteries in the Chinese capital, Ch'ang-an, housed some genuine relics from India.[9] Schafer calculated that 'there were teeth of the Buddha in four temples of the capital city, each with its special festival which attracted hordes of believers, who offered medicines, foods, fruits, and flowers and, in fragrant clouds of incense . . . tossed cash like rain toward the storied hall of the Buddha's tooth' (1963, 267).

As objects of public worship, Buddhist relics should never have become commodities for sale, for giving up holy objects for profit was a sacrilege. However, transactions in relics had been going on for centuries, though under certain conditions. Pious emperors would not let the finger bones go for any price, just as the kings of Sri Lanka would not let the tooth of the Buddha go out of the country for fear that the whole island would be swallowed by rākṣasas. Meanwhile, anti-Buddhist emperors also would not let the objects be traded in the market for fear that the bones would

[8] In 637 the ruler of Kapisa gave in tribute some relics in addition to good horses to the T'ang court (TFYK 970/8a; Kuwayama 1990, 433).

[9] There were relics under the stupa of the Hua-yen monastery (Tuan 249); there were bones and a tooth in the Ta-hsing-shan monastery (KHMC v. 15; Tripitaka v. 52, 203b).

become valuable in transactions. Relics, either bones or granules, had no absolute use value. They were precious only because of the sacredness attached to them. Therefore, on his way back to China, to thwart the greed of robbers, Hsüan-tsang sent someone ahead of the procession announcing that the items they carried were only Buddhist texts, images and relics (Hui-li 114). The robbers, he thought, would not care for relics because their authenticity would be in doubt. However, the relics that were transferred by respected pilgrims had great value. A successful transference meant that the relics themselves were willing to go to the new owners and carried good fortune with them to their new destinations. Commenting on the failure of Ming-yüan to steal the tooth from Sri Lanka (c. 664–65), I-ching felt that the translation could have succeeded only with divine permission (WPW 68).

Pilgrims and traders were well aware of this special, though abstract, value of relics, and the status, and perhaps wealth, the relics would bring them once they reached their destinations. An anecdote of the pilgrim, Wu-k'ung, illustrates the special value of relics. Once when travelling in a caravan along a Central Asian route, Wu-k'ung carried his texts and the Buddha's tooth that he had received as a gift. Along the way a dangerous storm threatened their lives, and the head of the traders announced that there must be someone who was carrying either relics or special treasure which had invoked the greed of the dragon in a nearby lake. Whoever had these should throw them into the lake in order to protect the whole caravan. Now Wu-k'ung prayed fervently and promised to allocate part of the merits gained by the translation of the relics to the dragon. The storm finally passed, and Wu-k'ung was convinced that his sincere prayer had moved the dragon (Tripitaka v. 51, 980b–c).

In the case of Wu-k'ung, as in the cases of the other pilgrims who brought relics, the Chinese emperor granted official positions and honours (Tripitaka v. 51, 981a). But on other occasions, the buyers had to pay silk or cash. The small parietal bone that Wang Hsüan-ts'e brought from Kapisa in 661 was worth four thousand bolts of silk. Wang bought the bone in Kapisa with the exact amount of silk (FYCL v. 38; Tripitaka v. 53, 587b; Kuwayama 1990, 280). The rulers of Kapisa determined this price on the basis of their previous trading experiences. In 637, when the king sent an envoy to the T'ang court with relics and horses, the emperor rewarded him with silks.[10] When the sacredness of the relics hindered their transactions on certain occasions, it raised their value in people's eyes, and therefore the market price as well. Once the rulers bought and sold holy objects, the objects gained in market value, because no government monopoly could be absolute. In the T'ang capital, a finger of the Buddha which looked just like a 'rusty nail' could be sold for ten million coins. A high official and a member of the royal family, the prince and the minister, Li Lin-fu, donated such a relic to a monk on a ritual occasion as a reward for his performance (Tuan 253). The disappointed monk who received the finger bone was later shocked by the price offered by a buyer in the market.

The above instances show that the holy bones of the Buddha entered the Chinese market in different forms of transaction: as gifts, as rewards, as tributes and simply as commodities. The force that supported the transactions was the belief of the Indian and Chinese populace in the religious power and the efficacy of the relics in helping them solve their difficulties. In the world of commodities, this power and efficacy were often evaluated and exchanged with another kind of precious and even more widely accepted commodity—silk.

[10] The *Chiu T'ang Shu* recorded that the T'ang emperor rewarded the Kapisa envoy who brought good horses with silks; TFYK cites a tribute of both relics and horses in the same year. The two records probably refer to the same event (CTS v. 198, 5309; TFYK 970/8a).

Chapter II

Silk and Buddhism

The close connection between the famous Silk Route and the spread of Buddhism is a historical fact. Much of the scholarship on the Silk Route deals with Buddhism, and mostly with the historical developments of Buddhist iconography. I have analyzed the causal relationship between commercial transactions in silk and theological developments in Buddhism, and between the Buddhist rituals and the demand for Chinese silks in India from the first to the sixth centuries (Liu 1988, 68 ff). This demand continued to exist after the sixth century even though India had developed its own silk industry. The flow of Chinese silks into India had probably even increased. A few important factors sustained the silk trade. First, the demand of the ruling elite for exotic foreign luxuries did not diminish, even though the growth of fiefs caused a decline in domestic trade. Secondly, communication between India and China and Central Asia increased because of the increasing popularity of Buddhism in the latter countries.

While Tantrism and related popular cults accelerated the process of deviation from the original Buddhist philosophical system and social discipline, they also made Buddhism accessible to a larger populace, and Buddhist concepts permeated all walks of life. Tantric rituals supplemented witchcraft in dealing with birth, death and other major events in human life. More cults were available for different purposes of worship. Among these activities, Buddhist institutions specialized in funeral rites.

Silk and silk clothes were essential components in burials in China, even before the advent of Buddhism, as is evident from the well preserved silk textiles in the tombs of Ma-wang-tui in Hunan Province (late second century BC), and those of Chinese Central Asia. The Buddhists' involvement in funeral rites naturally created a deep affiliation of silk with the religion. This affiliation between Buddhism and silk soon expressed itself in relic worship. Because relic worship or stupa worship originated in funeral rites, a transference of relics was intended to reduplicate the funeral ceremony of the Buddha in order to transfer the religious power of the relics to the new location, or to invoke their religious power on a special occasion for a specific purpose. Buddhist devotees in China instinctively adopted the same instruments. to show their piety towards the sacred bones of their ancestors. As the tombs and temples symbolized the point of departure into the unknown, the sacred relics of the Buddha and the stupas were like the gate as well as the bridge separating this life from, as well as linking it to, future lives. Making an investment at this juncture was considered very useful and lucrative for one's own future and for the future of one's offspring. As silk was the most common form of wealth in China and Central Asian countries, and a commodity very much in demand in India, religious investment was often made in silk textiles and clothing. Therefore, sacred relics often functioned as the key to silk transactions.

Silk in India

Indian artisans produced silk from wild cocoons from very early times. But they did not learn the art of raising mulberry silk cocoons and the technique of unravelling thread from boiled cocoons until the time of the Delhi Sultanate (thirteenth to the fifteenth centuries) when immigrants from Central Asia introduced the technique. Before this time, Indian silk was very different from that of China. The two kinds of silk looked so different that the Korean monk, Hui-ch'ao, after travelling throughout India, claimed that there were absolutely no silk floss and fabrics in all the five parts of India (Tripitaka v. 51, 976a). Hui-ch'ao, of course, was wrong. Hsüan-tsang referred to Indian silk by its indigenous name kauśeya and described it as 'silk of wild silkworms' (HT 176). This kind of silk was not as soft and shiny as the mulberry silk. The cocoons were collected after the silkworms had gnawed through them. Silk yarn was spun from floss made of the broken cocoons. Thus kauśeya was much heavier and rougher than Chinese mulberry silk.[1] This does not mean that

---

[1] The indigenous silk found at Navdatoli, Northwest Deccan, dated to the

kauseya was not beautiful and desirable to both Indians and foreigners. kauśeya was widely used by Buddhist monks 'in all four sects all over the five parts of India' (I-ching, Tripitaka v. 54, 212c). King Harṣa donated a large quantity of kauśeya clothes to monks at ceremonies held in Kanauj and Prayāga (HT 441; Hui-li 111). Indian silks in this period probably reached China. A Chinese document found in a tomb dated 574 in Turfan, Central Asia, names a kind of silk textile 'deva brocade' (*t'i-p'o-chin*) (67 TAM 84:20, Turfan v. 2, 207). Though the name does not reveal anything about the textile itself, it sounds Indian, with some religious connotation.

An explanation of this technique which prevailed in India was that Hindu textile workers were reluctant to kill the worm in order to protect the length of the cocoon filaments (Leggett 1949, 101). During the seventh century or later, this was also an issue for Buddhists. There was not much silk in the days of the Buddha and the period immediately following. The clothes of the monks at that time were made of cotton, the most easily available material in India. From the Gupta period, silks became fairly common in India, and monks accepted them without much dispute, as I-ching tells us. However, I-ching described the silks used by the monks of the five parts of India as 'rough silks' (*shih-chüan*) (Tripitaka v. 54, 212c), indicating that these silks were made from broken cocoons, which absolved Indian monks from the guilt of killing worms.[2] Meanwhile, Chinese monks, who were well aware that the Chinese method of processing silk killed worms, preferred to follow the strict rules in *vinaya* texts specifying that they wear cotton. Hsüan-tsang wore cotton all the time (Hui-li 223). But cotton was such an expensive imported material in T'ang China that not many monks could afford it. Facing this dilemma, I-ching tried to persuade his fellow Chinese monks to accept silk. He argued that since Indian monks used silks, Chinese monks need

early agricultural phase, was probably kauśeya (Ghosh, A. 1989, vol. 1, 16.1, p. 319a; 16.16, p. 334b).

[2] In modern India, when silk with a long filament was available, silk textiles made from broken cocoons at holy centers such as Benares were highly priced textiles for Vaishnavite Hindus and Jains. In general, however, in spite of the fact that people are aware that silk processing involves killing, silk textiles have been treated as the ritually purest textiles and have been widely used on religious and ritual occasions (Bayly 1986, 289).

not confine themselves to the very scarce fine cotton cloth when silk was easily available (I-ching, Tripitaka v. 54, 212c). He explained that kauśeya was also a kind of silk (ibid., 213a). But he may not have been aware of the differences between Chinese and Indian silk processing. As for the problem of killing silk worms, I-ching argued that only deliberately killing them would create one's karma—the negative score for one's future lives. 'Even a layman should not witness the killing of silk worms.' But, he argued, 'if a donor takes the silk to you with good intention, you should just happily accept it and wear it to protect your body in order to nurture merit' (ibid., 213a). The Indians Buddhists were not aware of the problems their Chinese counterparts were concerned with.

In the seventh and eighth centuries, silk became a popular textile in India, both among the rulers and the commoners who could afford it. There was a rich vocabulary for silk fabrics. During the time of King Harṣa, aṁśuka was a kind of silk which was almost as common as dukūla, a textile probably made of plant fibre. Cīnāṁśuka was made in China or made with silk yarn from China. Paṭṭa was a kind of silk of a natural golden colour. Netra was white silk and pinga or pṛinga was coloured silk (Agrawala 1969, 104–5). In addition to the kauśeya, which was described by Hsüan-tsang, patrorṇa was another kind of wild silk. Bleached silk was called mahādhana, and kṛimirāga was a silk dyed a red colour (Chandra 1973, 55). Indians imported silks not only from China but also from other countries. Stavaraka was a kind of heavy and costly silk from Iran (Agrawala 1969, 105). Pṛinga was probably imported from Central Asia (ibid., 106). The Central Asian style of clothing, such as caps, tunics and boots influenced Indian attire which often appear in the art works of Ajanta (Chandra 1973, 88–9). Though no appreciable silk samples have survived, colourful literary and artistic expressions of silks appeared so frequently in the Gupta era and the following period that various silk textiles must have been familiar materials in India.

However, Indian silks were not the most famous items of export from India to other countries. The Romans and Arabs bought silk, cotton and linen from the Indian coast in early times, but silk was probably mostly of Chinese origin. Upto the time of Mas'ūdī, who was in Cambay in the year 916, and Marco Polo who visited there in the thirteenth century, India was more famous for its cotton textiles than for anything else (Chandra 1973, 130; Serjeant 1972, 216). Therefore, India seems to have been mainly a silk importer in ancient and medieval times in spite of her domestic production.

The domestic market for silk was quite large. Consumers ranged from the most sacred and elitist personnel to those of low social status. Silk was considered good enough for clothing deities. The goddess Lakshmi is described as wearing a white silk scarf in the *Harṣa Carita* (Agrawala 1969, 84). Kings and royal members enjoyed wearing silk, as is evident from the textiles which formed part of the rich dowry and wedding decorations for Rājyaśrī, the sister of King Harṣa. But servants, especially female servants, and low status persons like dancers could also wear silk. Agrawala identified the costumes of both a sun god and a dancer ?s the costly Persian silk stavaraka (104–5). In cave XVIII at Ajanta, one may notice a royal attendant wearing 'silk brocade with a floral design or a maid servant with a skirt of striped silk' (Chandra 1973, 86, 95). In South India silks were freely used by whoever could afford them, even at the time when classical Tamil works, such as *Shilappadikaram* and *Maṇime-kalai*, were collected.

It seems that there were no sumptuary laws regulating clothing according to official or social status in ancient and early medieval India. Actually it was impossible to have this kind of law issued by any Indian monarch because the so-called law code, the *dharma*, was never enacted by any Indian ruler but compiled and interpreted by various schools of Brahmans according to prevailing customary laws. While monarchs were supposed to follow and enforce dharma, it was the Brahmanical or Hindu social system that enforced all the regulations prescribed by the dharmas. The *Arthaśāstra* and its commentaries were more like manuals containing knowledge of how to rule for kings and their ministers than dharmas. Neither the *Arthaśāstra* nor the dharmas could cover the practices of the whole society, as the Buddhists and Jains had monastic rules and guidelines for their laity.

In dharma literature, there were regulations about how one should wear which kind of garment on ceremonial occasions, but there were no references about which material should be worn by different kinds of people. The *Arthaśāstra* contains references about the production of textiles and their provenances, for the

purpose of taxation, but it gives no advice on who should wear
what. The Buddhist Pali *vinaya* and Sanskrit *Prātimokṣa Sūtras*
stipulate certain conditions under which a monk could receive
donations of clothing. The *Prātimokṣa Sūtras* are much more
lengthy and elaborate on clothing than the *vinayas*, because society
and textile products in the early centuries AD, when the Sanskrit
texts were compiled, were much more complex than during the
time of the Buddha and later, when the Pali monastic rules were
formed. The *Prātimokṣa Sūtras* of Mahāsāṃghikas ruled that no
monk should own rugs made of sheep's wool mixed with silk,
while that of Mūlasarvāstivādins ruled that a monk should not
own a rug made of silk (Prebish 1975, 68–9). These rules were
probably intended to prohibit individual monks from owning
expensive property rather than to oppose the use of silk. Neither
sect had stipulations about silk garments. Jain canon also listed
many textiles that a monk or a nun should not wear because of
their high prices, including a variety of silks such as *paṭṭa*, *malaya*,
aṃśuya and *cīnāṃśuya* (Chinese silk) (Jain 1984, 173–4).

In spite of the absence of secular and monastic rules regarding
styles and materials for clothing, people did pay attention to what
they wore. I-ching in the eighth century observed that four different schools of Buddhism distinguished themselves through
different ways of wearing their under-garments and belts (Tripitaka v. 54, 214a). Some Chinese pilgrims who went to India
with clothes that were not in fashion were so embarrassed that
they tore them up and discarded them as rags (ibid.). Chinese
pilgrims had the strong impression that clothes and decorations
were important for distinguishing status in India. Hsüan-tsang
noticed that kings and their ministers not only wore fine clothing,
but also adorned themselves with fine jewellery. Rich and influential traders could only wear bangles (HT 177). In Kashmir, Hui-
ch'ao saw kings, chiefs and the wealthy wearing clothes similar to
those worn in Middle India, but the commoners simply wrapped
themselves in blankets so as to cover their bodies (Tripitaka v. 51,
976c). Other Chinese sources mention that in India, kings and
ministers mostly wore brocade and woollen textiles (CTS v. 198,
5307; HTS v. 121, 6237). This might have been limited to
ceremonial occasions, as I-ching noticed that secular nobles normally wore two pieces of white cotton fabrics and the poor people
wore only one piece (Tripitaka v. 54, 214b).

The rulers and the elite surely wore better clothes than did the poor people. Nevertheless, in ancient and early medieval India, the upper level of society did not seem to care whether the people of a lower status transgressed their boundary by wearing good clothes. This is especially interesting because India was a very status conscious society. Yet textile materials and colours were more often used for ritual symbols than for status. Colours such as ochre, white and black were of symbolic importance. I-ching surprisingly observed that Indians did not use a true purple colour (Tripitaka v. 54, 216a). This absence seems quite marked because purple was the colour which distinguished status in T'ang China in both secular and religious circles. Based on a study of the cave murals of this period, Moti Chandra suggests that status was expressed more by headdress than by clothes (ibid., 1973, 84). For whatever reason, Indian rulers did not monopolize silk. Therefore the wide use of silk for clothing and the popularity of silk, especially Chinese silks, made India an open market for silk imports. China was a famous silk producing centre in the ancient world including India. As late as in the twelfth century, Mahā-sollāsa listed Mahācīna as a centre for silk production along with Indian producers (Chandra 1973, 123).

With all the domestically produced kauśeya, Indian rulers and the elite still desired Chinese silks. The terms cīnāṁśuya or cīna-paṭṭa, i.e. Chinese silk, are also found in the literature of this period. In the biography of King Harṣa, Chinese silks are mentioned more than once.[3] Envoys from the kingdoms of northwest India which were linked by Central Asian routes to T'ang China as well as from the south which was linked by sea routes, were often sent to the T'ang court with gifts from South Asia (CHL v. 6, 64–5). They probably came back with bolts of silk, some with robes of brocade, varying in colour according to the rank of the status in the T'ang hierarchy, as well as with certain belts, bags, etc., totalling altogether seven items which symbolized the forging of diplomatic relations with T'ang China. In 719, the king of Kapisa sent lions and parrots to the T'ang court. 'In rewarding the tribute from so far away, the emperor Hsüan-tsung entertained the envoy who returned with five hundred bolts of coloured brocade' (TFYK 971/3b). In 746, a ruler from the same region

[3] For example, in chapter 7, p. 55, line 22; chapter 5, p. 31, line 32.

again sent envoys (TFYK 971/16a). During the seventh century the people of Kapisa were so eager to acquire Chinese silk that they even traded their precious relics, the parietal bone and some minor relics, for silk. Though Chinese silks were treasured, the ruler was willing to donate them for religious purposes. A Kapisa king once gave five bolts of 'pure silk brocade' to Hsüan-tsang (Hui-li 36) which was obviously not kauśeya made in India. Chinese pilgrims, though disputing about whether monks should wear silks, were well aware of the demand for Chinese silks and unhesitatingly deemed silks carried to India the best gifts to the Buddha or the currency paid to monasteries.

Silk in Central Asia

For centuries, many nomadic groups controlled and passed through the Central Asian steppe. Trading horses with silk with the Chinese was one of the major provocations for warfare. The right and privilege to participate in the silk and horse trade was a symbol of sovereignty among the nomadic tribes (Matsuda 1936, 134). After the Hsiung-nu empire collapsed, Scythians, Hephthalites, various Turkic tribes and Arabs occupied and passed through various parts of Central Asia at different periods. The nomads among them could not master the art of silk production because they were constantly on the move. But their desire for Chinese silks never waned.

When Hsüan-tsang visited the court of Yabgu Khan, the king of the Western Turks, he was impressed by its grandeur:

Wearing a robe of green damask, exposing his hair, the Khan bound his head with a piece of silk about one *chang* in length. The two hundred or so advanced officials (*ta-kuan*) surrounding him all wore robes of polychrome silk, and braided their hair. All lower officers and soldiers wore fur and wool. . . . The Khan lived in a great camp, decorated with golden ornaments. Its splendour was so brilliant it caused people to wince. All advanced officials were seated on two long rugs, their polychrome silk attire was impressive. . . . Even though he was only a nomadic king, his court was quite elegant (Hui-li 27–8).

By the sixth or the seventh century, Khotan was already famous for its textiles (HTS 221a, 6235). Here again, the silk was *shih-yu*, a kind of rough textile, and *ch'ü-shu*, a woolen or silk rug.' Khotanese law forbade the killing of moths for fear of wiping out silk worms (HTS 221a, 6235). Kucha and Kashgar polychrome silks were well known commodities in Central Asia (e.g. Turfan v. 1, 181; v. 2, 18). Sericulture in the Turfan region, before and under T'ang control, prospered (Ch'en Liangwen 1987).

As in India, Central Asian domestic sericulture and weaving could not replace Chinese silk. Establishing diplomatic relations with the Chinese was still the main channel for acquiring silk. From the sixth century local kings received the seven items including a silk robe from Sui and T'ang emperors in return for sending gifts or tributes to China (TFYK 975). They often also received grants of Chinese silks. For example, Wakhan (in northeast Afghanistan) obtained the seven Chinese items in 720, including a purple silk robe, the highest ranking robe, and fifty bolts of coloured silk. They then either traded this Chinese silk or produced some of their own, as 3000 bolts of silk were sent annually to the Arabs as tribute (TFYK 964/14b). The kings of Sogdiana wore various kinds of silks ranging from the finest damask and gauze to heavy polychrome, woven and embroidered, in addition to fine cotton (SS v. 83, 1848). In Udyana, rulers wore robes of brocade, while the poor wore cotton (HTS v. 221b, 6253).

Silk was an important tool of diplomacy in Central Asia. When Hsüan-tsang left Turfan, the ruler there wrote twenty-four letters to the kings of the states along his route and every letter was attached to a bolt of damask. To the most powerful king, Yabgu Khan of the Western Turks, the king of Turfan sent five hundred bolts of damask and plain silk and two carts of fruit. In addition to these gifts, he gave gold, silver, all kinds of silk clothes, plus five hundred bolts of damask and plain silk to Hsüan-tsang himself as his travel fare (Hui-li 21).

Hsüan-tsang needed thirty horses and twenty-five labourers to carry these gifts and treasures (Hui-li 21). Though a bulky commodity, silk continued to be the best medium of exchange in Central Asia. Chinese documents dated from the fourth century to the ninth century, found in tombs in the Turfan region, provide

4 I-ching described *ch'ü-shu* as a kind of sleeping rug woven with silk (Tripitaka v. 54, 213a).

abundant evidence of the use of silk as currency. People used silks almost exclusively to make payments before the T'ang empire extended its control over Central Asia in the mid-seventh century. Even after Turfan became one of the prefectures of the T'ang dynasty, silk was used as currency at least as much as were officially cast coins. In a region where trade went beyond borders, copper coins may not have been as acceptable as silk. Moreover, the supply of copper coins and gold was limited. Chinese authorities from the T'ang to the Sung dynasties tried many times to ban the use of gold, iron and copper coins in foreign trade for financial and military reasons (Chang Kuang-ta 1987, 756). Though this rule may not have been implemented effectively, it certainly encouraged the use of silk as currency. In the year 721, Emperor Hsüan-tsung even issued an edict to punish those who refused to accept silk as payment (Lei-Hsüeh-hua 119).

In recent years, gold and silver coins from Byzantine, Persia and the Arab empires have been found along the silk routes and China interior. But except for the region around Turfan where silver coins may have circulated for a while, most coins were used as bullion or decorations (The Institution of Archaeology, CAAS, 1984, 563). The Arabs also mentioned that the T'ang government forbade foreign merchants to trade in gold and silver coins. For the purpose of market regulation and tax collection, all the accounts in T'ang China were settled in Chinese copper coins (Sung Hsien 1987, 220). This restriction on the use of gold and silver coins was also applicable in Chinese Central Asia, where people used silks to buy horses (e.g. Turfan v. 5, 107; v. 8, 88; v. 9, 48) and slaves (e.g. Turfan v. 4, 266; v. 5, 108). A female slave cost only forty bolts of plain silk in the year 732 (ibid., v. 9, 29) and a horse cost eighteen bolts of plain silk in the year 733 (ibid., v. 9, 48). People used silk as payment for labour (ibid., v. 6, 66), as salary for soldiers (ibid., v. 6, 71), as rent (ibid., v. 6, 223) and as a substitute for horse tribute (ibid., v. 8, 67). The most common use of silk, of course, was the tax paid to the government. Inventories of private property and accounts of moneylenders also show that silk fabrics and clothes were the most common form of property (ibid., v. 1, 195; v. 4, 158; 186; v. 6, 81; 316 ff).

At the same time that people used silk as currency in their mundane life, silk gradually became the currency in the afterlife. Many of the documents found in Astana tombs were there because they were used as paper clothes and shoes and were buried with the dead for unknown ritual reasons. The only documents deliberately put in the tombs were inventories of goods, mostly clothes and textiles, that the dead would take with them to the other world. This was a tradition from the earliest dated tombs, i.e. the tombs of those who died in the fourth century during the rule of the Liang state. Ma Yung noticed that before the establishment of the rule of the Ch'ü family in the kingdom of Kao-ch'ang (499–640), there was no mention of Buddhism in the inventories, even though Buddhist influence had reached this region much earlier. He was of the opinion that in the earlier period Buddhism circulated only among the upper social strata and only after it became a popular religion did it play a role in burial rites (Ma Yung 1986, 33). In the beginning, the inventories named only a few pieces of clothes, probably those worn by the deceased during his lifetime, but not all the named items were actually buried in the tombs. Since many of these tombs have been disturbed by archaeologists or local residents, it is very difficult to check the items in the inventories against the buried items.

In many cases the goods listed were more than those actually buried. It is possible that some of the listed items were buried but are now missing. The inventory in tomb Astana 173, dated 633, lists a 'face-cover made of Persian brocade, a bed-cover made of Persian brocade'. Another face-cover made of Persian brocade was dated c. 641 (Ast. 15, Turfan v. 4, 32). As a face-cover was only for the dead and as there was only one piece of face-cover on the list, we may assume there was a real face-cover made of Persian silk in the tomb.[5] Art historians have studied quite a few face-covers of compound silk weaving in the Sassanian style from these tombs. However, face-covers were probably, if not the only kind of real item, one of the few kinds of goods buried with the dead. Yoshihisa Oda's study of the inventories and the excavated items showed that in both an early tomb where the inventory was short and looked realistic and a later tomb where the inventory was long and seemed exaggerated, the listed items did not match with the excavated items. In the tomb dated 436 (Ast., TAM 62), only the

---

[5] *Yu-yang Tsa-tsu* mentions the custom of people covering the dead with a face-cover in T'ang China (Tuan, 173).

item of 'a pair of shoes' listed in the inventory matched with a
pair of paper shoes in the list of excavated items. In the tomb
dated 596 (Ast. 66, TAM 48), the long list of inventory was almost
completely different from the goods actually buried (ibid., 1976,
92). Therefore, the inventory was not a list of the goods buried
but was another burial item for ritual purposes.

The format and phrasing of the inventories changed with time.
From these changes one can sense that people's vision about the
world after death became clearer. An inventory dated 437, after
naming the clothes of the dead, lists 'a bundle of yellow silk yarn
thirty feet long in his hand', followed by the Chinese geomantic
symbols: 'black dragon on the left, white tiger on the right, red
skylark in front, Hsüan-wu behind'[6] (Turfan v. 2, 62–3). If the
thirty foot long yellow silk yarn looks strange here, its purpose is
revealed by some later inventories. For instance, a rather typical
inventory dated 548 goes:

ten thousand gold coins,
one million silver coins,
one thousand pieces of brocade,
ten thousand bolts of damask,[7]
one thousand catties of silk floss,
ten thousand bolts of plain silk,
1,000,090,000 foot long silk yarn for climbing to the heaven.
A disciple of the Buddha, monk Kuo-yuan, moves the great deity of the
five states[8] for the disciple of the Buddha Kuang-fei who passed away
in the big city of Kao-ch'ang, who had been observing the five absten-
tions, making the ten merits, but unfortunately had to pass to the five
states. Please do not detain her. The witnesses are those present at the
time of Chang Chien-ku and Li Ting-tu. Whether she wants to go to
the end of the east sea, or the end of the east (sic, probably 'west') sea,

[6] Hsüan-wu was an imaginary animal, a combination of a turtle and snake.
[7] Ta-ling, a silk textile thinner than brocade, similar to damask, hence referred
to as damask in this book. Here the name is not associated with the city
Damascus.
[8] Wu-tao-ta-shen, a Buddhist deity, who was either an officer or a general in
the retinue of the ten kings who were in charge of the purgatory. The five states,
gatis, refer to the five forms or realms of being: being in hell, being an animal,
a ghost, a human and a god. There was also a sixth state, where the being of
asura, something between a ghost and a god, was added (A Dictionary of Chinese
Buddhist Terms, 128).

no one should stop her. Immediately follow the statutes and ordinances! (Turfan v. 2, 62–3.)

Though the listed amount of gold, silver, textiles and clothes was extremely large, and growing larger all the time, the inventories often claimed that these items were all personal belongings for the dead to carry to the other world (e.g. Ast. 210, Turfan v. 6, 64; Ast. 327, Turfan v. 6, 124). Here we see a Buddhist monk helping a devotee to go over to the other world, hopefully one of the heavens, with the instrument—the silk yarn—to climb up to heaven ready at hand. Meanwhile, the great deity of the five states had to be taken care of by the Buddhist monk. Compared with the 'yellow silk yarn thirty feet long in his hand', the '1,000,090,000 foot long silk yarn for climbing to the heaven' gives a much clearer picture of what the deceased would do after the funeral.

During the T'ang dynasty, Buddhism became more involved in funeral rites. A more detailed inventory evolved which listed not only clothes and wealth under personal belongings as well as currency accumulated, but also the merits gained. An inventory dated 673 contained a will which was addressed to the Buddha. The man who had drawn up this will explained that he had had an image of the Buddha and two of bodhisattvas made, and that he had recited the *Ullambana Sūtra*. He planned to spend the merits he accrued from these efforts in the other world, along with the numerous silver coins, silks and specifically named female and male slaves who were his personal property (Turfan v. 6, 402, Ast. 4).

Some inventories of merits were drawn up by the relatives of the dead. A woman listed the merits of her mother-in-law to include the payments she had made to monks to recite sutras as well as her donations to monks (AD 674, Turfan v. 6, 500, Ast. 201). Another woman listed among the many merits of her father-in-law the sutras he had recited, the silk banners he had made and the silk clothes he had donated. This extremely long list recorded the many things done to try to buy him back from death during the year he had been ill (Ast. 29, Turfan v. 7, 66 ff). The old man nevertheless passed away. Though these credits were not enough for him to recover his health, they could be used as his property to pass beyond this world. In the tomb of a certain official, the inventory only lists the merits he gained by reciting sutras, namely the *Saddharmapuṇḍarika*, *Vajra Prajñāpāramitā*, etc. as the wealth he wanted to carry over into the next world. Nothing of material consequence was listed, either because the deceased had been an honest official and was thus poor or because it was inappropriate for an official to claim much wealth (Turfan v. 7, 528). From these inventories, one sees a combination of material wealth, particularly in the form of silks, and the Buddhist merits to be carried to the unfathomable beyond, either heaven or hell. The religious practices among Chinese residents or sinicized Central Asians in Central Asia signalled a new form of Buddhist participation in silk trans-actions, leading to an accumulation of silk in Buddhist institutions in China and in other parts of the Buddhist domain.

Silk in China

Silk and linen were the major textiles produced in T'ang China. As sericulture and silk weaving were part of the agricultural ac-tivities of peasant households, plain tabby silks were one of the major taxes paid to the government. Therefore, silk was always an essential part of state revenue, only slightly less than linen. For example, in the mid-eighth century, during the heyday of the T'ang Dynasty, the annual revenue included 7,400,000 bolts of silk, 1,800,000 t'un[9] of silk floss and 10,350,000 bolts of linen (HTS v. 51, 1346). Because of its use value and exchange value, silk was widely used as a medium of transaction in China even though the T'ang government had established a sound coin currency system.

Silk had an advantage over other commodities in foreign trade. Even the plainest tabby silk weave was considered precious outside China because the long filaments made it unique in the world at that time. Profits in the silk trade were high. In the mid-eighth century, a bolt of plain silk valued at around 200 coins in the interior, commanded as high a price as 450 or 470 coins in the western frontier (Ch'en Liang-wen, 124). No doubt, the price abroad was even higher.

The T'ang government, being aware of the value of silk in foreign trade, encouraged its production over other textiles. A notice in 687 from the revenue ministry ordered local officials in the prefectures that produced both linen and silk to allow the

---

[9] T'un was a special weight unit for silk floss. One t'un equalled six *liang* or approximately 200 grams.

people who wanted to substitute silks, silk floss and rough silks for linen to do so (72 TAM 230:46/2a, Turfan v. 8, 136–7). In the early days of the T'ang government, Emperor T'ai-tsung issued an edict in 626 to the custom stations to the east of the T'ung Gate[10] to abolish all restrictions on the trade of silk textiles such as damask, tabby patterned with twill, as well as gold and silver utensils (TTCLC 108/8a). This policy clearly aimed at encouraging silk production and trade.

This situation changed with the flourishing of commerce and social prosperity of the T'ang empire. When rich commoners, including traders, became ostentatious, the rulers found it necessary to enforce sumptuary laws. Since the Han Dynasty, the issue of who was qualified to wear elaborate silk textiles had always been the major topic of public discourse. In the seventh century, the T'ang court issued a series of sumptuary rules to cut down on the use of luxury silks. In 674, Emperor Kao-tsung issued an edict ruling that officials and commoners should wear clothes appropriate to their status. In 714, Emperor Hsüan-tsung issued two edicts banning jewellery, jade, brocade and embroidery (TTCLC 108/9a, 109/1b–2a).[11] He also issued an edict on the rules of apparel in the same year, and ordered government workshops to stop producing many kinds of luxury silks (TTCLC 188/10a). Meanwhile, he forbade the sale of the most exquisite silk products to foreigners: polychrome patterned silks, damasks, gauzes, crepes, embroideries and other fancy silks, and yak tails, pearls, gold and iron (THY 86/1581, Schafer 1963, 24). Keeping in mind that Hsüan-tsung was the most extravagant emperor of the T'ang Dynasty, and the splendid cultural achievements under his rule, one can understand that his utterances about leading a thrifty life were really only meant for certain kinds of people.

However, regulations on materials and styles of clothing in T'ang China aimed at a different purpose and therefore had a different effect than did the sumptuary laws of former dynasties. The sumptuary laws on silk clothes in the Han Dynasty were simply meant to differentiate the rulers from the ruled. In the few

10 T'ung Gate (T'ung-kuan) was a strategic pass between Ch'ang-an and Lo-yang.
11 A fragment of one of the edicts was incidentally found in a tomb of Turfan (Turfan v. 8, 172 72 TAM 230:96).

centuries following the Han Dynasty, many ethnic groups invaded or migrated into Chinese society, and brought with them different hair styles and clothing patterns. Meanwhile, the old Chinese aristocracy observed strict endogamy and certain rituals to keep their blood pure during the turmoil accompanying political changes. After unifying China again, the Sui rulers started to regulate apparels in order to ensure a certain social order. The T'ang rulers maintained this policy but clearly not in order to maintain the social hierarchy by protecting the old aristocracy. The aim was to build a bureaucratic hierarchy. The long and bloody process of fighting with the old aristocracy and the question of whether it resulted in a pure bureaucratic system in the T'ang Dynasty are topics that are beyond the scope of this work. But the process of establishing a new bureaucratic hierarchy was certainly reflected in the efforts of maintaining and continuously revising a code of clothing based on status.[12] In one of his edicts about clothing issued in 681, Emperor Kao-tsung made a clear statement about the code of clothing: 'The purpose of issuing special clothes from the court is to distinguish nobles from commoners, to make difference between promotion and demotion, and to encourage and reward (those who made achievements)' (CTW chapter 13, p. 159).

After several revisions, a comprehensive code of clothing was enacted to give detailed regulations on materials, colours and styles for the whole echelon of the T'ang bureaucracy, from emperors down to commoners. It was established that the official exclusive colour for the emperor's apparel was yellow. Officials at the three highest levels wore purple robes, followed by crimson, green and black (CTS 45/1952 ff, TS 24/526–7). While the ceremonial robe of the emperor was yellow, his daily robes were purple (CTS 45/1952). The novelty here is that purple and crimson (*fei*) were upgraded from being low status colours to high status ones. Colours had always had important connotations in the Chinese hierarchy. Purple and crimson were considered low status colours because they deviated from the purity of Chinese red (*chu* or vermilion). Though occasionally some unorthodox rulers demonstrated their boldness by wearing purple, Confucius condemned this immoral behaviour saying that purple

[12] For the evolution of the code on clothing in the T'ang Dynasty, see chapter 24 of HTS and chapter 45 of CTS.

overstepped into the position of the pure red (Huang Neng-fu 1985, 23). In order to have all the official costumes made under government supervision, the T'ang government had to have a special department which was in charge of twenty-five workshops, divided into four divisions of function, in the capital city (Wang, R. 1988, 45).

These sumptuary laws, as is true of all sumptuary laws in history, were never totally successful because the rulers themselves did not follow them. This was especially true in the T'ang Dynasty, as the bureaucratic hierarchy allowed a certain social mobility. It was possible for commoners to reach a certain status through their own merits, examinations or achievements in the civil service or on the battlefield. While the court granted costumes to certify the status and reward the achievements of successful officials, others who were not so successful but who considered themselves equally good would imitate the style of clothing of the former. The rich merchants in Ch'ang-an city, envying the high officials who wore purple and crimson clothes, also had purple and crimson clothes made for themselves. In the edict of 681, Emperor Kao-tsung referred to this problem:

It is said that some officials and commoners do not follow the rules (about clothing) in public, but wear tight jackets of crimson, purple, black, and green under their robes. They even dare to show those clothes when they are in lanes or in the country. This kind of behaviour blurred the distinction between the nobles and the masses, and eroded the moral standards. From now on, everyone should wear clothes according to his own status. Those holding high status may wear clothes designated for the low ones, but those of low status are not allowed to wear clothes above their status. The office that is in charge of this affair should enforce this rule and never let such aggressions reoccur (CTW 13/159).

Though the emperor tried to enforce these rules, frequent revisions of the clothing code caused confusion. Empress Wu Tse-t'ien, probably the T'ang ruler who fought most fiercely with the old aristocracy, granted so many different kinds of costumes to those who supported her politically, that the historical compiler of this period did not bother to record the variations in costume under her rule (CTS 24/529). In the later T'ang period, the court issued so many official costumes that even the merchants did not desire them (Ge 1988, 54).

Nevertheless, despite all the flexibility and adjustments in implementing the clothing code, punishments could be severe. Violations of clothing regulations could also be taken as a sign of more substantial infractions which incurred harsher punishments. Ho Si-chih, an officer who served in the reign of Empress Wu Tse-t'ien, and who was notorious for his illiteracy and uncouthness, was accused of the crime of preserving silk brocade, surely of the forbidden kind, and was beaten to death at court (Chang, Chuo 32). Although the official history of the T'ang Dynasty gives another version of the story,[13] the preservation of forbidden textiles was considered a severe crime. At least in the early days after sumptuary laws on silk textiles were imposed, those who did not deserve the purple robes but wore them suffered for their transgressions. According to a T'ang legend, a friend of Emperor T'ai-tsung, who in his youth desired the status which would grant him the right to wear a purple robe, requested for this honour and swore that he would be happy even if he were to die the day he received the honour. The emperor granted him the status out of affection but the receiver died the same night (Chang, Chou 148). Whether or not this story is true, it shows that the early T'ang people believed that transgressions on purple robes, the symbol of nobility, were severe sins which could incur punishment from the world beyond, if not from the secular powers in this world.

Both the case of Ho Si-chih and the story about the friend of T'ai-tsung reflect an extreme point of view. The transgressions were considered severe crimes only when they encroached on the bureaucratic hierarchy. Actually, even the T'ang law did not impose death penalty for owning forbidden silks. According to an authoritative commentary on the T'ang law (*T'ang-lü Shu-i* 8/176–7), the punishments for privately owning brocade and damask and for exporting other silks were mostly confiscations of the goods in question and several years in exile (ibid.). It is not surprising that a privately owned and managed silk industry and trade developed in spite of these restrictions. A low official

---

[13] According to the official history of the T'ang, Ho, only an illiterate and low level officer, was so aggressive that he was bold enough to ask for the hand of the daughter of a man of status. This request really angered a prime minister who had him beaten to death (CTS 186a/4844; HTS 209/5910).

in the Ting prefecture opened hotels next to the three government post offices under his supervision to host traders and ran silk workshops with a capacity of 500 weaving machines for damask (Chang, Chuo 75). Damask was not supposed to be privately owned and producing it privately would be an even more severe offense. However, with the development of silk technology, many workshops outside government supervision produced fancy silks for the domestic market as well as for export.

Similar to practices in Central Asia, silks were commonly used as clothing and for burial in the interior of China. Archaeological evidence in the interior of China is not as well preserved as in Central Asia, but literary sources suggest that some customs, such as using silk face-covers on dead people, were common in the T'ang period.[14] I have mentioned earlier that the famous stupa of Hsüan-tsang was financed by the clothes of the dead in the imperial harem (Hui-li 160). In the ninth century, a monastery in Ch'ang-an preserved six pieces of clothing that belonged to the former empress Wu Tse-t'ien (r. 684–705), including a shawl of golden weaved tapestry with a dragon pattern, a jacket and an embroidered shirt (Tuan 260). Here it is interesting to see the way that Buddhism and silk were connected in conceptions of the afterworld. On the one hand, it is conceivable that devotees gave their best belongings to the Buddha. On the other hand, items used by the deceased persons were considered impure, which prevented others, at least those in the same social circle, from using them again. Donating these beautiful silks to Buddhist institutions served two purposes. It brought merit to the dead and helped them in their future lives. The items became usable wealth after being purified in a religious institution which was powerful enough to overcome the pollution of death. The quality of the clothes that had been worn by the women in the palace must have been high, and their quantity, enough to cover the cost of a big construction project, must have been large. Since the monks could not wear the clothes, they had to sell them through financial

[14] In the chapter regarding the death and funeral of the Yu-yang Tsa-tsu, Tuan Ch'eng-shih has listed the face-cover as a customary burial item for women (p. 124) but a story in the same book also refers to a man wearing a face-cover for burial. In a hurry to open a mouth slit on the face-cover before burial, a maid cut the lip of the dead. It was said that after twenty years, the man in the other world still suffered from the injury (p. 205).

institutions attached to the monastery. No wonder the sumptuary laws could not stop commoners from wearing fancy silk clothes.

If silk clothes could serve as currency in the other world, why were not all the clothes of the dead buried with them? Surely the rich and those connected with the rich, such as the palace women, were buried with at least a set of decent silk clothes in addition to a few personal items. But the inventories of clothes from Turfan tell us that at that time people wanted to carry much more on their journey beyond this life than the few things buried with them. The manner in which the inventories evolved shows that Buddhists in the T'ang period gradually came to the realization that the currency they needed in the other world was the merit they had accumulated. Though they could purchase merit with silk, changing them to a foreign currency had to be through an agency or medium—Buddhist institutions and rituals. A devotee could donate silks and silk clothing to a monk or monastery to have sutras recited, to have a statue carved or to have a stupa built to store relics for his benefit.

The most direct way to buy merit was to donate silk to relics on ritual occasions. I have mentioned that the relic-worship cere- mony was a repetition of funeral rites for the Buddha or other Buddhist deities. Relics in the Fa-men monastery were frequently taken out for worship by the monks and emperors. In 1987 excavations revealed stele inscribed with records of such cere- monies and donations. According to one of the inscriptions, after performing a rite of bathing the relics in the year 649, the monk, Hui-kung, donated 3000 bolts of silk to the relics in the year 656 (Hou Jo-ping 1989, 88–9). An inscription of 874 recorded all the donations made by generations of emperors, empresses, princes and others who were qualified to do so (Wang Ts'ang-hsi 1989, 30). Archaeologists actually found more than seven hundred pieces of the silk clothes listed in the inscription, though most of them were carbonized beyond recovery (Lo Ch'ang-an 1987, 4). An inscription dated to 741 from another site of relics, the Ch'ing- shan monastery, reports that the relics were covered with exquisite silks (P'ang, Chin 1989, 37). Even though the excavated silk items from the Fa-men monastery are quite large in quantity, they obviously do not represent all the donations. Most of them prob- ably were used to cover the cost of building and maintaining the stupas, or they simply became the property of the monastery under the name of the Buddha. This association of silk with Buddhism, as a material expression of the religious function of relics in the life and death cycle, brought silk textiles and clothes into Buddhist institutions, including those beyond the border of T'ang China.

Pilgrimage and Silk Trade

For the purpose of acquiring relics, or just to see and worship relics, pilgrims carried with them large quantities of silks—banners, pieces of brocade or tapestry, ritual robes or bolts of plain silks. Buying precious relics with silk, as the envoy Wang Hsüan-ts'e did, or rewarding a tribute of relics with silk, as in the Kapisa case, are the most direct instances of the affiliation between silk and relics. In most cases, however, we do not know how the pilgrims obtained their relics, but we do know that they carried much silk towards the 'Western Land'. Although devotees and monasteries provided pilgrims with free food and lodging, the travel costs were high. While worshipping the parietal bone in Nagarahara, Hsüan-tsang donated fifty gold coins, one thousand silver coins, four silk banners, two pieces of brocade and two sets of ritual robes. He then sprayed flowers, for which he presumably had to pay (Hui-li 37). On reaching north India, Hsüan-tsang had already spent all the gold, silver, silks and clothes given to him by the king of Turfan. The pilgrims along the sea routes also spent large sums. A disciple of the Chinese pilgrim, Hui-ning, travelled to Canton from India with the new text on relic worship. On his way back to India to resume the pilgrimage, the disciple carried a few hundred bolts of plain silk for his teacher in Kalinga (WPW 77). When he reached the Mahabodhi monastery in Bodha Gaya, I-ching made a ritual robe of the same measurements as the Tathagata statue here from the silk donated to him by the monks and lay devotees of Shantung, China. He also presented tens of thousands of gauze silk canopies to the monastery in honour of his friend, the Vinaya teacher, Hsuan from P'u-chou (WPW 154). These pilgrims were often agents of transactions in silks and merits. While Hsüan-tsang donated the silks he received from the Turfan king to the stupas on his routes, he received five pieces of pure silk brocade from the king of Kapisa. Again, one may assume, he would donate these brocades to other sacred sites. By giving silks to monks or envoys on pilgrimage to India, the donors earned merits for themselves. By donating the silks on their journey, pilgrims earned merits both for themselves and their patrons.

Even after they reached back to China, these Buddhist teachers sent silks to India through Indian monks. In his career which spanned the regimes of two T'ang emperors, Hsüan-tsang received more than ten thousand pieces of silk ranging from plain silk to damask and brocade, plus a few hundred pieces of clothes and ritual robes. But he never accumulated anything for himself. Except for spending on building stupas and making images, he gave these silks to the poor and 'foreign Brahman guests', i.e. Indian guests (Hui-li 215). Knowing his fondness for fine cotton materials, his Indian fellow monks indulged him with gifts of cotton materials. In two of his letters to Indian friends, Hsüan-tsang mentioned sending back gifts in return (ibid., 164, 165). He did not specify the gifts, but judging from his habit of giving silks to foreigners, one may assume that he sent silk to his Indian friends.

Many Indian Buddhist monks resided in T'ang China. Numerous records tell of emperors who rewarded these monks with silks or silk ritual robes for their religious services, translations and preaching activities. For example, Parabhagramitra (Po-lo-p'o-ka-lo-mi-to-lo), a monk from central India, received many bolts of silk from the court during his career in China, including a ritual robe made in the palace workshop (HKSC v. 3; Tripitaka v. 50, 439c–440c).[15] The Tantric teacher, Amoghavajra, received so many yards of all kinds of silk from the emperor, that they piled up like a hill, and Buddhist sources report that he never kept these for himself (Tripitaka v. 50, 294b). It is not easy to judge whether this statement is true or just an eulogy. But a Buddhist monk was not supposed to have children of his own and because Amoghavajra was a foreigner, he probably had no other legal inheritors of his property in China. Unless we assume that all the yards of silk were returned to royal treasuries upon his death, there remains the question of what happened to all the silk. Did some of it go to India via his relatives? This question may never be answered,

15 Other examples are Budhapāli (Fo-t'uo-po-li, SKSC v. 2; Tripitaka v. 50, 717c–718a) and Prajna who received a purple robe in addition to silks from the T'ang court (SKSC v. 3; Tripitaka v. 50, 722a–b).

but given the heavy traffic between India and China at the time, there is a distinct possibility of his having sent back silk to India. The use of silk as material for Buddhist rituals began at the latest by the fourth century. From the fifth century, in both India and China, silk banners were essential for ceremonies. The custom of emperors' granting ritual robes to monks gained significance during the T'ang Dynasty, though it probably started in the sixth century. The quality of the silk robe granted became a status symbol among Buddhist monks and other religious figures. In the year 648, Emperor T'ai-tsung gave an audience to two famous monks. Both wore fine ritual robes which they had inherited from their teachers, who, in turn, had received them from Emperor Wu-ti of Liang (503–50). The emperor discerned faults in the robes and showed the monks an exquisite robe made in his palace workshop. Both monks expressed, by composing poems, their desire to have the robe as a gift. But the emperor gave them only fifty bolts of silk each and saved the robe for Hsüan-tsang (Hui-li 151). After Hsüan-tsang's death, the robe was displayed in his funeral procession (ibid., 226). About two hundred years later, the people of Ch'ang-an city still remembered the robe of Hsüan-tsang: 'That robe, worth a hundred gold pieces, was so well done that one could not see the trace of sewing' (Tuan 262).

Though exquisite in every detail, there is no description of the silk weaving and tailoring that went into the making of this robe. Hsüan-tsang received another precious ritual robe in 656 for his prayers for the empress who had a difficult childbirth. Hsüan-tsang described the robe as 'superb apparel with golden thread' (Hui-li 196). This was at the time when Persian silk textiles with woven golden yarn became famous in China. Among the treasures found in the stupa of the Fa-men monastery, there are a few pieces of purple silk with golden embroidery. The silk fabric used to wrap a relic bone has been described as silk embroidered with golden thread (Lo Ch'ang-an 1987, 4). One wonders what kind of silk Hsüan-tsang's 'superb apparel with golden thread' was. Was the textile of Persian woven gold? Or was the golden embroidery locally produced?

Amoghavajra was probably the most favoured Buddhist monk in the T'ang court next to Hsüan-tsang. This Tantric teacher from a Brahman family in north India and brought up in Central Asia, often received hundreds of bolts of silks, dozens of embroidered

silk banners and other silk items such as beddings, for his performance of Tantric rituals. In the year 746, as a reward for his
successful prayer for rain, the emperor granted him two hundred
bolts of silk as well as a purple silk robe. Emperor Hsüan-tsung
personally placed the robe on his shoulders (Tripitaka v. 50,
293a–c). From the mid-T'ang period, purple robes were established as the highest badge of honour that monks could receive.
Many outstanding Buddhist monks received purple robes from
the court. Preachers of other religions, namely Manicheism and
Christianity, were also bestowed the same honour (CHL v. 1, 121,
TFYK 975/13b; CHL v. 4, 159). However, the granting of silk
robes to Chinese and Indian monks in China was not enough to
show the emperors' piety. In the early period of the T'ang Dynasty,
T'ai-tsung frequently sent envoys to the Mahabodhi monastery
in Bodha Gaya with donations of ritual robes (Tuan 176). During
the reign of Kao-tsung, one of Wang Hsüan-ts'e's missions to
India (in 657) was to send a robe for the Buddha (FYCL chapter
16; Tripitaka 53/405a). This tradition continued into the eleventh
century, when two Chinese monks donated a gold embroidered
kaśaya—a Buddhist ritual robe—to spread over the throne of the
Buddha in Mahabodhi on behalf of the Sung emperor (Cunningham 1892, 72–3; Chou Ta-fu 1957).

The fashion of presenting monks with purple or gold woven
and embroidered silk robes extended to Buddhist deities. Images
of Buddhas and bodhisattvas clad in splendid robes penetrated
into the literature and art of the time. In the Pao-ying monastery
of Ch'ang-an, a famous portrait of the Maitreya shows him wearing a purple Kaśaya (Tuan 251). In the T'ang records of the
miracles in India, a passage from Fa-yüan-chu-lin contains the
information that when Śakyamuni reached nirvāna, he left the
golden woven robe made by his aunt to Maitreya, the future
Buddha. His favourite disciple, Mahākāśyapa, was entrusted with
the task of delivering the robe. Twenty years later, Mahākāśyapa
climbed a mountain to wait for the Maitreya to inherit this robe
(Tripitaka v. 53, 504a). Such legends in Chinese literature, set in
India, accurately project the religious behaviour of Chinese Buddhists and to some extent that of Indian Buddhists of the time.

Chapter III

Silk in Byzantium

At the time that T'ang China (AD 618–907) was exporting a large quantity of silk to the countries of the early medieval world, another important centre of silk industry and trade arose in the eastern Mediterranean area. The silk industry of the eastern Roman empire was established in a society dominated by aristocrats and in a land where Christianity was growing into a state religion. This was the period when the eastern Roman empire was shrinking into a relatively small state. Having experienced a temporary territorial expansion under Justinian, this empire began to lose its territory to the Sassanians, Arabs and later to the Turks in the east and to the Bulgars in the north, even as its Italian cities became more and more autonomous. Byzantium, a civilized Christian state, had to constantly grapple with conflicts in both the civilized non-Christian states to the east and the less civilized Christian states to the west. As the earliest Christian state, Byzantium naturally assumed the role of the chief propagator of the Christian religion and strove to contain traditional Roman cultural supremacy within the boundaries of the rather barbaric but Christianizing Europe. It was against such a background that a full scale and high quality silk industry developed.

Establishing the Silk Industry in the Byzantine Empire

The silk industry in the Byzantine empire developed with new fashions in clothing. A set of customs that stemmed during the transitional period when the Roman empire, from being a republic became an imperial state, was further stylized with oriental inspiration in the Eastern Roman Empire. This combination of eastern and western traditions was exemplified in the use of the colour purple on silk textiles as the highest emblem of status. Silk textiles as an emblem of status became more and more elaborate in the period the Roman-Byzantine empire became more and more totalitarian. While improving the artistic and aesthetical quality of the silk textiles, Byzantium's articulation on various shades of purple colour and weaving-embroidery technology served to designate increasingly complicated bureaucratic and clerical hierarchies.

Purple dye made from *murex*, a shellfish found in the eastern Mediterranean, had been a symbol of status from as early as the second millennium BC in the Near East (Reinhold 1970, 8). Since the cost of extracting the dye from a large quantity of shellfish was extremely high, and purple was the only fast colour known to the ancient Mediterranean world (ibid., 11), it became the most durable status symbol in history. Even though the colour had been associated with royalty and divinity from a very early date in the Middle East, purple was not established as a specific colour exclusively used by certain social groups in either Greek cities or the Roman republic. Up to the early empire, Roman citizens still had the freedom to wear purple according to their means. It was the introduction of the silk industry that signalled the change.

Silk weaving started in the eastern Mediterranean area in the Roman period. As I have mentioned in the first chapter, the Roman empire, later the Byzantine empire, relied on imported silk yarn for centuries, even after Byzantium developed its own sericulture.[1] During the reign of Justinian or one of his successors, a law was enacted to put a ceiling price of 15 *nomismata* on the sale of one pound of raw silk within the empire. Only imperial

---

[1] Most western scholars are of the opinion that the Chinese carefully guarded their technology of sericulture. This is based on the legend that the Khotanese smuggled the eggs of silkworm from their east neighbour (HT 1021–22) and the Nestorian monks smuggled the eggs of silkworm from Serindia, as recorded by Procopius (VIII, xvii, 1–14). However, technology transfer was probably much more complicated than these legends indicate. The history of the later Han Dynasty (AD 25–220), written in the fifth century, recorded that the Roman empire had a flourishing sericulture and that people wore embroidered silks. At least in the fifth century, the Chinese thought that the Roman empire was a strong and vast country similar to China. Naturally there should be sericulture in that country (HHS 88/2919). Later Chinese historical sources continued to repeat this description of the Romans. If the Chinese thought that sericulture was already established in the Roman empire, there was no point in keeping its technology a secret.

officials with the title of *kommerkiarioi* were authorized to buy raw silk from foreigners (Oikonomides 1986, 34).

This policy aimed at protecting the state monopoly of the entire silk supply in the sixth century. By the late ninth century, when sericulture had become an essential part of Byzantine industry, the strategy of the government also changed. The *Book of Eparch* ruled that 'individuals who have come to lodge with raw silk in the caravanserais have no fee to pay for selling it. They shall only pay their rent and for the right of sojourn. Nor shall those who buy raw silk be required to pay any fee' (Freshfield 1938, VI 5, 241). It also permitted that 'silk dressers shall purchase the quantity of foreign raw silk which they are prepared to dress' (ibid., VII 1, 243). Now the tax exemption encouraged merchants to transport raw silk, and there were no ceiling prices or designated state officials to ward off private purchasers (Lopez 1945, 14). Though imported raw silk continued to be used in the weaving industry, domestic sericulture changed the strategic position of Byzantium vis-à-vis the Eurasian silk trade. Instead of fighting with private entrepreneurs for raw materials, Byzantine rulers, with the abundant domestic and foreign supply at their disposal, could manipulate the weaving, the patterns and the dyeing in government workshops to produce fancy silk textiles. Silk textiles plus purple dye became a powerful weapon for the emperors to consolidate imperial order and deal with constant frontier disturbances.

During the reign of Justinian (AD 527–565), important events occurred that determined the course of the silk industry. His painstaking efforts to procure raw silk and then sericulture, and his legislation monopolizing the silk industry and trade helped the silk industry in Byzantium to gain in strength and to assume a social function similar to that of T'ang China. Byzantine emperors had made efforts to develop a raw silk supply network even earlier than had Justinian. Under the reign of Justin (AD 518–27) Byzantium supported the Ethiopian war against the Jewish Himyari kingdom of Yemen in the name of Christianity. Historians agree that the struggle between the Christians and the Jews was on account of the silk trade. The Jewish king, Dhu-Nuwas, started his anti-Christian campaign by killing Byzantine traders travelling on the silk route through Yemen (Starensier 1982, 61–2; Procopius I xx, 1–8). While continuing with his policy of aligning himself with Ethiopia to procure a continuous silk supply, Justinian drove private merchants out of the silk market by fixing the highest sale price on silk at eight gold pieces per pound (Procopius VI xxv, 16, 17).[2] No private merchant could afford to sell silk at a price lower than the purchasing price from Persia. The government agent then took the opportunity of bidding a higher price because he was not subject to the restriction. According to Procopius, this policy was disastrous for the private silk industry..Many artisans lost their means of livelihood and either sought employment in state workshops or immigrated to Persia (ibid.).

Though it was during Justinian's reign that Byzantium started sericulture, and domestic raw silk supplies enabled the revival of the private silk industry in later centuries, the Byzantine silk weaving industry in Justinian's lifetime had to rely on imported materials. The government monopoly on the limited foreign material was enough to ruin private weaving shops. The damage to the private silk industry in the sixth century provided an opportunity to the Byzantine government to establish its monopoly on certain silk textiles and to put state workshops in a commanding position in the whole silk industry. The silk textiles under government monopoly were silks dyed in purple or embroidered with gold thread. Restrictions on silk, purple and gold embroidery had been coded in the early fifth century by Theodosiasius (Code Theod. x, 21, 1, 2, 3; Lopez 1945, 10) but the reissue of the law in the code of Justinian put it into effect. Roman citizens treasured the freedom of wearing purple, thus distinguishing themselves from the barbaric kingdoms who used purple as royal insignia, and it took hundreds of years for the later Roman emperors to fight this defiant attitude (Lopez 1945, 10). Only under Justinian, when the private silk industry in the territory was virtually extinguished, did the government monopoly on silks in purple and with gold embroidery become effective. Purple dye-houses and silk workshops became key government departments, occupying the same level as the imperial treasury, and came under the administration of the minister of finance (Starensier 1982, 76).

Byzantine military power ceased to grow after Justinian. Threatened by the Avars and Slavs at home, and the Persian and

---

2 This ceiling price must have been imposed before the 15 gold pieces per pound ceiling price was coded. See Oikonomides 1986, 34, note 6.

later the Islamic states to the east, the empire lost its richest agricultural and industrial provinces—Egypt and Syria, and its great harbours and towns—Alexandria, Gaza, Antioch and Beirut. However, the silk industry in Byzantium thrived in spite of the loss of territory containing the early silk weaving centers. As silk industry was crucial to the regime, the government made every effort to guarantee its growth and the silk industry grew into the most essential component of Byzantine state economy. As mentioned earlier, in the early sixth century, state designated official traders—kommerkiarioi—were in charge of the supply of raw silk. During the sixth and the early seventh centuries these kommerkiarioi concentrated their activities to the eastern part of the empire—Antioch and Tyre—where silk imports were received and the early silk textile industry flourished (Oikonomides 1986, 42). Their seals with the imperial effigy, stamped on bales of merchandise, were a guarantee of quality and an authority for sale (ibid., 37). After the eastern territory, i.e. Syria and Phoinika, lost to the Persians (AD 613–27) and then to the Arabs (AD 638), Byzantium also faced the threat of losing its sericulture and domestic silk supply. To maintain its silk industry, Byzantium had to shift its sericulture to the northwest. A study of the seals of the kommerkiariois shows that the positions of these officials cum traders were always located in the area of silk production. Their jurisdictions in the seventh century were still quite close to the early centres of the silk industry. In the eighth century their positions shifted to the western part of Asia Minor. By the early ninth century, the seals of the kommerkiariois were found only in the territory west of Constantinople (Oikonomides 1986, 43–7). In this period, the kommerkiariois were probably agents to promote sericulture in the de-urbanized areas (ibid., 43). By the ninth and tenth centuries, the kommerkiariois had nothing to do with the silk trade. The supply of raw silk was abundant in the Mediterranean world. Muslim traders carried silk textiles to Constantinople. They were the most privileged foreign merchants residing in Byzantium. Byzantine emperors even maintained a mosque in Constantinople for their benefit (Lopez 1945, 29, 31). There was a special guild of merchants in Constantinople that dealt in manufactured goods, mainly silks imported from Syria and Baghdad (Freshfield 1938, 19 ff). Egyptian silks were also available in the Byzantine market (Starensier 1982, 255). In short, in spite of losing territory to the Arabs, silk from these areas continued to come in through trade.

With an increase in the supply of raw silk, the Byzantine state preserved the prestige of its silk textiles through an elaborate weaving technology and the purple dye. Having deprived its own citizens of the right to wear purple, Byzantine rulers never let the secret of making the purple dye pass to others. It seems all purple dye-houses were concentrated in Constantinople from the reign of Justinian. After Tyre and Beirut (the ancient centres of purple dye technology) fell to the Persians and later to the Arabs, this knowledge did not spread outside Byzantium (Starensier 1982, 78).[3] The government monopoly on purple was so strict that after the fall of Constantinople in 1453, the production of sea purple stopped totally. In place of the purple for church vestments, Pope Paul II declared the scarlet dye from cochineal kerms to be the colour for clerical robes and hats (Reinhold 1970, 70). Of the five shades of purple mentioned in the *Book of Ceremonies* (mid-tenth century), only a pale violet colour was allowed to be manufactured outside the imperial workshops, according to the *Book of Eparch* (Starensier 1982, 236). A private silk dyer risked having his hand cut off were he to dye 'raw silk with blood[4] or converts it into parti-coloured purple, double, triple or two-thirds red' (Freshfield

---

[3] It is also possible that the Muslims of the time, just like the Indians, did not care for the purple colour. An Arabic writer in the mid-ninth century was amazed at the strenuous efforts of the Byzantine emperors to keep the monopoly of *al-furfir* (purple) silk. He mentions that those who dared to violate the rule lost their heads (Ibn Khordâdhbeh, 116). The reader may remember that when Chinese Buddhists were busy making purple robes for the statues of the Buddha and outstanding priests, the pilgrim I-ching was surprised at the fact that Indian monks never wore purple clothes. As Muslims had frequent contact with Christians, we may assume that they were aware that purple was the prestigious dye in the Christian world. That was another good reason for Muslims to ignore or dislike this colour. It was unlikely for two antagonistic neighbouring political entities to adopt the same symbolic system. Therefore the monopoly on certain luxury items was only meaningful for those who desired and treasured the product, either because they respected the cultural value of the monopolizer, as in the case of the Christians in west Europe who desired purple silks as this luxury represented both high culture and the Christian religion, or because they took a fancy to exotic things from far away and made use of their rarity to symbolize a high status.

[4] A synonym for murex, which was the source material of purple dye.

1938, VIII 4, p. 26). To further guard the secret of the purple dye
from foreigners, it was ordered that 'every dyer who sells a slave,
a workman, or a foreman craftsman, to persons alien to the city
or the empire, shall have his hand cut off' (ibid., VIII 8, p. 26).

   While the imperial workshops produced the most strictly controlled purple silks and gold embroidery, private guilds under the
jurisdiction of the eparch wove silks for the lower strata of society
which were not necessarily lower in quality. The quantity of their
products was probably much larger than that of the imperial
workshops. These guilds not only sold their goods in the market
but also provided garments for low level officials (Lopez 1945,
21). On ceremonial occasions, their public obligation was to
decorate the city with precious silks (Starensier 1982, 226).

   As mentioned earlier, due to domestic and imported raw silk
supplies, the production of silk textiles in both imperial workshops
and private guilds and the influx of silk textiles from lost territories,
silk products in the Byzantine market continued to increase after
the seventh century in spite of the shrinking territory. However,
the increased supply did not bring down the price of silks. Silk
was still an extremely valuable commodity because the demand
for silk from the ruling classes and ecclesiastical institutions continued to grow. We will now examine the role of the Byzantine
government as both a producer and consumer of silk textiles.

Silk as a Means to Strengthen the Imperial Order

When Constantine restructured the Roman empire with the construction of a new capital, he had to get rid of Roman legacies.
By granting Christianity the status of a legal church, he hoped
that this religious institution would help him stifle residual republican traditions among the citizenry. As mentioned above, the
Roman citizens used to be proud of their freedom to wear purple
and silks according to their economic means. This does not mean
that the Romans were not status conscious people. They wore
purple textiles to show their social status and affluence, and as
badges of political and priestly positions. But they were also
strongly critical of oriental luxuries which they viewed as a sign
of degeneration, and frequently used purple and silks as targets.
It is well known that Pliny blamed the drain of the Roman treasury
on imported luxuries, including fine textiles such as cotton and

silk, spices, pepper and gem stones (Pliny XII, 41, 18). While both silk and purple were not used exclusively by the ruling elite, silk was somehow related to femininity.

In the later Roman empire, during the period that the monarchy was consolidated, i.e. the period between the reign of Constantine and that of Justinian, the purple colour was established as a royal insignia. Imperial heirs were 'born in purple', i.e. in a chamber made of purple-coloured porphyry, and imperial family members were 'buried in purple', the sarcophagus being made of porphyry (Reinhold 1970, 62). The most important medium to display the association of purple with royalty was silk attires. The highest position occupied by purple silk garments in the hierarchy of Byzantine clothing developed in the process of the maturation of the imperial order. In the year 325, Constantine appeared in an assembly of bishops 'clothed in a garment which glittered as though radiant with light, reflecting the glow of a purple robe' (Starensier 182, 32).

Consolidating monarchical rule through silk clothing and decorative silk hangings was not a Byzantine invention. With the shift of the capital city from Rome to Constantinople the political centre came closer to the homeland of Christianity and to the zones of other eastern cultures. Byzantine emperors deviated from many Roman traditions by imitating the customs of eastern empires. Before the seventh century, the closest possible source of eastern influence was Sassanian Persia, even though the Sassanians and Byzantines were arch enemies. Sassanid was another important producer of silk textiles outside China, but few literary sources about its silk industry are in existence. The material evidence of the glorious Sassanian silk textile is a small corpus of fragments found in graves in Central Asia and Egypt and church treasuries in Europe (D. Shepherd 1983; CHI III 2, 1109). Based on the few samples and reliefs at Taq-i-Bustan and frescoes in Central Asia, scholars have established a pool of Sassanian motifs. Based on this knowledge of Persian motifs, we know that with the import of Persian silks, Byzantine weavers imitated some typical Sassanian patterns such as equestrian figures and animal motifs with or without medallions or pearl roundels surrounding them (Dalton 1961, 590–4). The penetration of Persian motifs reflects the influence of far-flung civilizations on one another through trade or other forms of exchange. The more profound idea of using silk to

mark differences in status at ceremonial and ritual occasions probably came from further east, i.e. the homeland of silks. In the early
fifth century, at the baptism of Theodosius II, Constantinople was
decorated with silk hangings (Bury 1889, i, 204; Dalton 1961,
584). As discussed earlier, silk banners were essential decorations
and regalia during Buddhist and other religious ceremonies in
China, India and Central Asia in this period and in earlier periods.
Chrysostom has also mentioned that at this time the silk raiment
of Emperor Theodosius was embroidered with golden dragons
(Dalton 1961, 578).[5] According to literary sources, dragons appeared on banners even earlier. Without any material evidence of
the origin of the dragon motif in western tradition, Starensier tried
to identify the dragon in Byzantine literature with the Persian motif
simurgh (1982, 118 ff).[6] Perhaps there is another possibility. If one
considers the basic shape of the imaginary animal to resemble a
gigantic reptile, the simurgh motif bears little resemblance to a
dragon. The big tail on a simurgh motif looks like the tail of a
peacock motif in early Indian art. Without the characteristic horns
of a dragon, the head of a simurgh looks like that of a dog. The
simurgh is more like a combined mammal and bird than a gigantic
reptile. Thus even though material evidence is lacking, I suggest
we look further east. The dragon emerged in Chinese art as an
imaginary animal in early times and was associated with royalty.
Even though envoys of the later Han Dynasty never reached the
Roman empire, Chinese silks and other art works with various
imaginary animal motifs were no doubt known to the Roman
world. The Chinese silks found in Palmyra, a Hellenistic caravan
city in Syria, bear the motif of an imaginary animal.[7] Though the
floating animal motif with horns does not look completely like a

[5] According to Starensier, the guards surrounding the emperor wore garments
of silk ornamented with dragons (1982, 118).

[6] Krishna Riboud identifies a caftan excavated from northern Causasus with
the simurgh motif and three related samples as post-Sassanian (1976). But
Starensier has attributed them to Byzantine workshops (1982, 121–31).

[7] Pfister identified this piece as Han silk and linked it to the Han silk found
at Lou-lan and Noinula by A. Stein (Pfister 1934). In her 'Textile through the
Sassanian Period', Phillis Ackerman simply classifies this piece as Parthian without much discussion (Pope 1938, reprint 1981, 689). Pauline Simmons points
out this obvious mistake of Ackerman in her review of the studies of Chinese
textiles (1956, 23 ff).

reptile, it bears, in my opinion, more similarity to a dragon than a simurgh.[8]

After speculating on motif-transfer and the details of designs on textiles, we could look at the overall similarity of the clothing hierarchy in both Byzantium and T'ang China. In the chapter on silk in T'ang China, I mentioned that there was a whole set of rules guiding the clothing of emperors and the royal families, as well as those of officials of different ranks. Their silk robes varied in weaving, colour and pattern according to their ranks in the bureaucratic system. While the emperors considered yellow to be the traditional supreme colour, signifying the royal insignia on ceremonial occasions, purple was the highest in rank among the colours designated to officials as well as for the daily robes of the emperor, since the seventh century. Though the prestige given to the colour purple in seventh century China was probably inspired by western practices, the hierarchy of clothing had long imperial traditions. The rulers of the T'ang Dynasty, however, not only needed to change and adjust some specific items to make their court look different from that of previous dynasties, but also needed to built a comprehensive code of clothing to facilitate the transition from an aristocratic to a bureaucratic hierarchy.

In contrast, Byzantium had to establish its hierarchy of clothing against resistance stemming from the legacy of Roman republican traditions. Although sumptuary laws concerning the colour purple and purple silks were formulated in the early days of the later Roman empire, it took a few centuries for the emperors and their entourage to articulate the details and finalize the rules. The *Code of Ceremonies* compiled in the mid-tenth century was the result of these efforts.

Similar to the rules on clothing in T'ang China, according to the code compiled by the Byzantine emperor Constantine VII Porphyrogenitos (born in purple), the wardrobe of the Macedonian emperors and the costumes of the officials included robes and crowns for different occasions. Not only was the official set of clothing different from that of parade dresses, different colours and patterns were designed for religious festivals such as Easter (Starensier 1982, 184, 190 ff). The basic shades of the imperial

[8] See Totto Maenchen-Helfen (1943) for a comparison of animal motifs on Palmyra silks and dragon motifs on Chinese jade items and bronze mirrors.

garb were a deep purple and gold (ibid., 193). Following Augusta (empress) and Caesar (the younger son of the emperor), all the imperial ranks had their designated dresses for various occasions (ibid., 200 ff). In addition to purple, some motifs such as the eagle, ram and grapes were reserved for emperors (ibid., 240). Various officials and dignitaries wore robes with patterns of ivy leaves, white lions with coloured figures, red and green eagles, oxen, eagles in circle, marine creatures and white lions (ibid., 240). To make the scene of the court even more grandiose on diplomatic occasions, the court was decorated with silk hangings with patterns of griffons, plane trees, peacocks, equestrian figures and eagles (ibid., 221, 240). The dazzling display of fine silk apparels and decorations must surely have impressed foreign missions. To receive and to impress a delegation of Tarsus from the Islamic world:

The apsidiole into the sanctuary of the Theotokos Pharo was hung with crowns; that into the Oratory of H. Theodore with silk ornamented with lion/griffons; that into the Pantheon with thrice dyed purple silk with a design of plane trees; that through the Kaballarios, the emperor's equestrian entrance, with hangings with equestrian figures; that into the dining hall with important tapestries or rugs; that into the living quarters with peacocks; and the apsidiole of the Silver Door with two hangings, one with peacocks, another with eagles. Above the Silver Door itself was hung a gold sagion called the Caesarean (Starensier 1982, 222).

The *Code of Ceremonies* was compiled at a time when the T'ang Dynasty had already disappeared in China. As this code reflected a custom formulated over a few centuries, the whole concept of using silk textiles for projecting the grandeur of the court started in China. We may recall that when the Chinese pilgrim Hsüan-tsang travelled along the Central Asian routes in the seventh century, the tent court of the Western Turk with its splendid display of silk decorations and apparels greatly impressed him. The Arabs carried fancy Chinese silks, probably T'ang silks, to the Byzantine court in the tenth century (Dalton 1961, 586). Most silks that reached Byzantium, however, were probably silk materials and plain textiles waiting for further processing. This, rather than a few pieces of precious silk that reached the Byzantine territory, is indicative of cultural influences from the Orient which gave birth to the idea of using silk textiles to aggrandize the majesty of the court and mark differences in the bureaucratic hierarchy.

To preserve the uniqueness of the Byzantine court, sumptuary laws against its own citizens and the prohibition of commercial exportation were necessary. Up to the tenth century, the gold embroiderers, state clothiers, tailors and purple dyers worked in the proximity of the imperial palace (Starensier 1982, 235). Only once, at the end of the ninth century, did Emperor Leo VI allow scraps of purple silks to be traded in the domestic market:

I do not know for what reason emperors of earlier times, considering that they themselves were entirely garbed in purple, were induced to decree that not even trimmings of purple be allowed on the market, and not permit anyone to sell or buy that colour. And indeed, if they prohibited whole cloth to be sold, they would perhaps seem to have had a reasonable motive for doing this. But inasmuch as they prohibited to be on the market stripes and small pieces which might provide utility and use not unsuitable to either seller or buyer, with respect to this, what worthy reason do they allege in this decision of theirs, what envy of their subjects lurks therein? For as to the possibility that it may either affront the eminence of the Imperial Majesty, or may degrade it into common use, why, I ask, does it exist for those reasons? Accordingly we, not acquiescing in that decision, decree that fittings and strips which might provide our subjects with an elegant appearance or with other not prohibited use be permitted to be both sold and bought. For it is proper that his Imperial Majesty, since he bestows other varied benefits upon his subjects, should not begrudge them elegance (*Constitution LXXX*, quoted in Reinhold 1970, 69).

Though as late as in the first few centuries AD, purple was still readily available in Mediterranean markets, the combination of purple dye and silk weaving made government monopoly quite effective, even more effective than the monopoly on pure gold. In this respect, the Byzantine rulers were probably more successful than those of T'ang China.[9] Purple silk textiles and gold embroidery on silk were combinations of rare natural sources, technology, artistic creativity and ideological expressions. They were

[9] Starensier points out that the large quantity of Coptic textiles excavated from tombs in Upper Egypt, dated from the second to the ninth centuries, contained no single garment or hangings of whole silk (1982, 178). There may be other reasons inhibiting Egyptians from burying their dead with luxurious clothes. But the lack of silks in tombs with rich collections of textiles, compared to the abundant silks in Chinese Central Asian tombs, was an indication that in this part of the Byzantine empire, silks were not so common that commoners would bury them with their dead in spite of all prohibitions.

products of a civilization. Threatened with growing military might to the east and west, Byzantium clung to its last prestige. One can understand why, in the tenth century, the Byzantine customs' officials told Liutprand, an envoy of Otto I, when they confiscated the purple silk robes that he had tried to smuggle out of Byzantium, that only Byzantines deserved the silks, 'as we surpass all other nations in wealth and wisdom' (Lopez 1945, 41, *Legatione* LIV, Wright 1930, 267–8).

State Church and Silk in Byzantium

Byzantine emperors, though reluctant to let purple and gold embroidered silks be traded in domestic and foreign markets, were quite generous in donating these luxuries to churches and priests. Christian churches, both inside and outside Byzantine territory, may not have enjoyed immunity from sumptuary laws but they did receive many special gifts. Sharing prestigious silk vestments with the Christian church was only one of the ways in which Byzantine emperors sought to enhance their political power through the church. However, their relationship with the church was far from simple and straight forward. From the time that Constantine legalized the Christian church to the reign of Justinian I, fundamental social changes occurred in the eastern Roman empire. Archbishops became permanent local leaders. While eparches as state officials sent by Constantinople stayed in office for only short terms and had few local contacts, archbishops held their episcopates for long periods, if not life terms, which enabled them to build local ties (Cormack 1985, 75). With the weakening of state functionaries and the breakdown of civic structures, local wealth flowed into religious institutions. Cormack's study of Thessaloniki, a city in northern Greece, shows that in the seventh century, aristocrats donated their wealth to the church of St. Demetrios to build a haven of peace and safety, instead of giving money to maintain public and civic facilities as they used to do (Cormack 1985, 94).

   With the expansion of the Christian church, there were more and more bishops. The bishops held judiciary powers for civil suits; the churches owned properties. The clerical hierarchy was based on the state administrative structure. While metropolitan bishops were seated in provincial capitals, county bishops or presbyters took care of places of worship and prayer in rural areas

(Walter 1985, 184–5). From Constantine to Justinian, Byzantine emperors encouraged the expansion of the Christian church not only because their religious faith required them to do so, but also because an ideologically unified religious institution could serve as a powerful weapon for defending and expanding the empire.

However, in spite of their patronage, the emperors who wanted to assume leadership in religious matters found it increasingly difficult to handle the mature Christian church. Even Justinian failed to secure his leadership, though he was famous for not only founding the cathedral of St. Sophia, but also for enhancing church property and defending Christian orthodoxy. Procopius accused him of ruining his subjects to enrich the church 'for he thought that justice consisted in the priests' prevailing over their antagonists. And he himself, upon acquiring by means which were entirely improper the estates of persons either living or deceased and immediately dedicating them to one of the churches, would feel proud in his pretence of piety . . . ' (Procopius, VI, xiii, 4–10, p. 159).

Yet, it was not easy to choose the right side when the Christian church itself was entangled in the struggle to build its orthodox theology. In order to establish a unified church armed with an orthodox theology accepted by all Christians, conferences were held in succession to suppress heresies and expel condemned heretic groups from the church. Depressed and puzzled by the fierce debates between Arius and Athanasius, Emperor Constantine called for the council of Nicaea, which condemned the Arians as heretics (Placher 1983, 75). The council of Chalcedon in 451 condemned both the Monophysites in Alexandria and the Nestorians in Antioch as heretics (ibid., 80). In the sixth century, to establish himself as the leader of a unified Christian empire of the five patriarchates—Rome, Constantinople, Alexandra, Antioch and Jerusalem—Justinian outlawed paganism and persecuted various heresies (Walker 1985, 177). He was severe, perhaps ruthless, when trying to achieve his goal 'for in his eagerness to gather all men into one belief as to Christ, he kept destroying the rest of mankind in senseless fashion, and that too while acting with a pretence of piety. For it did not seem to him murder if the victims chanced to be not of his own creed' (Procopius IV, xiii, 4–10, p. 159). Justinian was more confident of his knowledge of Christian theology than was Constantine and so he actively precipitated controversies in order to bring different sects into his fold. However, he failed miserably and it was during his rule that different theological sects developed into churches in Syria, Egypt, Armenia, Ethiopia and Persia (Meyendorff 1968; Walker 1985, 179). In the next century these nationally based churches paved the way for Byzantium's loss of control over these provinces. The Monophysites in Egypt were more willing to accept Arab rule than that of the Byzantines (Walker 1985, 182). A strong Nestorian church held its ground in a large area from Syria to China for centuries. In spite of all his efforts to hold the orthodoxy, Justinian died a heretic according to the orthodox priests of the time (Gibbon IV, 148). In contrast, the Pope in Rome always triumphed in these debates. To the dismay of the Byzantine emperors, in the centuries after Justinian, the patriarchate of St. Peter gradually gained supremacy among the five patriarchates and eventually assumed the leadership of the entire Christian world.

The rise of divine power and the decline of imperial power was paralled by a change in the mentality of Byzantine citizens. They attributed their successes—military victories and accomplishments in other endeavours—to the grace of God and help from saints, and their failures to the scourge of God and saints as a punishment for their sins. Constantinople became the city of the Virgin. In 717, the patriarch attributed the failure of an Arab attack on the city to the Virgin instead of to the military campaign of Leo III (Cormack 1985, 107). The accumulated wealth and spiritual influence of the church were the cause of tensions with the imperial power, which ultimately led to the iconoclasm of the eighth century.

The apparent argument of the iconoclasts was that icons did not represent god and that icon-worshippers degenerated into idolatry. But the thrust of the movement was aimed at Christian institutions. The Christian community in the eighth century was no longer a group of believers who was only concerned with its salvation. It was a huge institution encompassing many peoples and social groups with vested interests. Whatever were the direct causes that led Leo III to remove the icon of Christ from the Chalke Gate in 726, and whatever the other events that triggered the surging and falling of iconoclastic waves in the following century, Byzantine citizens witnessed a religious persecution that resulted from this iconoclasm: icon-worshippers were imprisoned, tortured and exiled; monks were ridiculed and forced to marry; monasteries and their properties were confiscated (Walker 1985, 233). Meanwhile, the Byzantine empire did experience a stable imperial rule with iconoclast emperors and patriarchs in power. Both the temporary termination and the final termination of iconoclasm in the years 787 and 843 took place when junior emperors were on the throne (Cormack 183, 117). Military humiliations on the frontiers of Sicily, Crete and Asia Minor by the Saracens and in the Balkans by the Bulgars during the regency of the widowed queen Irene and her iconophile successors made the political situation of the country even worse (Walker 1985, 258). When the iconoclast tides finally receded, the Christian church in the empire emerged as an even more powerful ideological force and institution and wrested greater autonomy from the monarchy. Meanwhile, imperial power suffered a further loss. Having suffered another failure in the struggle with Rome because iconoclasm was condemned as heresy, the Byzantine emperors also lost the loyalty of the army when they returned to icon-phil (ibid.). The church assumed control of social and administrative functions in inverse proportion to the loss of control by the imperial system.

During the theological and political struggles that lasted a few centuries, the one advantage Byzantine emperors had over their western rivals and dissatisfied subjects was the cultural and material superiority of their people. The eastern part of the Roman empire was the homeland of Christianity. Byzantium owned the 'True Cross', the robe, the shroud, the girdle and the swaddling clothes with the marks of the milk of the Virgin (Baynes 1949, 175) plus the corporeal relics of numerous saints. Even during the age of iconoclasm, these relics were rarely touched. The 'True Cross' had been distributed through the entire Christian world for centuries. The Christian calendar and liturgy—the worship of Christ and Virgin, the festivals celebrating the Annunciation, the Nativity, etc. and the solemn and awesome rites and heavenly decorations in the basilica—started to take form since the time of Constantine in the eastern part of Christendom and then spread to the western section (Walker 1985, 193). No less important was the material culture which made this liturgy possible. It is hard to over-estimate the impressive effect of the grandeur of Constantinople in converting people to Christianity. In the year 988, when

Prince Vladimir of Kiev in Russia sent delegates to choose the best religion for his country, Byzantine's enthralling liturgy captured the hearts of the delegates: 'We know not whether we were in heaven or on earth. For on earth there is not such beauty and we are at a loss to describe it. We only know that God dwells there among men, and their service is fairer than the ceremonies of other nations. For we cannot forget that beauty' (quoted in Placher 1984, 103). So the Russians chose to follow Christianity. In West Europe, Byzantine culture reached most places through the relics of saints, covered by symbolic Byzantine silks, often in the form of a relic pouch. Relic pouches made in Byzantium have been found at many archaeological sites in West and North Europe (Muthesius 1982, 264 ff).

Only in this context can we realize the significance of the Byzantine rulers' patronage of the Christian church with silk textiles. Since Constantine gave a robe 'fashioned with golden threads' to Bishop Macarius of Jerusalem for use on the occasion of Baptism (M. Shepherd 1967, 63), figured silks made in imperial workshops continued to be used for liturgical purposes such as for church hangings and alter covers. Purple silks, gold-woven silks and whole silk continued to be given to Christian priests (Starensier 1982, 161, 178). To portray themselves as patrons of Christianity, Emperor Justinian and Empress Theodora had their images appear on the alter cover made of silk and gold in Hagia Sophia, along with that of Christ and the Apostles (ibid., 174).

Soon purple silks became sacred vestments for the church. On sacred art works, Byzantine court costumes covered the bodies of the images of Christ, Mary and the angels (Reinhold 1970, 65). Here again, we may recall the story about Sakyamuni Buddha leaving his gold woven ritual robe made by his aunt to the future Buddha Maitreya, and the mural portrait of Maitreya clad in a purple robe in a T'ang monastery (chapter III). On a beautiful silk tapestry in the Vatican, depicting the Annunciation (*Encyclopedia of World Art*, XIV, pl. 11), the Virgin is seated beside a basket of 'purple' (Lethaby 1913–14, 145). There is also an apocryphal literature on this subject. It is said that the Virgin spent her youth spinning purple (thread) in a temple. Around the year 670, a pilgrim in Jerusalem saw a tapestry showing Christ and the Apostles which was allegedly woven by the Virgin (Starensier 1982, 454). Here another phenomenon similar to the one that took place in

Buddhism occurred. The association of precious silks with divinity not only elevated the status and value of silk, but also increased the demand for silk throughout the Christian world.

Silk Was the Most Prevalent Currency

Many factors in early medieval Europe made silk the most preferred form of wealth, and therefore the most prevalent currency in transactions. China first discovered the advantage of trading silks for exotic goods from the West. The labour, technology and artistic value embodied in silk textiles made them more reliable and precious than copper coins, and more special than gold and silver. With human resources at hand, China commanded an inexhaustible source of wealth for foreign trade. We know that in both T'ang China and Central Asia, silks were the common currency. Byzantium learned this through its experiences in obtaining silk textiles and raw materials. In their struggles with Persia for the raw silk yarn, Romans realized how profitable it was to control this resource. Even after Byzantium developed sericulture, it could not monopolize raw silk because both the Persians and Arabs had access to Chinese silk supplies, and later to the technology of sericulture. However, Byzantium successfully monopolized purple silks and silk weaving through an imperial order. Byzantine rulers considered these silks to be a financial resource as important as gold, and the administration of silk production was under the ministry of mint since the fourth century. Later changes in administration never really separated the silk industry from the fiscal department (Starensier 1982, 492).

On the whole, inter-cultural trade did not prosper in the early medieval world. The monetary system in Europe, as well as in Asia, was not comprehensive. Even in Byzantium, silver coins stopped being minted around the sixth century (Postan 1987, 788). Even though silver coins in Sassanian Persia were quite valuable, they were rarely exchanged with Byzantine gold coins (Frye 1972, 361). In West Europe, from the seventh century onward, gold coins were not used for another five centuries (Postan 1987, 792 ff). As Postan describes it: 'The disappearance of the coinage system of antiquity, like the disappearance of the Roman senatorial aristocracy, took many generations. It was none the less complete' (ibid., 794).

The discontinuity of coins in Europe and the lack of interaction of different coinages in the early medieval world helped make silk one of the best gifts and a very useful weapon in diplomacy. The dazzling effect of silk displays in parades and court ceremonies aimed at impressing both Byzantine citizens and foreigners. With the diminishing of military glory, Byzantium depended more and more on manipulating foreign relations to keep its trade going, to defend its borders and even to get support for domestic power struggles. In the year 705, Justinian II regained the throne with the aid of the Bulgarian, Khan Tervel. As a token of his gratitude, the emperor presented silk cloth and purple leather to the Bulgarians in addition to an export license for controlled Byzantine goods (Lopez 1945, 32). This was a strategy the empire often employed to buy off barbarians along its borders (Starensier 1982, 290), similar to the Chinese who often had to buy off Hsiung-nu and other nomadic peoples along their borders since the Han Dynasty.

But Byzantine had more diplomatic problems than the Chinese of the Han and T'ang Dynasties had. To the east was the equally civilized Islamic world. To the west was the culturally inferior co-religious German states. Both had a stronger military presence than Byzantium. For making allies and enemies, silks were among the most prestigious gifts. For different purposes, silks were sent as gifts to Islamic rulers or as dowries to German kings. From the eighth to the twelfth centuries, about sixteen marriages between the Byzantine and German empires were negotiated or arranged and Byzantine envoys invariably carried silks as gifts (Muthesius 1984, 250). In 1100, the Byzantine emperor, Alexis I Comnenus, paid 100 purple garments to a German king (Reinhold 1970, 70). Sometimes the Byzantine rulers hid their humiliation by presenting their gifts as religious donations. In 1261, Emperor Michael VIII donated an altar frontal featuring the saints Lawrence, Sixtus and Hippolytus, all patron saints of Genoa, to the city in gratification for its aid in recapturing Constantinople from the Latin emperor, Baldwin II (Starensier 1982, 349). This is only one example of the numerous religious donations that brought Byzantine and eastern silks to western churches.

Chapter IV

Cult of Saints and
Christian Expansion

Most silk samples from the early medieval world, whether Byzantine, Persian, Central Asian or even Chinese, have survived in the graves of saints and church treasuries in Europe. The association of exquisite silks with the relics of saints and religious institutions was a component of the rise of the cult of saints and the Christianization of Europe. This phenomenon appeared in a period when Christianity, born in an urban environment, was spreading to a basically rural society. The demise of the Roman empire in the fifth century meant the final collapse of civic structures after centuries of conflicts and assimilation between the Roman civilization and barbarians. In Geary's words, it brought about the 'substituting Romanized barbarian kingdoms for a barbarized Roman Empire' (Geary 1988, 38). During the centuries that it took for the Romanized barbarian kingdoms to build a civic structure in Europe, governmental administration was weak and the Christian church functioned as the key institution in the civilization. Yet the Christian church had to establish itself in the whole of Europe through many proselytizing efforts. In this process, the cult of saints became the major vehicle of cultural influence spreading from the more civilized and already Christianized territory of the former Roman empire to the less civilized and Christianizing western and northern Europe. Silk textiles preserved in western and northern European churches are material evidence of the religious and cultural infiltration. Before going into detail regarding the silk trade and Christianity, we will look at the significance of the Christian church and relic-worship in the process of Christianizing and civilizing the European countries.

Significant Functions of the Christian Church

The de-urbanization of western Europe under the Franks continued into the ninth or tenth century. This was a period when even in the Byzantine empire de-urbanization was taking place. While Merovingian rulers still lived in cities, Carolingian kings could stay only on their rural estates (Geary 1988, 228–9). As public services no longer provided career opportunities, the Roman elite sought their fortunes either in the courts of barbarian kings or in ecclesiastical institutions. The Christian church was the unifying force in a divided and violent Europe. When military lords were busy feuding, the clergy assumed public responsibilities. In the sixth century, the clergy dwelled in cities, and its services in civic affairs maintained a thread of continuity in urban life from Roman times. Bishops gave alms to the poor according to the cities' poor roll (Geary 1988, 100). In the Carolingian period, when ecclesiastic institutions spread to most rural areas, churches served as community centres for peasants. After mass, people made contracts, with the priest serving as the drafter and the notary (Riché 1973, trans. McNamara 1978, 109). In a world where the state functionary was inadequate to maintain social order, urban and rural priests of good character sometimes acted as the protectors of the weak and delivered social justice, however limited, to their communities. Gregory of Tours described how a local priest tried to protect the marriage of two servants of the infamous Duke Rauching, though he did not make it to the spot in time to prevent the duke from burying the young couple alive, which led to the eventual death of the girl (Thorpe 1974, v. 3, p. 256).

Christian religious institutions, which provided some cohesion in chaotic late-antiquity and early medieval Europe, were mainly vassals of the feudal lord. Their clergy were related to aristocrats by blood. In the Merovingian period, perhaps most of the bishops in the Frankish kingdom were old Roman aristocrats. Gregory of Tours (AD 573–94 as bishop) was of distinguished senatorial stock from both sides of his family. In his antagonism with his sub-deacon, Riculf, Gregory boasted: 'The poor fool seems not to have realized that apart from five, all the other bishops who held their appointment in the See of Tours were blood-relations of my family' (Thorpe 1974, v. 49, p. 321). Under Carolingian rule, Frankish aristocrats often entered monasteries or joined the clergy.

Unfavoured royal members and young nobles without a definite
future would be educated in monasteries which were centres fo:
learning and the arts (Walker 185, 247).

From the early stage of their conquest, Frankish leaders had a
vassalage relationship with ecclesiastical institutions. Clovis (481–
511), according to Gregory of Tours, had converted to Christianity in the battle against Alamanni, when his army was almost
annihilated. In despair, he had invoked Jesus Christ and had
promised to become a Christian (Thorpe 1974, II, 30, p. 143).
Viewed from a broader context, one may suppose that the military
leader converted to orthodox Christianity to enlist the support of
the local Gallo-Roman aristocrats, and his conversion led his entire
army or his people to become Christians (Geary 1988, 85 ff).

The Merovingians strengthened churches and monasteries by
making endowments of big landed properties and donations of
precious goods. From Dagobert to Charles the Martel, Merovingian kings and nobles made St. Denis the largest property-holder
in the region of Paris (Geary 1988, 213). St. Denis became the
very necropolis for Frankish families. In incessant political struggles, ecclesiastical institutions were refuges and property-keepers
of elite Frankish families. Some of the nobles joined the church,
while others became saints. Those who were raised and educated
in the church voluntarily or involuntarily served the interests of
their families. The Pinide lineage was saved from political decima-
tion because two members of that family achieved sainthood and
became cults of worship (Geary 1988, 193–4).

To the resentment of Gallo-Roman priests like Gregory of
Tours, the Merovingian kings not only decided who would be
bishops, but also often made instant bishops out of laymen, such
as when Chilperic (561–84) assigned Badegisil, a Mayor of Palace,
as bishop of Le Mans (Thorpe 1974, VI, 9, p. 340). In many cases,
candidates who brought treasures to kings received their bishoprics
(e.g. Thorpe 1974, III, 2, p. 163; VIII, 21, p. 454). Gregory of
Tours accused King Childebert of naming a layman as the Bishop
of Eauze, in spite of the king's own oath that he would never
appoint a layman as bishop again, 'but to what will not the cursed
lust for gold persuade the heart of men' (ibid., VIII, 21, p. 454).
In the Carolingian period, bishoprics became such an honoured
prize that Notker the Stammerer, a monk in the Benedictine
monastery of Saint Gall, who lived in the ninth century, noted

that many people with status would come to Charlemagne when a bishop died, requesting the position for their candidates (Thorpe 1969, 4, p. 97).

Charlemagne was a great patron of the catholic church. According to Einhard, an adviser and friend of Charlemagne, he ordered bishops to restore all the ruined churches and shrines in his territory (Thorpe 1969, 17, p. 72). He built the magnificent Cathedral of Aachen with marble columns from Rome and Ravenna (ibid., I, 26, p. 79). 'He donated so many sacred vessels made of gold and silver, and so many priestly vestments that when service time çame even those who opened and closed the doors, surely the humblest of all church dignitaries, had no need to perform their duties in their everyday clothes' (ibid., I, 26, p. 80).

Charlemagne's political influence and patronage extended to St. Peter's in Rome. Between his four trips to Rome and his interference with the papacy, he donated a vast amount of wealth to the Apostle church and the Pope (Thorpe 1969, I, 27, pp. 80–1). In his will, Charlemagne left most of his valuables—gold, silver, jewels, regalia—to the twenty-one metropolitan dioceses, with Rome receiving the most. The archbishops administered the distribution of the valuables in their dioceses (ibid., I, 33, p. 88).

Military victories enabled Frankish kings to patronize the Christian church with luxury products. Even at the time of Charlemagne, the European economy was still quite backward. Agriculture was primitive, trade and industry were minimum, and surplus from production was limited. Valuables came mostly from war booty, as is evident from Einhard's statement that impoverished Franks suddenly became rich after defeating the Avars (Thorpe 1969, I, 13, p. 67). The Franks often sent part of their booty to churches and monasteries in thanksgiving for victories, as in the case of Charlemagne who, according to Notker the Stammerer (ibid., II, 2/1, p. 137), distributed the booty from Pannonia among his bishoprics and monasteries. On the other hand, the bishops and clergy of ecclesiastical institutions had to serve their lords, sometimes suffering humiliation at the hands of their lords, as their position was commensurate with that of vassals.

Frankish military leaders often seized church property to distribute among their followers (Geary 1988, 206). Church treasuries were used for emergency financial need (Fichtenau 1984, 77). Pipin II·of Heristal (d. 715) and Charles Martel (d. 741)

seized church property for their war needs (Walker 1985, 229).
Charlemagne was more careful about his relationship with the
church. Instead of meeting his financial needs by confiscating
church property, he took full advantage of the political and social
functions of ecclesiastical institutions. The clergy he appointed
carried out his policies and served as his envoys on diplomatic
missions (Riché 1973, 85). While monasteries and shrines often
provided asylum and refuge to rebels and dissidents, the rulers
also used monasteries to imprison their enemies or adversaries who
were related to them through blood or marriage. Charlemagne
put his son Pipin in the monastery of Prum after the son was
discovered in a plot against the father (Thorpe 1969, I, 19, p. 75).

The mutual dependence of Frankish lords and the Christian
church meant that proselytizing often followed the sword. After
conquering western Frisia, Pipin, the Frankish mayor of the
palace, encouraged Archbishop Willibrord to preach there at the
end of the seventh century (Bede, V, 10, p. 280). One of the
reasons Einhard gave for the Franks conquering the Saxons was
that 'they are much given to devil worship and they are hostile to
our religion' (Thorpe 1969, I, 7, p. 61). The war ended with the
condition that the Saxons would accept Christianity, and 'once
they had adopted the sacraments of the Christian faith and religion, they were to be united with the Franks and become one
people with them' (ibid., I, 7, p. 63).

In the British isles, strong support from kings was also necessary
for the spread of Christianity. In the year 616, when the people
of London preferred their idolatrous priests, King Eadbald could
not restore Bishop Mellitus to the See of London because royal
authority in the region was not strong enough (Bede, II, 7, p. 114).
Wilfrid could convert West Saxon to Christianity in AD 686
because he supported Ceadwala in his power struggle there and
the latter became his patron (Webb 1988, 143).

However, in a region even more rustic than Gaul after the
retreat of the Roman garrison, civilizing influences did not immediately follow proselytizing. Christianity gained root in Britain
first through rural-based monasteries, not urban-based bishops.
Early Christianity saw the spread of monasticism among the
peasantry of the non-Hellenistic populations of Egypt and Syria
(Walker 1985, 155). Between the fifth and the sixth centuries,
monasteries became centres of religion and culture in Britain

(ibid., 222–3). Irish monks advocated an anti-urban, austere life-style, and spread this to England and even the continent. The pristine form of Irish monasteries gradually receded when Western Europe, including both the continent and the British isles, started to appreciate the urban civilization which was represented by the Christian church and the material culture of Rome and beyond. Only by the ninth and tenth century, did trade and urban life start to revive in Europe, accompanied with the even more vigorous religious activities surrounding the cult of saints and the translation of the relics of saints.

Cult of Saints and Relic-Worship

The cult of saints appeared at an early stage of Christianity. After Constantine legalized Christianity, many churches were built throughout the Roman empire. These churches were of two types: cathedrals dedicated to Christ and the martyria to commemorate certain events or saints (M. Shepherd, 1967, 71–3). The martyria, analogical to the funeral buildings of pagan heroes in architecture, were built in the cemeteries of Rome and Constantinople (ibid., 72–4). To identify himself with the saints, Constantine planned for his tomb, first in Rome, and later in his new capital, to be conjoined with the martyrion. He prepared twelve sarcophagi for the relics of the apostles in the church of the Holy Apostles (ibid., 75).

As St. Peter was the protector of Rome and later of the papacy, the new capital also needed a protector. Jesus Christ would provide protection of a superior kind than St. Peter, but Jesus had left the world physically. It was felt that secondary relics related to his life could be a source of protection. Constantine wrote to the bishop of Jerusalem inquiring about the True Cross on which Christ was nailed, and legend has it that Constantine's mother went to Jerusalem to obtain it (Bentley 1986, 48). However, eventually, the Virgin Mary became the protector of Constantinople. In the fifth century, the robe of the Virgin was taken to the city, presumably with the consent of her heavenly being, along with her shroud, her girdle and the swaddling clothes 'in which Jesus had rested against his mother's breast' (Baynes 1949, 174–5).

If the origin of the cult of saints had some links with hero-

worship, the Christian cults underwent a fundamental development from the fourth to the fifth centuries. Most of the earliest
sacred relics were secondary. Though Jesus did not leave body
relics to his devotees, the saints did. The early Christians buried
saints and worshipped them at their tombs. From the fourth
century, Christians began to dig up the corpses of saints (Bentley
1985, 41). Modern historians, perplexed by this strange behaviour, try to determine the logic behind relic-worship and the
Christian view of the afterlife. A conventional view on the cult of
saints and relic-worship is that with the spread of Christianity to
uncivilized peoples, the general mass just substituted saint cults
for their pagan deities. The cult of saints may have reflected a
compromise between a monotheist religion and a polytheist religion, whether the polytheist religion comprised hero-worship
from the Roman culture or the worship of pagan deities of nature.
However, the compromise still does not explain the transition
from the ceremony at the graves of saints to the worship of the
corporeal relics of the saints enshrined in churches. As Peter Brown
has pointed out with sagacious wisdom, relic-worship caused deep
resentment in Rome during late antiquity, where hero-worship-
pers certainly resisted this abhorrent practice (ibid., 1981, 7). The
two-tiered model, i.e. the elite and the populace having different
religious practices, not only failed to explain the change in practices, but also could not explain the fact that both the elite and
the general mass of people in early medieval Europe shared these
religious practices (ibid., 181, 18–19).

The causes of the transition to relic-worship are multiple. In
the context of Christian institutional expansion, the rise of local
community centres as a consequence of the cult of saints may have
caused tension between the central Christian leadership and the
elite patrons of the local centres of worship and prayer. This
tension was reflected in the debate about superstition among
Christians and the propriety of feasting at the graves of family
members and the tombs of martyrs in the late fourth century and
early fifth century. At the beginning of the debate which lasted a
generation, bishops condemned the funeral ceremonies that were
patronized by the local lay Christian elite as pagan superstitions.
By the end of the generation, Augustine, one of the greatest
Christian thinkers, applauded the miracles taking place at the local
shrines of saints (Brown 1981, 26–7, 32–3). Now the bishops

managed to use the cult of saints to rally Christians to build local communities (Brown 1981, 37; Geary 1988, 137).

However, a profound change occurred in the concept of death and the afterlife which made people no longer abhor the dead body and be willing to engage in relic-worship. Early Christianity, like Judaism, emphasized the goodness inherent in this world, arguing that the world after life, whether heaven or hell, was too remote to be concerned with (Placher 1984, 53). However, in the late fourth century, Christians began to create a clear structure of the world beyond (Brown 1981, 63). Sin and final judgment became their greatest concern. This concern was the genesis of various specific Christian theological points which led to relic-worship. Geary thinks that because Christians believed in the resurrection of the dead body, they kept the relics of saints as a pledge that the martyrs would pick up at the final judgment (Geary 1978, 33). According to Baynes, the Byzantines believed that honouring the holy dead would make the saints speak to God on their behalf (Baynes 1949, 167). Bentley gives an example of the relics of a saint transforming the horror of death into hope of attaining heaven. Since the saint's soul was in heaven, the relics were links between earth and heaven (Bentley 1985, 27). Both Geary and Bentley point out that the relic cult was a religious expression shared by both Islam and Buddhism (Geary 1978, 32; Bentley 1985, 191–4). This common religious expression may have been inspired by a similar view of the afterlife shared by the major religions, though the exact picture of the afterlife varied greatly among the various religions. The fact that most early saints were martyrs and Jesus himself was a martyr makes one wonder why those who could not defend themselves when alive would be trusted to protect others after death. However, if there is an afterlife, those who were faithful in this life and died heroically would certainly be in a superior position in the other world, and thus could wield supernatural power over those alive. Whatever the rationale behind this custom, it prevailed among both the Buddhists in Asia and the Christians in Europe in the same period.

The Romans used to bury their dead out of the city, on the roadside, or later in catacombs. Even the saints shared their tombs with commoners, whether Christian or pagan, in these cemeteries (Aries, 1985, 5). Before the seventh century, the bishops of Rome had to make a trip to the catacombs to worship the relics of martyrs. It was only in 648 that these relics were first brought into the city and enshrined in churches (Bentley 1985, 59). Since then, many translations have taken place. The heads of St. Peter and St. Paul, enshrined in the Lateran, became the centre of worship for the entire Christian community (ibid., 60). The Pope was the guardian of the body of St. Peter who had been entrusted with the key to heaven by Jesus Christ, and who was considered the first Pope of Rome. This legend thus provided legitimacy to the Pope to win the leadership of the Christian world.

The Role of Relics in Christianizing Europe

Outside Rome and Constantinople, in the Frankish kingdom and Britain, apparently the local cults of saints replaced cults of woods, rivers and groves during the early Christian period. By the sixth century, the tombs of saints became centres of religious life. Tombs and altars joined with churches being built on old cemeteries. This was because the local saints were originally buried there, and because it was a privilege for common Christians to be buried near saints as the latter would facilitate their entrance into heaven. Therefore, chapels were built on pre-Christian cemeteries and cemeteries changed into Christian necropolis (Geary 1988, 109). In this process, the church replaced the family in taking care of the dead (Brown 1981, 31).

In the spread of Christianity to western Europe, the vision of the afterlife and the ways to achieve salvation were the decisive factors in conversion. There were various approaches to salvation, including baptism, communion and penance. But the goal was either divine protection in this world or the bliss of heaven. Visions of the bliss of heaven, the ruthless torture of purgatory and the despair of hell urged people to seek a safe approach to the afterlife. In England, Bede (673–735), a monk of Jarrow and the author of the famous *Ecclesiastical History of the English People*, related how a man who returned from death after witnessing the procedure after death became a devout Christian (Bede, v, 12, p. 284). In AD 627, King Edwin of Northumbria in North England held a council with his chief followers to decide whether they should accept Christianity. One of his chief men supported the conversion with the argument that Christianity provided a better knowledge of the afterlife than did their original religion: 'Man appears on earth for a little while, but of what went before this life and of what follows, we know nothing. Therefore, if this new teaching has brought any more certain knowledge, it seems only right we should follow it' (Bede, II, 13, p. 130). When Northumbrians suffered a plague and many people resorted to praying to local deities and to witchcraft, Cuthbert (634–687), then a prior and later the bishop of Lindisfarne, preached with the promise of heaven (Webb 1988, 54). The logic was that if Christianity could not help its faithful escape death, it would help them to go to a better place after death. In 663, King Oswiu sponsored a debate between the pro-Roman bishop, Wilfrid, and the Irish bishop, Colman, on the proper way to observe Easter. After a long and vehement argument, Wilfrid finally convinced the king that his way was correct because it was the way observed by the Apostolic See, the See of St. Peter, who was the door keeper of heaven. The king accepted this argument as 'Peter is guardian of the gates of heaven, and I shall not contradict him. I shall obey his commands in everything to the best of my knowledge and ability; otherwise, when I come to the gates of heaven, there may be no one to open them, because he who holds the keys has turned away' (Bede, III, 25, p. 192). Thus the very idea that St. Peter was the door keeper of heaven rallied the English church to the side of the papacy.

Having converted to Christianity, largely due to their concern with the afterlife, aristocrats in the Frankish kingdoms and English isles did everything in their power to guarantee their access to heaven. From the seventh century, Frankish families built monasteries on their own property. The monastery not only received family members who chose a religious life, but also served as the necropolis of the family to pray for the souls of all members (Geary 1988, 173). St. Denis was the necropolis of the Frankish rulers. In Carolingian times, the clerks of kings guarded the relics of saints in palace chapels and provided religious services to the royal family (Riché 1973, 91–2). The Franks also made every effort to remind the living to pray for the dead. Lists of the names of the ancestors of aristocratic families were preserved in abbeys for prayers (ibid., 60–1). People formed prayer associations to say mass for their dead. A special mass would be said a month after the funeral of the dead. The next year, members would take turns to say the mass. After his death in 762, a member of the Synod of Attigny received a hundred masses and a hundred psalms in

addition to thirty masses by each bishop. The names of the dead
were carved on alters and churches exchanged lists for prayers
(ibid., 241 ff).

Prayer associations were first formed among the Anglo-Saxons
(242). Christians in the English isles feared death as much as did
the Franks. Nobles bought estates to build monasteries, even
though, as Bede complained, they were often filled with unworthy
monks (Bede, letter to Egber, 345). A Northumbrian king, Ethel-
wald, granted a piece of land to the priest Cedd in AD 659 to
found a monastery for him to pray and be buried (Bede, III, 23,
p. 181). His father, Oswy, dedicated his daughter, Aelffled, to a
monastery at Whitby. The St. Peter church in that monastery was
the tomb of Oswy, his daughter, his wife Eanfled, his father-in-law
Edwin and many nobles (Bede, III, 24, p. 184).

The earnest concern with the afterlife among the Christians of
Western Europe was natural considering the extremely difficult
and unstructured social conditions in which they lived. Warfare,
famine and plague constantly decimated the population. The
upper classes may have suffered less in times of famine, but
fratricide and feuds for power often wiped out entire families.
However, conversion never guaranteed happiness in this life.
Though saints, living and dead, wrought many miracles, only the
very fortunate were served by miracles. Most people, rich or poor,
noble or humble, succumbed to natural and human disasters. A
devout Christian ruler could lose his life in a battle against pagans,
as was the case of the East Angles king, Sigbert, who was killed
by the Mercians in AD 635 (Bede, III, 18, p. 172). The Mercian
king then, 'without fear of god or respect of religion', invaded
Kent and profaned churches (IV, 12, p. 224).

In their political struggles, Frankish nobles always trusted their
fate to churches and monasteries, even though they were often
betrayed by their faith. The royal members who were defeated in
battles or political intrigues, widowed queens and unfavoured
courtiers entered cathedrals or monasteries for refuge, yet they
were often killed there. Even a priest could be killed in front of
an altar.[1] Both the rich and poor deposited their treasure in

[1] Gregory of Tours blamed the priest, Proculus, for his own death; Proculus
was killed in front of the altar of his own church. According to Gregory, Proculus
must have done something wrong to St. Quintianus, the protecting saint of the
church (Thorpe 1974, III, 12, 172).

churches. But these treasures incited foreign invasions, which put even the warlike Franks in a defensive position. The stunning treasures that the Vikings took to Scandinavia were mostly from the churches of the English isles and the continent. Invasions by the Vikings in the ninth and tenth centuries caused monks to flee with the relics of saints since the saints could not ward off the invaders (Duby 1974, 116).

In early medieval Europe, diseases took many lives, both of the elite and the low-born, despite the curing power of saints and their relics. Before the Frankish king Clovis converted to Christianity, his son died just after being baptized in a white robe (Thorpe 1974, II, 30, p. 142). Clovis, nevertheless, received baptism, along with more than three thousand of his soldiers. His sister was also baptized but died soon after (ibid., II, 31, p. 145). The theological explanation for all the disasters falling on innocent and devout Christians was that the sins of the people incurred the scourge of God. Sin was inevitable; there was no way to stop other people from sinning, and hence the scourge was also inevitable. The only hope, therefore, was the promise of a better afterlife. St. Remigius, the bishop of Rheims, consoled Clovis upon the death of his sister with the assurance that since she had been baptized, she would certainly go to heaven (ibid.). On this matter alone, the Christian church never failed its faithful followers. Priests always baptized the living and always took care of the dead to prepare them for heaven. In the great plague of Auvergne in AD 571, bodies piled up in churches. In St. Peter's church in Clermont city, 300 bodies were buried on one Sunday. Rather than fleeing from the city, the priest, Cato, buried the dead and continued to say mass until he himself succumbed (Thorpe 1974, IV, 31, p. 226). Only an understanding of the fear of death and the hope of happiness after this life sheds light on the intensity of the devotion of early medieval European Christians and their great faith in a religion which did not always protect them from unhappiness in this world.

Roman Influence and Pilgrimage

As the Pope and Rome always sided with the winning party in theological debates in the Christian world, and as Roman churches were the keepers of the Apostles, Peter and Paul, the Patriarch of

Rome emerged as the leader of the Christian church in the western territory of the former Roman empire. He had the authority to send missionaries and settle disputes among the Christians in western Europe. Normally, Frankish rulers appointed bishops, but in cases of disputes, dismissed bishops could go to Rome to appeal their cases in front of the Pope.[2] In the year 722, when Pope Gregory II sent the English priest Boniface to the Franks, Boniface took an oath on the Apostle Peter. Frankish leaders considered Boniface, who brought Roman ideas and disciplines to Frankish churches, as having been sent by St. Peter (Walker 1985, 230). At the insistence of Pipin, Charles the Martel and Charlemagne, the Roman way of chanting prayers spread to all the churches in the whole empire (Riché 1973, 92).

Roman influence on the ecclesiastical institutions of the British isles was even greater. After the missionary, Augustine, set up his episcopacy in Kent, Pope Gregory I sent envoys to him in the year 601. 'They brought with them everything necessary for the worship and service of the church, including sacred vessels, altar coverings, church ornaments, vestments for priests and clergy, relics of the holy Apostles and martyrs, and many books' (Bede, I, 29, p. 90). In 664, the English kings, Egbert and Oswy, sent a priest, Wighart, to Rome to be consecrated as the archbishop. The candidate however died of plague soon after his arrival in Rome, and Pope Vitalian chose a Greek monk, Theodore, to be the archbishop of Canterbury. Theodore reached England in 669 with the decrees of Rome and became the first archbishop of all of England (Bede, IV, 2, p. 205). Theodore, well versed in both sacred and secular literature, visited churches and monasteries, and taught numerous students poetry, astronomy, calculation of the Christian calender, in addition to the holy scripture and sacred music (ibid.). As Gaul was more Romanized than was England, it served as a base for spreading orthodox Christian practices and knowledge (Webb 1988, 111). Pope Gregory I instructed Augustine, the bishop of Canterbury, to consult the bishops of Arles about problems related to the church (Bede, I, 27, p. 81). Bishop Wilfrid received his tonsure in the Roman style at Lyon. After his

---

[2] Two bishops dismissed from their positions by the Guntram because of their misbehaviour received permission from the king to appeal to Pope John III (559–72) (Thorpe 1974, V, 19, p. 285).

election to the episcopacy, he went to Gaul to receive consecration because the bishops there followed Roman rules (Webb 1988, 116). Due to his disputes with English kings, Wilfrid was expelled from his see. He made two trips to Rome to appeal his case in the Apostolic See. It was the support of Pope Agatho and Pope John that enabled him to finally be reinstated as the bishop of Hexham in England (Eddius Stephanus, *Life of Wilfrid*, in Webb 1988). To protect monastic property, Coefrid, the abbot of Jarrow from 682 and of both Wearmouth and Jarrow from 688 to 716, sent monks to Rome to get an indult from the Pope granting privileges to the monasteries, which was further confirmed by the synod of the English king, Aldfrid, and the bishops (Webb 1988, 201). To proclaim himself a true Christian, King Cadwalla of West Saxon went to Rome in 688 for baptism and was given the name Peter by the Pope (Bede, v, 7, p. 275).

The rise of the papacy and the increase of Roman influence in western Europe changed the sources of the saint-cult. Up to the seventh century, most of the saints worshipped by the Franks and English were local, either recluses who lead austere and pure lives or bishops who were successful missionaries. Even virtuous kings could become saints, such as King Oswald who became a saint to protect others after he died in battle (Bede, IV, 14, p. 229). However, as early as in the sixth century, relics from Rome or further east were treasured. Gregory of Tours sent his deacon to Rome to get relics in the year 590 (Thorpe 1974, x, 1, pp. 543, 547). Gundovald, pretender to the Merovingian throne, seized the relics of a saint from a Syrian merchant for protection (VI, 30, 413). The relics of Apostles were especially important for missionaries. When Willibrord received permission from the local prince to preach in Frisia, he hurried back to Rome to fetch relics (Bede, v, 71, p. 282). As mentioned earlier, Pope Gregory sent relics to the missionary Augustine in England. At the time of Bede, visiting Rome was viewed as a matter of great merit among the Christians of England (IV, 23, p. 245). Christians may have wanted to also visit Jerusalem and other sacred sites in the east, but Rome was a more practical destination and was prestigious enough to enhance the status of the pilgrims. Every time Wilfrid went to Rome on a pilgrimage or on business, he visited the shrines of saints and collected relics to take back for his church (Webb 1988, 110, 112, 140, 167). Benedict Biscop, the abbot of Weamouth and Jarrow, made five trips to Rome in the mid-seventh century to venerate relics, and brought back books, relics and silks (186, 188, 190, 194).

Initiated by the Pope, the translation of relics gained momentum and developed into a prosperous business during the rule of the Carolingians. Roman saints replaced local saints as major cult figures. Though many places already owned relics from Rome or the East, pilgrims continued to stream into Rome. In the ninth century, pilgrimages developed into a tourist business. In Rome, every national group, whether Anglo-Saxon, Frisian, Franks or Lombard, had its own hostel, which included a church, lodging and cemetery (Riché 1973, 283). Guidebooks helped the pilgrims to scout around the shrines for relics among the ruins and churches in Rome (ibid.).

The number of saints grew quickly and soon became overwhelming. By the eighth century saints were so numerous that under Carolingian rule, the kings started to regulate the cults. According to the Synod of Frankfurt in 794, no new saints were to be worshipped or invoked (Geary 1978, 44–5). However, this action was not taken from a feeling of hostility towards relics. Though there had been important theological debates between the iconoclasts and iconophiles in the eastern church, neither the western nor the eastern churches disputed the sacredness of relics. The second council of Nicea in 787, where the major aim was to reverse the iconoclast trend, ruled that all churches should have relics under their altars (Bentley 1985, 214). In the Frankish empire in the early ninth century, the council of Carthage ordered the destruction of all church altars without the relics of saints (Geary 1978, 43).

The extreme action of demolishing altars may appear contrary to the purpose of propagating Christianity. Nevertheless, considering that Christian preachers had to confront many local non-Christian cults, a tangible object for worship was necessary for recently converted pagans. When Pope Gregory the Great (590–604) commissioned Augustine of Canterbury to convert pagan England, these relics were especially useful in the contention with superstitious pagan rites. In his letter to Abbot Mellitus on the latter's departure for Britain (AD 601), Pope Gregory exhorted:

When by God's help you reach our most reverend brother Bishop

Augustine, we wish you to inform him that we have been giving careful thought to the affairs of the English, and have come to the conclusion that the temples of the idols among that people should on no account be destroyed. The idols are to be destroyed, but the temples themselves are to be aspersed with holy water, altars set up in them, and relics deposited there. . . . Because the English have been used to slaughtering many oxen as sacrifice to devils, some solemnity must be put in place of this, so on the feast days or birth days of the holy martyr whose relics were there deposited, close by those churches which were once pagan temples they may build themselves huts of the boughs of trees and hold a religious feast. Instead of offering beasts to the devil, they shall kill cattle and in eating them praising god, giving thanks to the giver of all things needful for food (Bede, I, 30, p. 92).

In this case, the Pope deliberately had saint cults replace many functions of pagan gods. The Christians treated the relics of saints in a similar way to that of gods. Relics were used as talisman in witchcraft. The queen of the English king, Ecgfrith, took away the reliquary full of relics from Wilfrid the bishop and wore it as a necklace (Webb 1988, p. 142). Frankish kings collected relics in their palaces for protection (Geary 1988, 188). When King Chilperic entered Paris in 583, he sent relics ahead of his retinue to avoid the curses he expected for breaking his agreement with his brother (Thorpe 1974, VI, 26, p. 355). There were so many feasts for saints that in 813 all-saints day started to be observed on 1 November (Riché 1973, 241). The rise and decline of the cult of a certain saint followed the rule of pagan deities. A deserted chapel would gain worshippers if people found it efficacious in curing sickness. This happened in one of the chapels of St. Denis in the early twelfth century. Abbot Suger quickly acted to restore and develop the chapel when he learned that candles were being burnt there (Panofsky 1979, 9).

The rituals accompanying superstitious sacrifices to devils and the feasts for saints did not differ much. Christians distinguished themselves from the pagans only by their objects of worship— relics of saints—and their praising of God. For the people who were not clear about the differences between their earlier cults and God, the relics were the only token of their conversion to Christianity. For this reason, Charlemagne intensified this focus on relics. Since a legitimate altar was supposed to have relics, the translation of relics was frequent. The importance given to liturgy

on the occasions of translation impressed the recently converted
Christians (Geary 1978, 43). After the disintegration of the Carolingian regime, the English succeeded the Franks as relic collectors
in the tenth century. Since there were not enough martyrs in
England to fill all the altars, King Athelstan and his successors
gathered many relics from the continent through various means,
ranging from diplomatic exchanges to purchasing them from
merchants or thieves (Geary 1978, 59 ff). From the perspectives
of the Pope and Byzantine emperors, the distribution of relics
helped propagate Christianity, showed the superiority of their
civilization and reminded barbaric states of their predominant
position in the religious sphere, if not in military power. But for
western European monarchs, whether Frankish, English or others,
collecting relics and establishing the norm that an altar with the
relics of saints was the centre of worship and ritual became a means
to obtain protector saints for their states and subjects and thus
consolidate their national states. One later example was the abbot
Suger of St. Denis who mobilized France to fight against Henry
V of Germany in the early twelfth century:

While the hosts were assembling, the relics of Saint Denis and his
Companions were laid out on the main altar of the Abbey, later to be
restored to the crypt 'on the shoulders of the king himself'. The monks
said offices day and night. And Louis le Gros accepted from the hands
of Suger, and 'invited all France to follow it', the banner known as the
'Oriflamme'—that famous 'Oriflamme' that was to remain the visible
symbol of national unity for almost three centuries yet, at the same time,
to proclaim the king of France a vassal of St. Denis; for the 'Oriflamme'
was in reality the banner of Vexin, a possession the king held in fief of
the Abbey (Panofsky, 1979, 5).

Therefore, the relics of saints assumed important economic and
social functions in early medieval European societies. In a period
when little communication existed between peoples and the means
to build trust was nonexistent, relics were used on important
occasions and during transactions. The early Christians were not
in favour of taking an oath. As Europe became increasingly rural
and the old social order disappeared, the council of Chalcedon in
452 allowed people in the eastern churches to swear on the Gospel
(Bentley 1985, 79–80). In the eighth century, the Pope made
oath-taking in front of relics not only legitimate but also necessary;

in 722, the Pope summoned the missionary, St. Boniface, to Rome to take an oath on St. Peter's relics before asking him to return to Germany to continue his work. With the support of St. Peter, Boniface successfully defeated the pagan cult of the tree. Then using the timber from the Oak, the object of tree worship, he built a chapel (ibid., 80).

As Germanic tradition was in favour of taking oaths on certain objects, it was natural for people to continue to do so on relics after they converted to Christianity. In 803, after Charlemagne ordered that 'all oaths be sworn either in a church or on relics' (Geary 1978, 44), taking oaths on relics became the norm. When nobles held a regional council to solve their disputes they swore on the relics of saints to promise peace (ibid., 24). The saint who could attract nobles to hold their council would also certainly enhance the reputation of the monastery or church that hosted him.

It is understandable that monasteries competed with each other for relics to win this kind of prestige. But relics of famous saints meant more than just spiritual superiority. They provided the very livelihood and prosperity for a monastic community or even the prosperity of the region.[3] The significance of a saint depended not only on his heroic behaviour as a martyr, but also on his miraculous powers in curing the sick and helping the needy. With numerous local saints competing for the patronage of pilgrims and worship, the latter quality became even more important. The powerful relics gained wealth for the monasteries and local communities. Initially donations were probably used for building cathedrals, embellishing churches and supporting monks. In a rural environment, agricultural products were donated—beasts, corn, oil, wood, etc. Once the miracles of saints became common knowledge, the donations also increased overwhelmingly. Monks began to organize fairs at the anniversaries of saints. These fairs were not only of benefit to monks and churches, but also provided blessings for the whole community (Bentley 1985, 101 ff). Since fairs were the hub of trade and cultural activities they gained in economic and cultural importance. Under the auspices of saints, churches and monasteries became rich. War booties went to

---

[3] See Patrick Geary for an illustration of the competition for the relics of St. Foy between Conques and Agen under the Frankish reign in light of the significance of relics in attracting pilgrims (1978, 72 ff).

churches in thanksgiving for the protection of saints during battles. The wealthy people deposited their treasures in churches for
safe-keeping by the saints. The accumulation of wealth was the
basis of building more brilliant shrines for saints and for bringing
more relics to shrines.

Translations of Christian Relics

In the Carolingian empire relics were necessary for all churches,
and hence the demand for saint relics increased. The problem
was how to increase the supply of relics, especially in Europe,
north of the Alps. Most early saints were martyrs because mar-
tyrdom was the most easily recognized standard for sainthood.
Yet there had not been many opportunities to produce martyrs
in the regions north of the Alps. Churches in the west naturally
looked to Rome for relics as martyrdoms mainly took place in
this city. Different kinds of transactions took place. Abbot Hilton
of St. Medicare of Soissons compelled the Pope to render him
the body of St. Sebastias in the early ninth century through
Frankish imperial power (Geary 1978, 47). The less influential
abbots had to rely on professional relic traders. These traders,
like other traders in medieval times, travelled in caravans, crossing
the Alps periodically and then the continent to supply goods to
England (ibid., 52). The famous relic merchant, Deusdona, obtained the bodies of St. Peter and St. Marcellinus for Einhard at
Mulinheim (ibid., 52–4).

Such important relics were not adequate to meet the demands
of the many churches in Europe. Secondary relics, though not as
good, bridged the gap. The clothes of saints, especially those
stained by their blood and the instruments used in the torture of
martyrs, were considered important relics (Bentley 1985, 42–4).
Theoretically these relics were as valued as the whole body. As
early as the fourth century, the Cappadocian father, St. Gregory
of Nazianzus, made it clear that even a drop of blood from a saint
or martyr was an efficacious relic (ibid., 51). Considering that
many martyrs did not leave their entire bodies to devotees, this
claim was quite practical. There was a whole nomenclature on the
different sets of relics in medieval Europe (ibid.).

Since relics were in high demand, all kinds of forgeries occurred. Relics of famous saints showed up at convenient times.

When modern historians calculated and added up the relics in different church inventories, they found that the sum of the parts exceeded the whole body. Mary Magdalene's relics add up to six bodies; St. Gregory the Great supposedly had two bodies plus four heads (Hermann-Mascard 1975, quoted in Bentley 1985, 29). These statistics may bewilder modern Christians, or even historians, who would find it difficult to believe that medieval devotees could blindly put faith in those relics. However, it is possible that in a society lacking communication, people may not have been aware that the body of a particular saint also existed elsewhere besides in their own church. The church clerks who were aware of the fact probably defended the genuineness of their relics in order to compete with other churches. The authenticity of relics depended on whether they wrought miracles, cured diseases and alleviated suffering.

Stolen relics seemed like a loss to the papacy. But Rome had a rich source of relics. Popes became increasingly aware of the rich asset that these relics were and started to manipulate their trans-lations. After Pope Paul I moved the relics of over a hundred saints to the city of Rome for safe-keeping in the mid-eighth century, the popes deliberately let some saints go to the Frankish church, to emphasize the central position of Rome in Christendom (Geary 1978, 64, note 39). The twelfth century anecdote concerning the English king Henry II clearly illustrates papal skill in manipulating sainthood in order to exploit human fear of the afterlife in a world of military power. Archbishop Thomas Becket, a long-standing enemy of Henry II, was murdered in the Canterbury Cathedral. Upon hearing this news on New Year's day of 1171, Henry II was terrified beyond measure (Bentley 1986, 72–3). He was aware that this form of death in a cathedral would make the archbishop a saint, and thus a supernatural power over himself. Pope Alex-ander III took full advantage of this occasion to humiliate the king by canonizing Thomas Becket as a saint (ibid., 73). The penance and humiliation that Henry II suffered is well known in history as a victory of the papacy. Here I want to remind the reader that this victory was possible because of the fear of saints and the supernatural power of saints, prompted by a common vision of the afterlife that was shared by many religions.

In spite of the many similarities between the cult of saints and popular deities, the Christian cult differed from primitive religion

fundamentally in its cultural connotations. As Peter Brown pointed out, the rise of saints helped to define the upper class and
urban culture as opposed to rustic society (Brown 1981, 124).
The patronage of saints not only structured the relationship
between secular and clerical elites, but also linked Christians to
the patriarchate of Rome. Individual Christians took on the
names of saints (ibid., 58–9). The church expanded to rural areas
from municipal bases, and Latin and Roman culture replaced
aboriginal languages and customs. Even cities could identify
themselves with Roman cities because they owned the relics of
the named Apostles of Roman cities (ibid., 41). In England, after
Wilfrid prevailed in the controversy on the observation of Easter
under the auspices of St. Peter, Irish monks retreated from north
England (Bede, III, 26, p. 193; III, 28, p. 197). Rustic monasticism
and austere recluses like Cuthbert who would not let monks wear
expensive clothes and enjoy any luxuries were in decline. Bishops
who were versed in both sacred and secular Latin literature and
who knew Roman ecclesiastical customs were beginning to shape
the Christian church in Europe along the lines of Roman spiritual
and material culture.

Chapter V

Christianity and Silk Trade

The rise of the cult of saints and the traffic of relics brought more wealth, including silks, into the already wealthy churches of western Europe. Silk textiles were preserved in churches in various forms: church decorations and hangings, altar covers, decorations and wrappings on reliquaries and shrines for saints, and shrouds and tomb covers for bishops and kings. It was a time when all the magnates, whether secular or clerical, were buried in ecclesiastic institutions. Churches stored silks in their treasuries as a form of wealth. However, initially Christians were not eager to give their wealth to churches. It took a few centuries for people to be convinced that to give their wealth to the church was a better way to help the dead than to bury treasures in graves. In Roman times, funerals were the show-places of family wealth and fame (Kyriakalis 1974, 49). Though the early Christian priests condemned the practice of burying the dead with rich clothes and ornaments and tried to convince the people that irrespective of how the dead were dressed, they ultimately faced God naked (ibid., 50), this approach seemed only applicable to common Christians. When the burials of commoners became simpler, more and more treasures went into the tombs of priests, whether they had led austere or lavish lives. In the fourth century, a bishop was buried with 'clean sheets, silk clothes, plenty of myrrh and perfume' (Kyriakalis 1974, 46). By the fifth century, Christian holy men were all buried with their finest liturgical vestments (Kyriakalis 1974, 51; Starensier 1982, 40).

The burial ceremonies of holy men and the re-burials of saints became increasingly luxurious, because of expectations of blessings in proportion to the donations made. The shift from burying luxuries with dead relatives to giving the luxuries to holy men or saints was a fundamental break from the traditional view of the afterlife. Like their Chinese contemporaries in Turfan, Christians began to also realize that their loved dead ones could not carry goods to the other world. On the other hand, if they pleased the saints by giving generous donations, the holy souls of these saints would help the dead in the other world. The commoners under the Byzantine kings probably followed the advice of priests. Both literary references and archaeological artifacts from Egyptian graves in the Byzantine period show that people did not bury their dead in their best clothes (Gervers 1983, 279). Silks were hardly ever seen in burials, even though silk production has been documented in that period (ibid., 296). This tradition continued into the late eleventh and twelfth centuries in Egypt under Islamic rule (ibid., 298–9).

If the Byzantines could not afford to bury their dead in all their finery, the poorer Latin Europeans were even more constrained. The Franks buried goods with the dead on the basis of status. Hence, silks and other tokens of veneration were reserved for a few rulers and quite a few saints. The rulers wanted to be buried close to the saints; Charlemagne was buried in the cathedral of Aachen and Charles the Bold was buried in St. Denis (Panofsky 1979, 71). The relics of saints made people want to bury their dead in churchyards, in the proximity of the holy power. The spacious and neatly planned cemeteries in the country were given up in preference for crowded churchyards. Churchyards became so popular as burial grounds that bones had to be piled up to make room for more corpses (Aries 1985, 20 ff). The scattering of the skeletons and bones of the dead did not bother the relatives since they felt that the remains of their loved ones had been entrusted to the church, God and the protection of saints. On the contrary, people felt at home in churchyards that were filled with human bones and churchyards became places for all kinds of religious and secular gatherings and activities (ibid., 19).

The difference between common human bones and those of saints was that the latter produced miracles. But to mark the difference in order to venerate and please the saint, Christians decorated the relics of saints. From the sixth century, the lay people regarded silk clothes placed over a tomb as testimony of a canonized saint (Starensier 1987, 450). Gregory of Tours described the silk covers on the tombs of St. Denis and St. Goar (Muthesius 1982, 286). By the eleventh century, the tombs of most bishops were covered with silks (ibid., 287). In England too, Byzantine silks covered the corpses of eminent holy and secular persons in churches (Dodwell 1982, 159 ff). As Byzantine silks depicting sacred images were not readily available in the West, country folks and rural saints were satisfied with whatever silks were available. Even Fatimid silk textiles with heathen images and Arabic inscriptions were used as shrouds (Starensier 1982, 452).

Most silks owned by churches were stored in church treasuries. But before the twelfth century, most churches and monasteries did not have treasuries, in which case reliquaries and altars were used for this purpose (Muthesius 1982, 264). Therefore, silks were inseparable from relics. The practice of using reliquaries as treasuries to hold luxurious donations started in Byzantium (Riché 1973, 72–3). In the Lateran Palace of Rome, through the grille front of the Sancta Sanctorum, medieval pilgrims could see a variety of reliquaries enclosing relics and silks (Muthesius 1982, 265). The shrine at St. Servatius, Maactricht, housed many silks including an Islamic lion silk dated to the tenth–eleventh centuries, and a piece of purple twill (266).

The affinity with relics made silk cloth a sacred object too. The altar cover was considered a sacred piece of silk in a church as the altar often contained relics. We know that Gregory of Tours regarded the altar cover as a sacred protection. Through his gifted vision Gregory predicted that King Guntram would rush to the church of St. Martin to catch Eberulf, a Frankish noble and an enemy of the king, who had taken refuge in the church. Gregory, in order to help the refugee, suggested that he take the silken altar cover for protection (Thorpe 1974, VII, 22, p. 404). Some of the altar clothes were from Byzantium with Greek inscriptions, as was the altar cloth at St. Mark of Venice, and cloth for bread and wine at Halberstadt Cathedral (Muthesius 1982, 280).

The relics of important saints often had to be divided into small portions for distribution in churches all over Europe. Silk pouches, specially made for relics, have been found in churches and archaeological sites. Some of the pouches were made of Byzantine silks, perhaps accompanying the relics from Byzantium (Muthesius 1982, 267). A relic pouch in Museo Sacro was made of the famous Samson silk, an eighth–ninth century Byzantine product (ibid., 266). In Sens Cathedral, a relic pouch was made of a lion silk in purple, sewn together with an olive green silk, both ninth–tenth century Byzantine products (ibid.). It seems that silks were symbols of sacred bones. Even the less important relics were associated with unpatterned tabby silks cut into small squares of a few centimeters (ibid.). Byzantine material culture permeated all of Europe along with the relics of saints.

Byzantine Silks and the Church

While the papacy in Rome gradually gained spiritual authority over the reckless secular rulers in western Europe, the Byzantine state claimed cultural superiority through its luxurious lifestyle and goods. As early as at the time of Constantine I, the emperors started to donate utensils and luxurious clothes which were reserved for royalty to the churches in and outside the territory of the later Roman empire. A robe with golden threads given to the bishop of Jerusalem by Constantine is one example (M. Shepherd 1967, 63). Following this tradition, Byzantine emperors regularly distributed silks to churches in the patriarchate of Constantinople, and, to show their superiority, to the 'patriarchate of Rome' (Starensier 1982, 274). The inventories of St. Peter documented donations from Justinian I, Theophilus, Michael the Drunkard, etc. (ibid., 484).

Both the eastern Roman empire and the Christian church had a hierarchical structure. In the process of establishing a highly hierarchical bureaucratic and social order, Byzantine state rulers tried to project their own social and political hierarchy in costumes on that of the church, thereby identifying the state with the church, to create the impression that they were rulers on earth and would be saints in heaven. This intention was explicitly expressed on the mosaics in cathedrals, such as those of St. Sophia in Constantinople and St. Vital in Ravenna. The famous mosaic of Justinian and Theodora with their retinues portrays the emperor and empress as donors to Christ. The royal couple is robed entirely in purple, while the attires of the other figures, some partly in purple, become lighter in colour from the center to the two sides. The visual emphasis on the central figures is obvious. The figures of the three magi on the robe of the empress identify the royal patrons with the ancient sages (*Encyclopaedia of World Art*, II, pl. 440, VI, p. 18). A mosaic in St. Sophia depicts the Virgin and Child standing between Emperor Constantine holding the city model of Constantinople and Justinian holding the church model of St. Sophia (II, pl. 443). Other examples are the mosaics of Emperor Leo VI (886–912) kneeling before Christ (pl. 442), the Virgin and Child flanked by Emperor John II Canneaus and Empress Irene (ca. 1118), and Christ flanked by Emperor Constantine Monomachus and Empress Zoe (eleventh century, pl. 448).

Easter was an occasion for the emperor to play the role of Christ. The purple garment designed for this festival was an elaboration of the purple garment worn by the crucified living Christ depicted in the Syriac Rabulla Gospels (ca. 586, Starensier 1982, 196–7). When discussing the purple silk robe in Chapter IV, I mentioned that when purple silk was used exclusively by the royal family and their retinue, the purple colour was associated with Christ and the Virgin in the artistic designs of the silk textiles. There are numerous examples of using the colour purple in depicting the clothing of sacred and celestial figures on mosaics and frescos. Whether the emperors imitated the style of Jesus Christ or projected their aesthetical value and concept of social order onto the ecclesiastical world, their ultimate aim and effect were to identify royal power with Christian divine power.

The royal largess of imperial silks to churches within the Byzantine empire promoted the image of an ecclesiastical world identical to the imperial order. Gifts to churches outside the Byzantine territory which did not accept Byzantine dominance nevertheless imposed Byzantine material culture in a less civilized Europe. Silks made in Byzantine state workshops carried the inscriptions of rulers to western European shrines, such as the lion silk in the shrine of St. Anno at St. Servatius, on which is inscribed 'during the reign of Ramanos and Christophoros the devout rulers' (AD 721–31) (Muthesius 1982, I, 16). For churches that could not obtain imperial gifts, the less prestigious silks made in private workshops were better than anything made locally (Lopez 1959, 77). With the revival of the private silk industry in Byzantium, this kind of silk continued to reach western church treasuries.

Silks in Christian Churches

As the papacy gained greater spiritual authority over the Byzantine patriarchate in western Europe after the mid-fifth century, and possessed a greater number of saint relics than the eastern church, the western rulers felt annoyed about the material wealth which enabled Byzantine emperors to be condescending to the church and the foreign rulers. If the Byzantines had their churches decorated in the most beautiful ways, missionaries in western Europe also needed beautiful shrines to impress their converts. Clotild, the queen of Clovis, had the church decorated with hangings and curtains for the baptism of her son, in order to arouse her husband's faith in Christ through the solemnity and splendour of the ceremony (Thorpe 1974, II, 29, p. 142). With their limited resources, the western rulers also wanted to show their generosity and piety to the church. When Pepin the Short (AD 751–768) received a gift of the 'Rider Silk', patterned with parried emperors riding on horses, from Emperor Constantine V, he donated it to St. Austremoines as a shroud (Starensier 1982, 146). It is said that the Frankish kings did not care for either purple or silks. Charlemagne used only luxurious textiles during festivals (Dalton 1961, 589). Charles the Bald incurred criticism for deviating from Frankish traditions by wearing a Byzantine robe after being crowned by Pope John VIII (Lopez 1943, 35). However, this may not be absolutely right. Clovis (AD 481–511), one of the early Frankish rulers, who was conferred the title of consulate by Emperor Anastasius in AD 507, was clad in purple when crowned in St. Martin (Thorpe 1974, II, 38, p. 154). Charlemagne, whose attitude was ambiguous, did not encourage his nobles to wear silk dresses, according to Notker the Stammerer (Thorpe 1969, Notker, II, 17, p. 167). He wore the national dress of the Franks, but his tunic was edged with silk, according to Einhard (Thorpe 1969, Einhard 23, p. 77). His wife, Luitgard, and his daughters, however, did wear silk dresses (Muthesius 1982, 289). Actually, the attitude of Frankish rulers to silks, the colour purple and other luxuries was ambivalent—resentment mixed with envy and admiration. Sometimes they tried to compete with the Byzantines. When envoys from Africa carried purple dye of Tyrean murex and other luxuries to the court of Charlemagne, the Frankish ruler paid them with corn and oil (Thorpe 1969, Notker, II, 9, p. 147). Interaction between the Byzantines and the Franks was frequent. As mentioned in Chapter IV, Byzantine and German rulers had many marriages negotiated or arranged. Envoys who went to the Byzantine court had to don silk clothes borrowed from imperial stores for the ceremony (Muthesius 1982, 289). Charlemagne could not afford to attire his entire court in expensive silk. On Easter day, he distributed clothing to the personnel who served in the court according to their ranks. 'To the more noble of their number he would order sword-belts to be distributed, or leg-wraps or the more expensive items of clothing fetched from the farthest confines of the empire. To the lower ranks Frisian cloaks of every hue would be handed out' (Thorpe 1969, Notker, ii, p. 171). For diplomatic visits, Charlemagne ordered his court to dress in fine clothes to impress the envoys of foreign countries (ibid., p. 141). After his death, Charlemagne was shrouded in rich silks, the symbol of sacredness and elevated status.

Also, in keeping with their spirit of competition with Byzantium, Frankish kings donated many silks to churches. Sabbe gives a long list of royal donations:

Charlemagne gave donations to a group of churches; among them the splendid collection of the church in Aix-la-Chapelle made Eginhard admire, in 790, the monastery of St. Goar which received two pieces of silk cloth from the emperor. The St. Riquier Abbey under the Abbot Angilbert (789–814) acquired several liturgical ornaments: 78 pieces of luxurious clothes, 24 silk dalmatics, 6 Roman albs (a white tunic), and brocade amices, 5 stoles and 10 oraires in brocade, 5 silk cushions, 5 mantles probably made in silk, 30 chasubles of silk, 10 of purple, 6 of styrax, one of peach colour, 15 of brocade, and 6 of sendal (a thin, fine silk), out of these certain number were definitely gifts of Charlemagne. In the period 823–833, Louis the Pious gave the St. Wandrille Abbey in Foutenelle 3 silk tissues with gold, 2 of styrax, one piece of Spanish cloth, 4 carpets, one tunic in Sacerdotal indigo, 4 chasubles in silk, 5 of purple, 3 of indigo sendal, 3 of green sendal, 1 of red sendal, 1 of purple, 2 Roman capes, one of them was red sendal and decorated with green fringe, another was in beaver fur; 1 oraire in brocade, 1 of styrax, 2 of sendal, some cushions in silk and one cross-belt in brocade. In the same period, he also offered one splendid vestment in rose silk, 5 chasubles in brocade, 12 in various coloured sendal, 3 dalmatics and 3 pieces of brocade, as well as 8 luxurious carpets to the abbey of Luxeuil, and 40 pieces of precious cloth, some chasubles and 30 pieces of sendal in various colours to the abbey of Flavigny (translated from French) (Sabbe 1935, 820–2).

These details show that donations to churches in the early medieval period were much more than have survived in the treasuries. Among the textiles, a few were explicitly designated as 'Roman' while most pieces were not. The supply from Byzantine imperial workshops was unreliable and limited, and, in addition, some of the designs on the silks available may not have been appropriate for western churches. Meanwhile, embroidery was an old technology which could produce sophisticated patterns without the complicated draw-loom; the palace women of the Carolingian and Ottonian royal houses embroidered sacred images on imported Byzantine or other eastern silks. As embroiderers they could raise themselves to the status of primary donors to churches (Starensier 1982, 329 ff). The work of the sister of Charles the Bald became the pillow of St. Remigius in 852 (330). The Ottonian court was even busier and produced more embroidered textiles for saints (ibid., 332 ff). While Byzantine emperors imposed their styles and preferences on the church, the Ottonians deliberately cut their royal ceremonial robes in the style of ecclesiastical vestments (ibid., 339). This effort was not only to emphasize the Christian nature of the state, but to also show the high cultural aspirations of the proto national states.

Meanwhile, popes in Rome also tried to demonstrate their independence of both the Byzantine and the western European states by distributing silks to churches. In the eighty year period from Pope Hadrian I (772–95) to Leo IV (847–55), five popes made numerous donations of silks to Roman churches (Muthesius 1982, 281–2). Following the Byzantine example, the Romans put silk hangings in front of the portraits of Christ and the saints as well as in the shrines of saints. Pilgrims from western Europe were impressed by the heavenly scene of dazzling silk hangings in the church of St. Peter and in other churches in Rome.

Popes also sent missionaries with gifts of silks to countries outside Italy. Pope Gregory sent altar coverings and vestments, and a pallium for ritual performances, presumably all made of silk, for Augustine in England (Bede, I, 29, p. 90). In the period when England converted to Catholicism, popes continuously sent palliums to archbishops there as tokens of honour and authority. In 624, Pope Boniface V sent a pallium with a letter to Archbishop Justus who had just assumed the position (ibid., II, 8, p. 116). In AD 634, Pope Honorius sent another pallium to Honorius who had succeeded Justus as the metropolitan archbishop of Canterbury (II, 18, p. 136). In order to convert King Edwin, Pope

Boniface sent him a letter, a tunic with a golden ornament and a cloak from Ancyra (Ankara), probably from Byzantium (ibid., II, 10, p. 123). Byzantine silks thus reached western European churches through the Roman patriarchate.

These grants from popes certainly did not satisfy the needs of English churches. English churchmen managed to procure their own Byzantine silk supply to decorate their churches in emulation of the heavenly scenes they had witnessed in Roman churches during their pilgrimage trips. Wilfrid brought back purple silk from his trip to Rome (Webb 1988, 167). He decorated the church at Ripon with 'silver and gold and every shade of purple . . . the altar with its bases was dedicated and vested in purple woven with gold' (123). Altar cloth of purple silks was probably the norm, as it is often referred to in literature, though there is some ambivalence as to the exact meaning of 'purpura', the Latin word for purple, in England.[1] Church documents refer to priests in London who owned patterned silk robes in the seventh and eighth centuries, the early days of Christianity in Anglo-Saxon England. The earliest sample is a small piece of silk in a reliquary dated to the seventh century. This piece was probably a fragment from a vestment buried with a saint, and therefore became part of the relics of the saint (Owen-Crocker 1986, 187). The shrine of Cuthbert preserved silks varying from the seventh century 'Nature Goddess' silk to the tenth or eleventh century 'Rider' silk (ibid.). The association of silk with ecclesiastic purposes was taken for granted, as indicated by the Anglo-Saxon use of the word 'godweb', meaning divine cloth, to refer to a kind of special precious silk. The word 'godweb' was used to translate the Latin word purpura (189). Both 'godweb' and purpura were certain kinds of silks of various colours used for ecclesiastical purposes. Whether the silks were purple or not, the association of 'godweb' with purpura indicates that silk liturgical vestments in England were considered to have come from Byzantium or from eastern countries. As the Byzantine silk supply was never sufficient, and the technology of weaving patterned silks was unavailable, English ladies, like their Frankish counterparts, also learned to embroider gold on silks for the church. The textiles were so heavy with gold

---

[1] According to Dodwell, purpura in England was a kind of shot silk, expensive, shiny, but not necessarily purple in colour (Dodwell 1982, 148).

that the value of gold exceeded the value of silk (Dodwell 1982, 174 ff).

Even popes adopted embroidered silk to overcome the limited supply of silk due to the unavailability of technology and Byzantine monopoly. There was a gold workshop in Rome which produced gold embroidered images on Byzantine silks. This technology enabled popes to give a silk fabric with the image of the patron saint embroidered on it to a particular church. During the iconoclast period of Byzantine history, these images of the saints distinguished the Pope's gifts from Byzantine imperial largess (Starensier 1982, 167).

Following the example of the Pope, archbishops, abbots and other high priests distributed luxurious goods to those churches which came under their pastoral responsibility (Starensier 1982, 486). Now even rural monasteries in Europe could enjoy the luxury of silks to decorate their saints. An affiliation between saints and silks was thus established in Christian Europe. Philip Sherrard's description of a modern festival celebrated in a monastery on Mount Athos in Greece, a Christian hermitage which has functioned since the ninth century, elucidates the practices of relic-worship in medieval Europe:

While the liturgy is in progress a row of benches is set up outside the church and covered with richly embroidered purple and golden cloth; on the benches are laid the monastery's most treasured possessions— miraculous icons, the skull and bones of saint and martyr. The service over, pilgrims crowd round to worship them with kisses and prostrations to the ground, offering them also their humble gifts. Then the treasures are carried round the court of the monastery, while barefoot workmen, black-clad monks and surplice priests chant the last hymns of the long office (Sherrard 1982, 141, quoted in Bentley 1985, 63).

With more silks available, silks in churches were not only religious items to sanctify relics and corpses and decorate shrines, but also stored treasures and valuable commodities. As an example, Benedict Biscop brought back two silk cloaks with good workmanship from his fifth trip to Rome. Later he used the cloaks to purchase three hides of land for his monasteries in Wearmouth and Jarrow (Webb 1988, 194). As Christian institutions in Europe became increasingly richer, the demand for silks, a scarce commodity most European states had not yet learned to produce, also increased steadily. The large quantities of gold, silver and silks stored in the church of St. Martin in Tours allured thieves (Thorpe 1974, VI, 10, p. 341). Although even as late as at the time of Charlemagne, austere priests such as Alcuin were critical about the clergy dressing in silk, silk vestments had become the norm. Notker the Stammerer referred to a bishop wearing precious silk and imperial purple (Thorpe 1969, Notker, I, 18, p. 112). An abbot who was in charge of the construction of the Aachen cathedral accumulated a vast store of gold, silver and silken cloth by embezzlement (Thorpe 1969, Notker, I, 28, p. 126). Between the ninth and tenth centuries, many churches set aside special sets of silk vestments for special occasions. Some of the archbishops owned purple of various shades for celebrating different festive occasions (Muthesius 1982, 269). The churches used every means to obtain such silks. The council of Aachen in 836 required those among the faithful who were lucky enough to possess silks to donate them to the church (Starensier 1982, 449). The church of St. Denis, which the Frankish king, Dagobert I (629–38), had built (Panofsky 1979, 87), received many hangings of 'tapestries woven of gold'. Silk collections and treasures in this church increased over time. Suger, an abbot of St. Denis in the twelfth century, maintained that there would be no graver sin than 'to withhold from the service of God and His saints what He had empowered nature to supply and man to perfect'. The basilica reconstructed by Abbot Suger was virtually a magnificent house of art treasures with 'vessels of gold or precious stone adorned with pearls and gems, golden candelabra and altar panels, sculpture and stained glass, mosaic and enamel work, lustrous vestments and tapestries' (ibid., 13–14).

It appears that the Christian priests in western Europe did not care about where the silks were made and what kinds of pattern they bore. As far as they were concerned, silk was a rare commodity in society, and only the churches and saints deserved to use it. It is also true that in the early medieval world, commerce was not the most respected of occupations and the status of merchants was quite low. To acquire a luxury in the name of the church sounded much better than to gain it for oneself and efforts to obtain silks in Byzantium were often made under the pretext of getting them for a church. Even so, only some met with success. When stopped by a Byzantine customs official, Liutprand, Bishop of Cremona, argued that the purple silks he was bringing out were for a church (Lopez 1945, 40–1, *Legatione* LIV, Wright 1930, 267–8) and yet his argument was not persuasive enough. Even church silks had to get through the Byzantine state monopoly.

Rise of the Silk Market in Europe

Whether using the church as a pretext or out of true devotion, European Christians did obtain all kinds of silks for their churches. In addition to the Byzantine imperial gifts and the golden embroidery added on plain silk textiles from the Byzantine market or elsewhere, there were patterned silks from other parts of the world. Whereas no patterned silk fabric dated to the Sassanian period has been found in Persia proper, Dorothy Shepherd catalogued sixteen Sassanian patterned silk samples in church treasuries, from the collections of Museo Sacco, Vatican; Cathedral Treasure, Sens and Aachen; and Musee Diocesain, Liege (CHI III, part 2, 1110).

Further east in Central Asia, a group of patterned silk fabrics called *zandanījī*, which was woven near the city of Bukhara, also survived mostly in Christian churches. Of the eleven silks first identified as zandanījī, nine were located in Europe, and only two pieces were found in Tunhuang, China, by Stein. 'Of the nine silks in Europe, seven were preserved in reliquaries associated with saints of the seventh, eighth and ninth centuries. The provenance of the other two, now in museum collections, is not known, but we may safely assume that they too were originally taken from reliquaries in European churches' (Shepherd & Henning 1959, 22). The locations of the churches—Cathedral of Toul in France; shrine of St. Lambert at Liege, Belgium; and the tomb of St. Landrade at Bilsen, Austria, etc. (ibid., 22–4)—show how far those samples travelled from the sites of production. Records about zandanījī by early Arab geographers indicate that the Bukhara region continued to produce this kind of silk under Islamic rule and that the silk trade also continued. One may assume that some of the zandanījī silks found in European churches were made under the Islamic regime. In her later studies of this topic, Dorothy Shepherd identifies 102 samples of silks as zandanījī, and classifies them into three major groups (Shepherd 1981, 118). Of the 102 samples catalogued by her, 34 samples were definitely associated with saints and relics in western Europe. Others preserved in western museums were probably also originally from some sanctuaries (Shepherd 1981, Table, 119–22).

While the zandanījī silk was woven in Central Asia, the silk yarn and dye probably came from further east, in China. According to Shepherd, the colours on these silks have faded terribly. On one well-preserved piece, the colours are seen to be a combination of chartreuse, orange and pink, which is a very unusual colour combination for Persian and Byzantine silk, but very common for Chinese silk. The difference is that on Chinese silks, the colours are always fresh. She thus suggests that even the dyes used by the Bukhara weavers came from China, but that they could not fix the dye properly without the appropriate mordant (Shepherd & Henning 1959, 28). Judging from the design, Michael Meister further suggests that their style, though not Chinese, indicates 'an attempt at some point in the development of the western pattern to translate onto western looms Chinese patterns of the sort seen in our Sui-period (581–618) fabric. Even the striping of colour noticeable in Chinese warp-faced fabrics where the patterning warps, fixed as they were to the loom, produce constant colour effects throughout the length of the fabric' (Meister 1970, 263). Imagine the long route that Chinese silk yarn, dyes and designs, transformed by weavers in Central Asia, travelled to reach western European churches! Here we finally see a link between the silk export of China and the western European market, though the link was not direct. Chinese silk materials were processed in Central Asia and then appeared in Europe. The producers and consumers were separated not only by distance but also by culture.

Asian silk, along with Byzantine silk, probably reached even further northwest to England and Scandinavia. Archaeological excavations reveal that some fragments of patterned silk were probably from Asia (Pritchard 1984, 70). But large quantities of Chinese silk did not reach Scandinavian churches until the thirteenth century. Actually it was only in the thirteenth century that the churches in Scandinavia were established enough to preserve exquisite silks. Before then, surely silks were traded and used there. In the burial grounds of the Viking city of Birka, the trading emporium of Nordic countries and the destination of the Apostle Ansgar, the excavations of some 1100 graves exposed Persian and eastern Mediterranean styled silks in about 45 graves

(Geijer 1983, 86). A small piece of Chinese silk dated to *c.* 900 was also found in a grave in Birka (Geijer 1951, 33–7). Compared to the many Byzantine and even Persian silks found in Europe, Chinese silk textiles were very limited. It seems that the high quality silk textile made in China only infiltrated, and not flowed into, Europe before the Mongol conquest.

The closest silk exporters to western Europe were the Islamic countries, especially those that formerly belonged to the Byzantine empire. Instead of closing down the imperial silk workshops in Egypt and Syria, the Arabs took them over to serve the Islamic state. Therefore these workshops continued to produce silk textiles in the Byzantine style and their imitation of Byzantine silks was naturally faithful. Anna Muthesius argues that a silk patterned with lions, at St. Servatius, Maasricht, may have come from an Islamic workshop, though it looks similar to the other famous lion silks from Byzantine shops (Muthesius 1984, 247–9, fig. 7). Even as far as Central Asia, Islamic countries produced silks with Byzantine artistic influences. Zandanījī II, also found in European churches, were silks made in Bukhara from the late eighth to the eleventh centuries, and shared Mediterranean influences in composition, colour and scheme (Muthesius 1982, 229).

Sometimes Arabic inscriptions on the silks found in European churches betrayed their origins. The Arabs did not maintain a strict control over their exports. At the beginning of their conquest, they allowed papyrus and precious textiles to be exported to the Christian countries, even with inscribed invocations to the Trinity (Lopez 1943, 23). Soon after they consolidated their rule, the Islamic formula in Arabic inscriptions replaced the invocation to the Trinity and the Cross (ibid., 24). However, to satisfy their voracious appetite for oriental silks, western European Christians did not bother about, or were not aware of, the religious symbols on imported silks. During festivals, clergymen and crusaders proudly displayed their ceremonial garments with inscriptions praising Allah (ibid., 37). The vestments of saints were made of Islamic silks with Kufic inscriptions (eleventh to twelfth centuries) (Muthesius 1982, 271). Striped silk garments, though not inscribed, but surely Islamic, found their way to many churches in England and Europe (ibid., 246).

A silk market gradually developed in the Mediterranean region from the ninth to the tenth centuries. Rome was a distributing centre for oriental and eastern Mediterranean silks. From Rome, European churches and probably nobles obtained, though at very high prices, silks with all kinds of designs. The typical Sassanian design of an animal motif in roundel, also imitated in Byzantium, was used for altar-coverings and church hangings (Dalton 1961, 588). Though there was no silk industry in Italian cities in the first millennium AD, the Frankish invasion of Italy did bring more silks to western Europe (Starensier 1982, 149–51).

The formation of a silk market spanned centuries and underwent different stages. In his critique of the evidence of commerce in the Dark Ages, Grierson points out that material transactions in this epoch took different forms than in the modern market economy. He gives the example of silk:

Gifts from the plundered Avar treasure were sent to English kings and bishops as well as to favoured recipients throughout the Frankish kingdom, and much of the plate and many of the silks and oriental embroideries which occur in ninth-century ecclesiastical inventories had probably passed through Avar hands (Grierson 1959, 131).

Nevertheless, the transactions of goods, textiles and silk in particular, gradually took the form of regular commodity transactions, though often still in the name of God. Considering that textiles and dye stuff were the main commodities in the Eurasian market in the later medieval period and that the European industrial revolution started with textiles, one has to look for the origin of this development in the silk market in the early medieval Mediterranean world. In this epoch, the silk market was very different from the modern one, because trade must have evolved in the name of God, with the aid of saints. Silks, as well as other wealth, were mostly kept in church treasuries, close to relics and shrines. From the ninth to the eleventh centuries, Italian towns undergoing reform stopped hoarding wealth in churches (Duby 1974, 150). The rise of Venice and other Italian trading cities exemplifies this transition in medieval silk trade.

Venice (Venetia) was a Roman province. After AD 568, the Lombards who poured into Italy drove the original inhabitants to the sand banks and islands in the lagoons. The refugees from Venetia built the city of Venice there which was under the sovereignty of Byzantium, while most parts of Italy were overrun by the Lombards. The subordination of Venice to Byzantium, despite the physical distance between them, lasted into the eleventh century, at least in name, with intermediate periods of obeisance to western emperors. This relationship with Byzantium was maintained from a need felt by both sides. Soon after Justinian assumed power, Byzantium began to lose its maritime strength, and frequently had to request Venice to supply ships in their struggle with the Arabs and for the transportation of messages and goods to western Europe (Lopez 1945, 38). In the time of Basil II (AD 976–1025) the Venetians assumed the duty of garrisoning the Adriatic (Lindsay 1952, 162). Meanwhile, the western empires felt that they would rather trade with Venice in oriental goods than be subordinate to the imperial claims of Byzantium. The treaty in 840 between the Carolingians and Venicians allowed Venice to sell oriental silks, •garments and spices in the Lombard city of Pavia (Lopez 1945, 36–7). The only weapon that Byzantium had to keep Venice, Amalfi and other Italian cities in a position of vassalage was its monopoly in the supply of silks (ibid., 38). When Venice recognized the overlordship of Otto II, Byzantium simply withdrew its citizenship which bestowed on them privileges in the trading of silks (ibid., 39). Venice managed to gain its autonomy in the conflict between the Frankish and Byzantine empires, between the Christian and Islamic states, and finally emerged as a powerful trading port and maritime state with the aid of saints.

Many factors contributed to the rise of Venice, but the Venetians carried out their expansion under the banner of a saint. In its struggle for autonomy, Venice adopted St. Mark as its patron saint. When Louis the Pious defeated the Greek church of Grado at the Synod of Mantua in 827, and ended centuries of dispute over the episcopal primacy between Aquileia and Grado, he made Venice subject to the Carolingian patriarchate (Geary 1978, 108–10). The Venetians responded by stealing the body of St. Mark from Alexandria, on the ground that the saint had been sent by St. Peter to convert northern Italy (ibid., 110). This action not only helped Venice gain ecclesiastical independence from the Franks, but also from Byzantium, since the saint was an Italian evangelist (ibid., 111). As soon as the body of St. Mark arrived in Venice, he was made the divine protector of the city. Meanwhile, Venice gained more and more privileges from the Byzantines, trade expanded, naval power increased and the city virtually became a commercial partner of Byzantium (Lopez 1945, 40). Finally, in 1203, in the fourth crusade, the Doge of Venice, carrying the banner of St. Mark, attacked and occupied the city of Constantinople (Hussey 1966, IV, part 1, 282).

The transference of the body of St. Nicholas to another Italian trading city, that of Bari, in the eleventh century had a similar commercial motivation (Geary 1978, 123 ff). The reputation of St. Nicholas in the modern commercial world has to be attributed to the merchants of Bari.

By the tenth and eleventh centuries, the commercial community in the Mediterranean world encompassed different religious groups—Christians, Jews and Muslims. Twelve variations of silks have appeared in the Geniza papers (Goitein 1967, vol. I, 222).[2] The silks originated from as diverse places as Spain, Sicily, Syria, Iraq, Iran, India and China (ibid.). However, despite the wide range of silks, there was a standard price set at two gold dinars a pound. Even when the monetary system was followed in the still feeble market, silk continued to be a stable factor in international trade. The fact that every trader carried silk made Goiten think that silk was used as capital investment, rather than a commodity (ibid., 223). Here silk was not necessarily considered a commodity, transported from its place of production to the place where there was a market demand for it, but in fact was regarded as a good to be traded for other commodities that would fetch a profit. In this sense, silk still maintained its character as a form of currency as in the old days.

[2] Documents deposited by Jews in the *geniza*, special storage containers for written papers in the medieval period. The Geniza papers found in Cairo have been catalogued and studied by Goitein (Goitein 1967).

Chapter VI

Rise of Islam and the Tiraz System

The Arabs were familiar with silk, situated as they were on the ancient silk routes. Trade in luxury commodities such as spices, precious stones and textiles was a source of profit for the commercial-nomadic society in the Arabian peninsular, but it also deepened social and economic tensions. The contrast between urban achievements as a result of this trade and the primitive material life of the Bedouins, and the tension between commercialism and tribal social values contributed to the birth of Islam.[1] The Islamic community, in its early phase, while sweeping into Central Asia and the Mediterranean region, had to constantly deal with conflicts caused by the overwhelming wealth garnered from conquests (which lifted the morale of soldiers) and the ideal of a prudent lifestyle advocated by learned religious figures. As silks, or luxurious textiles in general, comprised a major portion of property in the early medieval world, they represented the

---

[1] The crises caused by the interruption of Meccan trade in Oriental luxuries was believed to have given birth to Islam. Having screened most of the early Islamic literature, Patricia Crone refutes the legend of Meccan trade in luxuries and its connection with the origin of Islam. She argues that the Meccans dealt in basic primitive commodities available in the peninsula, and not in Oriental luxuries. She also points out that Muhammad was first accepted in Medina, not in Mecca (1987). The rise of a world religion cannot be totally attributed to one economic crisis. Nevertheless, Mecca was a caravan city; according to Richard Bulliet, 'the last of the caravan cities' (1975, 105). The site of Mecca was remote from the imperial forces of both Syria and Yemen but was in the midst of tribes that the Meccans had to dominate. Though the volume of trade was never as much as that of Petra and Palmyra, trade was nevertheless the very reason for the existence of Mecca (106). Meccans were merchants and Muhammad was a merchant. The early Islamic community was essentially a commercial society imbued with the values of the tribal system. This early feature shaped Islamic society, religious institutions, and the Islamic state very differently from other monotheist religions.

wealth sought after by Muslim leaders and commoners, and always figured prominently in the struggle to establish Islam and the Islamic state.

Islamic Sumptuary Rules on Textiles

Like other major religions, Islam also contained inherent contradictions. These aspects, though necessary for the development of the religion, were also the cause of confusion and frustration within the religious framework and provoked criticism from outside. Islam inherited a rich literary tradition from Arabic poetry. The composing and reciting of poems were an essential component of cultural life among the Arabs, especially the Bedouin tribes. Before the advent of Islam, poetry developed on the themes of attachment to women, warfare, feasting, and descriptions of camels, horses and other animals of the desert. As literature formed a major element in Islamic learning, legends of Bedouin heroism, embodied in Arabic poetry, permeated Muslim minds (Arnold 1928, 17). This poetry produced the classical Arabic language which was also the language of the Koran. The Arabic of the Koran, the words of the god, became the Islamic religious language which helped unify the Islamic empire over a vast geographical area. It conveyed the religious message of the Koran and that of Muhammad who was consolidating Arabian society through a monotheist belief. Totally different messages—mundane as well as religious ones—conveyed in the same language, were expressed in Islamic religious practices during rapid political expansions. As Muhammad did not have the time to solve the conflicting ideas between his religious messages and those from secular Arabic literature, which was also a part of Islamic culture, the various compilers of the Ḥadīth traditions had to grapple with the difficult task of discerning clear rules from the words of the prophet for guiding religious and political practices in a constantly enlarging social milieu.

In the space of a hundred years, Islamic power came to encompass many highly civilized countries—sedentary, urban areas of the Byzantine Middle East and Sassanian Iran—where many people with a more sophisticated cultural tradition than the Arabs became subject to the Islamic state. Though Arabic conquest was sweeping, not all the people who submitted to Islamic rule became Muslims immediately. The Arabs also needed to learn how to rule and benefit from the highly developed civilizations now under their rule. After the initial conversion of the animists, polytheist Bedouins and other tribal people to Islam, it took a couple of centuries to convert most of the Christians, Zoroastrians, Jews and Buddhists under Islamic rule.[2] There were no clear instructions provided for the way the state machinery was to operate in the Islamic empire. The Caliphs had to devise a set of rules for running the state machinery or had to learn how to rule from the conquered peoples. While the early Arab leaders tried to bring as many people as possible into the religious fold of Islam, they nevertheless had the fear of being assimilated into the civilizations under their rule. 'Umar (AD 634–44) tried to make the Arabs into a military elite group, separate from local people, by settling them in garrison cities, such as Basra on the Persian Gulf, Kufa on the Euphrates and Fustat on the Nile (Lapidus 1988, 42). His first concern was to keep the conquered people in the position of subjects, even if he failed to convert them. According to an agreement between 'Umar and the Christians of Syria, the latter promised: 'We shall not mount on saddles, nor shall we gird swords nor bear any kind of arms nor carry them on person.' They also had to refrain from teaching the Koran to their children, and from imitating Muslim clothing, hair styles and speech. They were not even supposed to use Arabic inscriptions on their seals (Lewis 1987, 217–18). The policy of distinguishing the Arab-Muslims from the non-Muslims gave the former a privileged status among the subjects of the Islamic state. On taxing non-Muslims, 'Umar declared his aim clearly:

Leave these lands which God has granted you as booty in the hands of their inhabitants and impose on them a poll tax (*jizya*) to the extent that they can bear and divide the proceeds among the Muslims. Let them till the soil, for they know more about it and are better at it than we are . . . For they are slaves to the people of the religion of Islam as long as the religion of Islam shall prevail (Lewis 1987, 224).

Among the early Caliphs, 'Umar stood out as the one for the

---

[2] According to statistics compiled by Richard Bulliet, it took until the mid-ninth century for half the population in Iran to become Muslims (1979, 23). Total conversion in Iraq, Egypt and Iran was achieved in the early eleventh century (Bulliet 1979). In other regions, the time taken for Muslims to comprise 50 per cent of the total population was even more.

cause of Islam, not of Arab aristocracy. The privileges given to Muslims were meant to encourage conversion. Meanwhile, with their limited knowledge of and experience in running a state, the Arabs could not afford to isolate themselves from their subjects. Following the models of Byzantine and Sassanian administrative institutions, they employed Persian or Greek-speaking clients (mawālīs) to run the state machinery for practical purposes. The clients who enjoyed a high status in their own society were willing to join the new elite by serving the Islamic state. As the clients became Muslims and vowed loyalty to the Caliph, a new generation of clients who spoke Arabic emerged around 700 AD (Lapidus 1988, 60–2). Meanwhile, the garrison cities quickly developed into prosperous urban centres which attracted all kinds of businessmen. The Arabs began to mingle with the non-Arabs to form a new religious elite, and a middle class of merchants, artisans, teachers and scholars emerged (ibid., 98).

Attracted by the new privileges offered to Muslims and motivated by the desire to retain their old privileged position, the old elite in the conquered lands tried to embrace Islam. Those who became Muslims claimed the same rights as the Arabs. Now, within the Islamic community the groups for an Arab-dominant empire and those for an Islamic empire clashed. The Arab military elite were not willing to give up their privileges. Under 'Umar II (AD 717–20) of the Umayyad Caliphate, the tide changed in favour of the mawālīs.[3] 'Umar II wanted all western Asian people to convert to Islam, and granted the same status and privileges to mawālīs as to Arab soldiers. After his rule, the tide went back and forth, and the new regime of Abbasid finally got rid of the supremacy of the Arabs (Lapidus 1988, 55, 63, 70). Soon the mawālīs of Greek and Persian origin gained an upper hand in the competition for administrative positions and cultural influence. This contention as to the superiority of the Arabs or non-Arab Muslims continued for centuries. An early ninth century non-Arab Muslim claimed that the mawālīs were superior to the Arabs:

We mawālī, as non-Arabs in the past, are nobler than the Arabs, and as Arabs in the present we are nobler than the non-Arabs. The non-Arabs

---

[3] Mawālī, literally client, meant non-Arab Muslims, often those from middle or high social levels and active in politics and in the social, economic life of the Islamic state.

have a past but no present, the Arabs have a present but no past, while we have both . . . (Al-Jahiz [AD 775–808] Rasā'il [1933], pp. 299–300, quoted in Lewis 1987, 200).

The Shu'ubiyya faction, a non-Arab Muslim group, articulated the opinion that the mawālīs had a superior culture than the Arabs:

The fact remains that non-Arab nations in every part of the world have kings who united them, cities which gathered them, laws which they obey, philosophy which they produce, and wonders which they devise by way of tools and crafts, such as the *making of brocade*, which is the most wonderful of handicrafts . . . The Arabs, on the other hand, never had a king who could unite their main part, draw in their outlying parts, subdue their wrong-doers, and control their fools. They achieved nothing at all in the arts and crafts and made no mark in philosophy. Their only achievement is in *poetry*, and this is shared by the non-Arabs (emphases mine). (Ibn 'Abd Rabbih Al-'Iqd al-Fàrīd, iii, pp. 317–19, 325, 326, 328, quoted in Lewis 1987, 202–3).

Yes, Arabs had poetry, their achievement in poetry was a source of national pride and a symbol of nobility.

Poetry is the mine of knowledge of the Arabs, the book of their wisdom, the master roll of their history, the repository of their great days, the rampart protecting their heritage, the trench defending their glories, the truthful witness on the day of dispute, the final proof at the time of argument (Ibn Qutagba [AD 828–889], 'Uyūn al-Akhbār, ii, p. 185, quoted in Lewis 1987, 173).

From the time of the prophet, most Arab scholars, Caliphs and nobles composed poems. Here I should remind readers that Arabic poetry carried messages that were not always compatible with the Islamic religious spirit. As Arabic poetry was the only cultural achievement recognized by the surrounding civilized people, its art form and hedonic contents naturally competed with and flourished alongside the cultural achievements—a sound administration, a judiciary and crafts such as brocade making—introduced into the Islamic empire by other civilizations. As leaders of a dominant but ethnic and religious minority, the Caliphs in Damascus and Baghdad, while holding the Islamic banner, strove to achieve a high cultural level in the court in order to adapt to and utilize existing administrative and material structures and to rank the Islamic culture with that of contemporary empires. Their patronage of poetry, philosophy, science, art, architecture and textile production represented not only their political authority in their own territory but also their aspirations for a culturally leading position in the civilized world.

Caliphs, as commanders of the faithful, were not invested with divine power. Though the Abbasids said that they were related to the prophet by blood, their claim was based more on their role as religious leaders and on their supremacy in military power and cultural achievements. The religious values they were supposed to propagate and the material wealth and cultural values developed under their patronage differed sharply. Mas'ūdī (AD 957) recorded an interesting anecdote that reflects the conflicting values of the rulers. After the fall of the Umayyad Caliphate in Damascus, Abd Allah, the son of the last Umayyad Caliph, Marwan (AD 744–50), fled to the country of the Nubians:

I had been in Nubia three days when the king came to see me. Although I had had a valuable carpet spread out for him, he sat on the ground. I asked him why he refused to sit on our carpet and he replied: 'Because I am a king and the duty of a king is to humble himself before the power of God, who has made him great.' Then he said to me: 'Why do you drink wine when your Book forbids it?' I answered: 'Our slaves and our followers have the audacity to do so . . . ' 'Why,' he went on, 'do you allow your cavalry to trample the fields when your Book has forbidden you destruction?' 'These are again our slaves and our followers, who have behaved thus in their ignorance.' 'Why,' proceeded the king, 'do you wear *brocade and silk and gold*, in spite of the prohibitions of your Book and your religion?' I retorted: 'As power fled from us, we called upon the support of alien races who have entered our faith and we have adopted these clothes from them.' (Emphases mine. Mas'ūdī, Lunde & Stone trans., 1989, 24–5.)

Responding to the accusations of the religious and austere Nubian king, the Umayyad prince could defend himself only by referring to the luxuries of his slaves, followers and new converts, who came under his regime as the consequence of Islamic conquest. For Muslims, the Koran held the ultimate authority on their thoughts, whether they were Arabs or not. However, the Book did not have ready solutions to many of the new problems. Actually, the Koran did not ban silk clothes. Perhaps the austere Nubian king assumed that the Koran would prohibit the use of silk as well as other luxuries. In the process of conquest, the new

Islamic community developed Ḥadīth traditions to cope with the task of ruling civilizations which were maturer than those of the Arabs, while maintaining the Arabic cultural identity and Islamic dominance in the religious sphere. One can see the evolution of new traditions through the rules governing the use of silks, one of the aspects of material culture that the Islamic empire inherited from the Byzantines and Persians.

There was no rule against the use of silk on any occasion in the Koran. Instead, because silk always represented a luxury item in sedentary societies, it was described as decorating paradise, and was equated with things desired by people living in the desert, such as fountains and trees. According to the Koran, people in paradise were clothed in silk.

Verily, God will make those who believe and do right enter into gardens beneath which rivers flow; they shall be bedecked therein with bracelets of gold and with pearls, and their garments therein shall be of silk, and they shall be guided to the goodly speech, and they shall be guided to the laudable way (XXII 22–4);

Gardens of Eden shall they enter, adorned therein with bracelets of gold and pearls; and their garments therein shall be silk (XXXV 30);

And God will guard them from the evil of that day and will cast on them brightness and joy; and their reward for their patience shall be Paradise and silk (LXXVI 12) (English translation by E.H. Palmer).

However, in the Ḥadīth traditions which developed after the Prophet, various rules were formulated against the use of silk, some harsh, others mild. The mild rules only forbade silks for men, the harsh ones did not recommend them even for women. The common expression was that those who wore silk in this world would not wear it in the next; that is, they would go to a lesser place than heaven (*Encyclopedia of Islam*, III, 209). According to Imam Malik Annas:

Yahya related to me from Malik from Nafi' from 'Abdullah ibn 'Umar that 'Abdullah saw a silk robe at the door of the mosque. He said, 'Messenger of Allah, would you buy this robe and wear it on Jumu's and when envoys come to you?' The Messenger of Allah, may Allah bless him and grant him peace, said, 'No-one wears this but a person who has no portion in the Next World.' Then the Messenger of Allah, may Allah bless him and grant him peace, was brought some robes of the same material and gave one of them to 'Umar ibn al-Khattab. 'Umar said, 'Messenger of Allah, do you clothe me in it when you said what you said about the robe of 'Utarid?' The Messenger of Allah, may Allah bless him and grant him peace, said, 'I did not give it to you to wear.' 'Umar gave it to a brother of his in Makka who was still an Idolater (Malik Ibn Anas, 387).

As for silk decorations, Hadīth traditions also differed greatly but unanimously agreed upon one principle, that silk could be used for covering the Kaaba. Whatever the rules, it seemed impossible to prohibit Muslims from wearing or using silks when they became the rulers of people who viewed silk as a desirable luxury. Eventually, a general guideline for regulating the textile industry and trade emerged. A robe decorated with a silk stripe that was less than two or three fingers in width or a cloth woven with silk warp but with the weft of other fabrics would not harm the wearer's future life (Al-Bukhari, *Kitab al-Libas* [B. 25]; *Kitab al-Fiqh'ala al-Madhahib al-arba'a* [p. 6], quoted in Marzouk, 1955, 63). Such rules may have emerged after half-silk textiles and textiles with silk stripes became available in the market. They were cheaper than whole silk textiles and were not considered luxuries. Such rules may have also been formulated in order to guide the production of silk in the Islamic world. There emerged a kind of popular half-silk textile, *mulham*, with silk warp, and many kinds of textiles with silk-decorated margins in Islamic countries. These rules, in addition to those prohibiting human and animal figures on silk patterns, formed the basic sumptuary laws on clothing and textiles in the Islamic world.

The sumptuary laws of the Islamic world, however, differed from those of China and Byzantium in their aim. Chinese and Byzantine emperors tried to enforce sumptuary laws on silks to protect their status as rulers and to differentiate the various levels of their bureaucratic echelons and social hierarchy. The Arabs, on the other hand, dazzled by the silk clothing of the kings and wealthy people they had just conquered, may have found it more difficult to impose sumptuary laws. Whereas the soldiers were attracted to the beautiful clothing they had never seen before, the learned ulamas, the scholars who studied the Islamic religion and who compiled and preserved the Hadīth, were concerned about the religious values of Islam. The Caliphs, as both military commanders and religious leaders, were responsible for rewarding soldiers for their bravery as well as for maintaining a cohesive Arabic society. Both were essential for the Islamic cause and both were highly valued in Islamic society. Furthermore, the Caliphs and Sultans, living in a world where rulers and religious leaders constantly displayed their superiority in material culture, could not resist the impulse to display their valour through their attire and indulge in a luxury that even their subjects, let alone competing kings, were entitled to enjoy.

Under the patronage of the Abbasid Caliphate, art, industry and trade flourished in Islamic cities. Baghdad, built in 762, developed into the largest city outside the T'ang empire, with a population of 300,000 to 500,000 by the ninth century. In addition to indigenous products—textile, leather, paper, etc.—there were many commodities available in its markets from international trade. Its residents comprised members of various religious communities—Jews, Christians, Muslims, pagans—and ethnic groups—Persians, Iraqis, Arabs, Syrians and Central Asians (Lapidus 1988, 69). Baghdad was visited by traders from remote countries; information could be exchanged easily due to the popularity of paper, the spread of writing and the use of a common language, and hence Islamic geographers' knowledge of the various customs and products of different lands was very good. A modern scholar in fact claims that in the medieval world only the Muslim geographers had a good knowledge of all the civilizations in the Eurasian continent (Spuler 1970, 20).

The Abbasid Caliphs, residing in their cosmopolitan city, viewed themselves as the centre of the world. They appeared before their audiences dressed in splendid clothes, as did the other great rulers. In a painting at Qusayr'Amra, the major rulers in the known world—the Shah of Iran, the emperor of Byzantium, Roderic of Spain, the Negus of Abyssinia, the emperor of China and the emperor of the Turks—are shown as greeting the Caliph as their master (Lapidus 1988, 83).

The most important material which contributed to the splendour of the Caliph's court, was textiles, either produced in Baghdad or brought in from distant lands. In the court, the Caliph's robe, the carpet and the curtain that separated him from his audience were of dazzling silk textiles. Mas'ūdī has mentioned that in the court of Caliph Amin (AD 809–814/193–198 AH) in

Baghdad there was a kiosk which was domed and decorated with silks and green brocades, woven with a pattern in red-gold and other kinds of silk stuff (Lunde & Stone, 1989, 138). Fine textiles, especially of silk, were major items in the treasuries of the Caliphs. This is revealed in the list of treasuries left by the great Caliph, Harun al-Rashid, in AD 809:

4000 embroidered robes
4000 silk cloaks, lined with sable, mink and other furs
10,000 shirts and shifts
10,000 caftans
2000 drawers of various kinds
4000 turbans
1000 hoods
1000 capes of various kinds
5000 kerchiefs of different kinds
500 (pieces of) velvet
100,000 *mithqāls* of musk
100,000 mithqāls of ambergris
1000 baskets of Indian aloes
1000 precious china vessels
Many kinds of perfume
Jewels valued by the jewellers at 4 million dinars
500,000 dinars
1000 jewelled rings
1000 Armenian carpets
4000 curtains
5000 cushions
5000 pillows (*mikhadda*)
1500 silk carpets
100 silk rugs
1000 silk cushions and pillows
300 Maysānī carpets
1000 Darabjirdi carpets
1000 cushions with silk brocade
1000 inscribed silk cushions
1000 silk curtains
300 silk brocade curtains
500 Ṭabarī carpets
1000 Ṭabarī cushions
1000 pillows (*mirfade*)
1000 pillows (mikhadda)
1000 washbasins

1000 ewers
300 stoves
1000 candlesticks
2000 brass objects of various kinds
1000 belts
10,000 decorated swords
50,000 swords for the guards and pages (*ghulam*)
150,000 lances
100,000 bows
1000 special suits of armour
50,000 common suits of armour
10,000 helmets
20,000 breast plates
150,000 shields
4000 special saddles
30,000 common saddles
4000 pairs of half-boots, most of them lined with sable, mink and other
kinds of fur, with a knife and a kerchief in each half-boot
4000 pairs of socks
4000 small tents with their appurtenances
150 marquees
(Ibn al-Zubayr, Kitāb al-Dhakhā'ir wa'l-Tuḥaf, 214–18, quoted in
Lewis 1987, 140–1.)

Of the 56 listed items, 30 are various textile products, ranging
from socks to marquees. Next in importance was the Caliph's
armoury, followed by cash, jewellery, perfume and fragrances, and
various utensils. Among the textiles, silk was predominant. Even
the textiles that were not designated as silk but were named after
their provenances were probably made of silk.

The Caliphs loved the feel of silk, and unlike their contemporary
emperors in T'ang China and Byzantium, they did not mind their
subjects also wearing silk textiles. In fact, the court often set the
fashion for the people. Zubaida, the queen of Harun-al-Rashid,
set the fashion for the women of her time. Her clothes were made
of 'a varicoloured silk called *washi*, a single length designed for her
cost 50,000 dinars'. Yet her expensive taste set the trend in fashion
designs (Mas'ūdī, Lunde & Stone 1989, 391). Caliph Mutawakkil
(AD 847–61) wore a shiny half-silk textile called mulham in public,
and in so doing spread this fashion among his people (ibid., 239).
Caliphs also showed their favour by showering their subjects with
silks and robes. Caliph Mu'tasin (AD 833–42) bought Turkish

slaves to build a new army. He dressed them in brocade with gilded belts (ibid., 229). In the court of Caliph Radi (AD 934–41), his courtiers invariably received money and robes from him (ibid., 411).

Islamic sumptuary laws, therefore, played no role in demarcating the ruler from the ruled. They were rather a compromise between the elite and the masses, between the concern for the afterlife and the practical, human desire for luxury, comfort and style, between asceticism in Islamic religious teachings and hedonism in Arabic culture, between the ideal of the equality of all Muslims for the purpose of mobilizing the masses for conquest and the need to differentiate the rulers and the ruled in political practices.

Restrictions on the use of silk did guide the development of the silk industry in many of the countries under Islamic rule. However, as Marzouk has pointed out, the silk industry did not decline but flourished despite, or because of, these regulations (Marzouk 1955, 63). The technological and artistic development of Islamic textiles which surpassed that of many contemporary civilizations was achieved through the *ṭirāz* system, an institution to implement the Islamic sumptuary laws on silks.

The Ṭirāz System

Theological discussions on how much silk yarn was to be allowed in garments worn by Muslims were not merely the speculations of ulamas, but practical problems related to silk production and trade. Actually many medieval Muslim scholars bore family names related to silk, such as silk-worker, silk-weaver or silk-merchant, while others engaged in silk production and trade themselves (Goitein 1967, I 104). After all, Islamic laws were made by middle class scholars who were familiar with practical problems, one of which was the degree of silk thread to be woven into linen or cotton textiles. As silk yarn was expensive as compared to other materials, there had existed many kinds of partial silk textiles for centuries. More specifically, the rules on the width of silken bands were applied to ṭirāz textiles. Ṭirāz, a Persian word for embroidery, denoted textiles inscribed with the specific political reign and the date of production on the border. The inscriptions were embroidered or woven with silk thread. Although inscribed textiles existed in Byzantium, inscriptions held a special meaning on textiles, as well as on other media of arts, in the Islamic empire. Since the regulation against using human and animal figures as a form of decoration developed in the Ḥadīth traditions, calligraphy and inscriptions became the most important form of decoration in Islamic arts, including textile designs. However, as the inscriptions had to be embroidered or woven with silk thread on the border of the textile, the width of silk allowed, i.e. how wide the band of inscriptions should be in accordance with the moral standard of the Islamic religion, was a serious issue to be discussed. Therefore, the debate on whether the silk band on linen or cotton textiles should be of two fingers' width or of four entered the arena of specific religious and technological instructions, and determined the production of fabric in ṭirāz factories (Kühnel 1952, 2).

Specific instructions were necessary because the Arabian empire inherited numerous textile workshops from the Byzantines and Persians. From Egypt to Persia, all kinds of textiles were sent to the capital of the caliphates—Medina, Damascus, Kufa, Baghdad and Samarra. As the production of, and transactions in, textiles were regulated by the Byzantine and Sassanian states, the Islamic state had to substitute the old regulations with a set of new rules to make the industry serve the new state. The institution of regulating the production of textiles in factories with Arabic inscriptions, the Dar al-Ṭirāz, was established after a series of conquests through the Islamic world. The ṭirāz system flourished and persisted into the thirteenth century, but reached its height during the Umayyad and Abbasidian caliphates, when the power of the Caliphs was at its apex (Serjeant 1972, 8).

As the ṭirāz institution represented Islamic religious and political authority, the name of the authority was inscribed on most textiles produced under the Islamic regime. The Arabs conquered Syria (AD 635), Mesopotamia (AD 635), Egypt (AD 641) and Sassanid Persia (AD 642) in the span of a few years. Islamic rule extended to Spain by AD 711 and to Sicily by AD 827. The ṭirāz system was imposed in all these regions. The Arabs inherited the Byzantine textile industry in Syria and Egypt and part of Mesopotamia, and that of Sassanian in Iran. The ṭirāz system reformed the silk and textile industry in these areas and made them produce an unprecedented high quality and large quantity of textiles, especially silks, and brought the industry to Spain and Sicily.

These achievements not only created the basis for the future silk industry in these areas but also affected the consumption and production of textiles in Christian Europe.

There were two kinds of ṭirāz factories in the Islamic world—those of the Caliph which produced garments for the Caliph and his family and the honorary robes for the inmates of the warehouse of the caliphate; and the public ṭirāz which produced garments for the public with the inscribed bands. The inscriptions began with the religious statement which appears at the beginning of most chapters of the Koran: 'In the name of God the Compassionate, the Merciful', followed by the name and title of the ruling Caliph, with a phrase in blessing, such as 'May God prosper him', or 'May God strengthen him'. On garments made in the ṭirāz shops of the Caliph, there would also be the name of the wazir, i.e. the prime minister who was in charge of the Caliph's ṭirāz workshops. The next phrase usually indicated that the piece was made in the Caliph's or in the public ṭirāz shop in a certain city, followed by the date according to the Islamic calendar (Britton 1983, 19–20). After the eleventh century, when the central power of the caliphate weakened, the format for the inscriptions became simple with one short pious phrase, such as 'victory from God' or 'the Kingdom of God' (ibid., 21).

The disintegration of the ṭirāz system began in the peripheral regions of the Abbasid empire where Sultans developed their own ṭirāz system. From the mid-tenth century even the ṭirāz in Baghdad was under the control of Buwayhid princes. The caliphate obviously could not stop the Sultan of the Fars in Iran from replacing the name of the Caliph with that of the Sultan on the ṭirāz (Serjeant 1972, 51).

Most extant ṭirāz fabrics are not luxury silks, but silken embroidered inscriptions on linen and cotton (mostly linen), even though literary sources have recorded luxurious silken ṭirāz produced all over the Islamic world. Probably literary sources tended to record outstanding achievements, while most ṭirāz fabrics were made of common materials. Furthermore, most of the ṭirāz that have survived are from Egyptian tombs thanks to the climate of this country, where linen fabric was famous and silk weaving was limited before its subjugation to Islamic regimes. Egyptians had long been accustomed to burying their dead in cheap clothes, and the linen clothes found in tombs often show signs of mending

(Gervers 1983, 288, 299). Of the eleven hundred pieces of dated or datable ṭirāz known of in 1935, over a thousand were made in Egypt, and 45 in other countries (Day 1937, 420). In the many years that have passed since then, more ṭirāz textiles have been found, but the whole picture has not changed. Statistics show that the current collections of ṭirāz certainly do not represent the ṭirāz system in the Islamic empire, but rather indicate customs dictated by nature as well as burial customs.

However, since the climate of Egypt has helped preserve their rich collection of ṭirāz, we can examine these materials to study the changes brought about by Islamic rule in the textile industry. Islamic power did not destroy the Byzantine government textile shops but took over the system and employed original Christian inhabitants, the Copts, as weavers. The continuity in technology and artistic style may suggest that the ṭirāz system was correspondent to the Byzantine state workshop, the *gynaeceum*.[4] However, the most obvious change was that silk replaced wool for embroidered or woven inscriptions or decorative bands since the time of the Abbasids (Kuhnel 1952, 2).

The ṭirāz institution probably started in the early Islamic era in the Delta of Egypt, as references exist in Egypt to the use of linen cloth with the ṭirāz at the time of 'Umar (Serjeant 1972, 12). The official inauguration of the Islamic ṭirāz institution in Egypt took place under the Caliph, Abdal Malik (AD 685–705), who, having noticed that the papyri, textiles and pottery from Egypt bore the Greek inscriptions of the Christian Trinity, ordered the governor of Egypt to cancel the Greek inscriptions on these products, and put Islamic inscriptions on the papyri. This action annoyed the Byzantine emperor, Justinian II, because Byzantium was the major importer of Egyptian papyri and textiles. Having failed to persuade the Caliph to restore the Greek inscription of the Trinity on the papyri and textiles, Justinian threatened to inscribe phrases against the Prophet on Byzantine gold coins which circulated widely in the Muslim empire. Malik responded by imposing an embargo on papyri to Byzantium and casting Islamic coinage. This resulted in a war between the two powers

---

[4] Gynaeceum was a place where the womenfolk spun, wove and embroidered. In the Byzantine period, it became an institution for making textiles for the royalty (Marzouk 1955, 47–8).

that ended in victory for the Arabs. A fully inscribed Arabic, Islamic coinage in gold, silver and copper replaced Byzantine and Sassanian prototypes (Serjeant 1972, 12–13; Lopez 1943, 23–5). This story may contain many legendary elements, but as it has been mentioned in both Arabic and Byzantine sources, one may safely say that in the late seventh century there emerged an Islamic sense of identity in religious, linguistic and visual expressions, and the Caliph asserted the power of the Islamic state in Egypt through inscriptions on papyri, coins and perhaps textiles. It is certain that the ṭirāz system was established in Alexandria under both the Umayyads and the Abbasids (Serjeant 1972, 14).

The variation in inscriptions also shows that there were ṭirāz factories for both the Caliph and for the public. The former were referred to as 'made in ṭirāz al-khassa in Misr (Egypt)' or 'made in ṭirāz Misr'. The latter bore the inscriptions 'made in ṭirāz al'amma in Misr' or 'made in Misr' (Marzouk 1955, 75–7). Both kinds of ṭirāz shops mostly employed Coptic weavers. Since they were not Muslims they had to pay higher taxes, a system which was considered oppressive by the Christian patriarch Dionysius in c AD 815.

Although Tinnis has a considerable population and numerous churches, we have never witnessed greater distress than that of its inhabitants. When we inquired into the cause of it, they replied: 'Our town is encompassed by water. We can neither look forward to harvest nor can we maintain a flock. Our drinking water comes from afar and costs us four dirhams a pitcher. Our work is in the manufacture of linen which our women spin and we weave. We get from the dealers half a dirham per day. Although our earning is not sufficient for the bread of our mouths we are taxed for tribute and pay five dinars a head in taxes. They beat us, imprison us, and compel us to give our sons and daughters as securities. For every dinar they have to work two years as slaves (Serjeant 1972, 138).

While the Caliph strictly controlled textile production in the Delta region through the ṭirāz system, the Upper Egyptian textile centres, such as Faiyum, had more freedom to maintain Coptic traditions, notably more freedom to decorate textiles with figural patterns. The weavers there perhaps did not understand Arabic inscriptions and so their inscriptions were more decorative and less readable (Kühnel 1952, 2). Coptic traditions survived and even revived in the south, and influenced the north. Thus animal motifs appear in the textiles found in the Delta region under the Fatimids (Cairo AD 969–1171). The Fatimids not only imported textiles from Persia, Iraq, Spain and Byzantium, but also workmen from these places (Serjeant 1972, 157). The imported samples and foreign workmen enriched the repertoire of textile designs and a new Islamic textile style evolved in the Fatimid period. Silk fabric became common in the opulent court. The ṭirāz institution was even more powerful now. The head of ṭirāz was a man of worth and enjoyed many privileges. His monthly cloth allowance included various silk textiles and clothes. He was also allowed to ride a horse given by the Caliph during his visits to Cairo, the capital (Serjeant 1972, 157f; Marzouk 1955, 68–70). Thus, with the ṭirāz institution, the textile industry in Egypt again found its own way of development independent of other Islamic countries.

Along the east coast of the Mediterranean where the Roman silk industry was first founded, silk weaving followed the Byzantine style even under Islamic rule. The ṭirāz factories in Damascus and other cities mainly worked on silk cloth (Serjeant 1972, 117). In Yemen, where the silk industry was famous from pre-Islamic times, the Umayyad caliphate owned factories which produced honorary robes (126). In Baghdad, the capital of the Abbasid caliphate, the ṭirāz institution was an essential part of the state machinery, similar to the mint (16–19). The Caliph would have his name inscribed on both the coins and ṭirāz textiles, and hence the tussle for control of the institution was part of court politics. The ṭirāz factories in Baghdad were models for those located farther from the centre. The earliest ṭirāz factories were located in the round city of the Caliphs until the reign of Rashid (AD 786–809, 16). All we know about the large ṭirāz institution and the textile industry in Baghdad is that there was a 'house of silk' and a 'house of cotton', and there was a ṭirāz street which belonged to the king (ibid., 25). To the east of Iraq, in the small province of Kuzistan at the head of the Persian Gulf, there were many ṭirāz cities. Situated on the trade route between Baghdad and China, residents of this region were familiar with silks from other countries. The ṭirāz factory in Sus, a city founded by Roman prisoners in the fourth century AD, produced 'precious kingly silks' (Serjeant 1972, 43). Sus silks were so beautiful that

Caliph Mu'tadid (AD 892–902) wanted to reserve them solely for his own use (ibid., 42).

In the former Sassanian territory, where the silk industry flourished before the advent of Islam, ṭirāz factories were established in many of the cities founded by Sassanian monarchs (ibid., 91). The ṭirāz factory in Khurasan may have been established as early as c AD 767 (ibid., 87). Even so, the entire silk industry was not under government control. Some cities and villages produced silks without ṭirāz inscriptions and exported them widely (ibid., 47).

The material civilization and cultural achievements of Sassanid Persia were too advanced to be subjugated to Islamic culture and to come under the control of the caliphate. Local governors often controlled too many resources to be obliged to obey the Caliphs. The powerful governors in the tenth century in Kuzistan controlled many ṭirāz factories. In the early tenth century, a governor had eighty ṭirāz factories under him which made clothes for his wardrobe (ibid., 42). A Sultan owned a ṭirāz factory in the city of Sūs (ibid., 44).

Further east, in Central Asia, ṭirāz shops were built after the early conquests to establish a link with the centre. There was a ṭirāz factory in Bukhara during the period of the Abbasids. The Bukharan people sent the same silk tributes to the caliphate as were sent to the Sassanians and Chinese (ibid., 97). But once central control weakened, the local dynasties and Sultans took over ṭirāz factories in the same way that they took over other state apparatus. The Shi'a dynasty of Ghaznevid took over the ṭirāz system built by the Abbasids in their part of Central Asia (ibid., 23). In Khwarizm, a local Amir had the title of Amir inscribed in ṭirāz textiles (ibid., 106). These local rulers imitated the Caliphs in announcing their regimes through textile inscriptions, though on a much lower scale.

Turning to the western part of the Mediterranean, one sees that the ṭirāz system played a different role there than in the east. Instead of reforming the established textile industry into a religious and state institution, Muslims brought this institution to the conquered land. The early Islamic capital in north Africa, Kairawan, had a ṭirāz factory, followed by factories in other cities in Maghreb (Serjeant 1972, 180–4). Tunis prospered under Islamic rule. There was a 'court of silk merchants' in the tenth century, and the Sultan there wore cloth with a ṭirāz border of silk (ibid., 184).

Many ṭirāz factories were founded in Spain. Embroidered garments were introduced in Spain in the early ninth century and by the late tenth century their ṭirāz products were even exported to traditional textile countries such as Egypt and Khurasan (Serjeant 1972, 165). The Spanish silk industry under the ṭirāz system flourished and even surpassed the industry in eastern countries. It was said that there were 800 ṭirāz factories that wove silk (ibid., 170). Silk textiles with human figures and gold tapestry produced in Spain gained fame in the medieval world and penetrated to the Christian north (Shepherd 1978, 128).

Sicily was another gateway for textiles entering Europe from the Muslim world. It was conquered in the year AD 827/211 AH. By the tenth century there was a ṭirāz market based on a well-developed textile industry. Its production included cotton, wool, goat hair, linen and silk. Sicily textiles found favour in the Fatimid court. An aunt of Caliph al-Hakim owned 3000 pieces of textiles from Sicily (Bierman 1980, 102–3). In the early eleventh century, the city of Palermo became a trading centre in the Mediterranean (Goitein 1973, 25) and under Norman rule (AD 1071–1133), the ṭirāz textile industry and trade continued to flourish. The Normans recognized the strategic location of the island for Mediterranean trade, and so did not use Sicily as a base to attack North Africa during their crusading march (Bierman 1980, 104). Consequently, Islamic textiles with ṭirāz borders found their way from Sicily to Christian Europe.

By the eleventh century, when the ṭirāz system extended to all parts of the Islamic world, the caliphate was gradually losing its power to the local rulers of peripheral countries. Many ṭirāz institutions in these regions now served the local Muslim state rather than the caliphate. The technique of weaving and the decorative patterns were also enriched through the transaction of goods and through communication with peoples of diverse cultures.

As mentioned above, the ṭirāz system did not include all the textile industries of the Islamic world, especially those in areas remote from the centre. Nevertheless, the vast amount of textiles that bore inscriptions recognizing the religious and political authority of Islamic rulers created a parallel institution to the numismatic system, whether it served the caliphate or the local sultanate, right down to the thirteenth century (Golombek & Gervers 1977, 82). 'It was the currency of mutual acknowledgement between the Caliph, as religious head, and the people' (Rogers 1983, 31). Under this system, i.e. under Islamic state patronage and regulations, the textile industry and trade made great progress through the transfer of technology and fashion. Although most of the surviving ṭirāz, or perhaps the ṭirāz ever made, were executed on linen and cotton cloth, it appears that more silks with inscriptions were made after two or three centuries of Islamic rule, especially in Persia and Spain, the oldest and the youngest silk producing regions under the ṭirāz system. We now turn to the redistributing function of the ṭirāz institution; how the ṭirāz institution promoted the silk industry and trade in the early medieval world is dealt with in the next chapter.

The Kaaba and Silk Redistribution

As the Kaaba in Mecca had been the religious centre for Arabic society long before the advent of Islam, and continued to be under Islamic regimes, the whole issue of inscribing rulers' names on the ṭirāz often became entangled with the issue of who had the right, and on what kind of material, to inscribe his name on the cover of the Kaaba. Before the spread of Islam, when the Kaaba was the object of worship for only the Arabs, the Tubba kings of Yemen used to supply the cover for the Kaaba, which was made of the famous Yemen striped material (Serjeant 1972, 123). Other regions also supplied coverings of precious textiles, though they may not have been given in the name of their kings. The Prophet saw that the Kaaba was covered with 'various coverings of striped Yemen stuffs, carpets, stuffs called kurr, silk and Iraqi carpets' (ibid., 34). Thus even before Islam spread to Mecca, the Kaaba was the political as well as religious symbol of the Arabs, and the fine textile coverings represented the powerful political patronage of the spiritual centre.

Under the caliphate, the Caliphs provided the coverings for the Kaaba by ordering precious materials from all the Islamic territories, with the name of the Caliph and the wazirs inscribed on the textiles. For centuries, Arabic writers keenly observed as to whose names were inscribed on the coverings (Bierman 1980,

19–20). With the diversification of Islamic power and the competition provided by local regimes, the arrangements for supplying
Kaaba coverings became complicated and adjustments took place
once in a while:

'Omar ibn al-Khattab and 'Othman ibn 'Affan clothed it in *qabati*[5]
cloth which was woven on behalf of the government treasury. Mu'awiya,
the first Umayyad Khalif, ordered two curtains, instead of one to be
made: one of qabati to be put on at the end of Ramadan, the 9th month
of the Mohammedan year and one of *dibaj*[6] to be put on in Muharram,
the first month of this year. Al-Mahdi, the Abbasid Khalif, clothed it
(873 AD/260 AH) with three curtains: qabati, *khazz*[7], and dibaj. The
Fatimid Khalifs clothed it with white cloth while the Abbasids supplied
a black one, and so did the Sultans of Egypt (Marzouk 1955, 56).

While representing the changes in quality and in the reputation
of textiles in various parts of the Islamic world, the different textiles
used for Kaaba covers also reflected political predominance. In
AD 892/279 AH, the governor of Egypt challenged the authority
of Baghdad by deleting the name of al-Muwaffak, the brother of
Caliph al-Mu'tamid and the man in power, from coins, prayers
and ṭirāz textiles. As the cover of the Kaaba was usually woven in
Egypt in this period, the action could have caused problems for
the caliphate. Therefore, the Caliph ordered the Kaaba cover for
the year AD 883/270 AH from Tustar in Khuzistan instead of from
Egypt (Serjeant 1972, 19–20).

With the spread of the ṭirāz system to the eastern part of the
Islamic world, these regions also supplied covers for the Kaaba.
In addition to Tustar brocade (Serjeant 1972, 40, 42, 43), another
Persian textile, *Khusrawānī*, was ordered by the Caliphs to cover
the Kaaba (ibid., 11). Khusrawānī means 'kingly', probably because this kind of silk textile was made in Sassanian royal workshops. Ibn Jubayr, who went on a pilgrimage to Mecca in 1183,
described the cover of the Kaaba:

The outside of the Ka'bah, on all its four sides, is clothed in coverings
of green silk with cotton warps; and on their upper parts is a band of
red silk on which is written the verse, 'Verily the first House founded
for mankind was that at Bakkah [Mecca]' [Koran III, 96]. The name of

---

[5] Qabati was the name used by Muslims for Coptic textiles made in Egypt.
[6] Dibaj normally meant brocade.
[7] Khazz was a kind of silk.

the Imam al-Nasir li Din Ilah, in depth three cubits, encircles it all. On these coverings there has been shaped remarkable designs resembling handsome pulpits, and inscriptions entertaining the name of God Most High and calling blessings on Nasir, the aforementioned 'Abbasid (Caliph) who had ordered its instalment. With all this there was no clash of colour. The number of covers on all four sides is thirty-four, there being eighteen on the two long sides, and sixteen on the two short sides (Broadhurst 1952, 79) . . . Thus the blessed Kiswah is sewn top and bottom, and firmly buttoned, being never removed save at its renewal year by year (ibid., 88).

Yemen and Egypt remained the most keen contenders to supply the coverings for the Kaaba. Even after the decline of the caliphate, the competition between Yemen and Egypt continued. Ibn Battuta reported that 'the king of Yemen used to provide the covering for the Kaaba until al-Malik al-Mansūr Kalāūn (the Mameluke) deprived him of that right' (quoted in Serjeant 1972, 128). In about the year AD 1262/660 AH, an Egyptian king 'made a mortmain for the covering of the Kaaba each . . . year, the name of the Sultan of Egypt was inscribed on the Kaaba covering. Thus the power of Baibars spread into the Hejaz' (ibid., 153). Since the Kaaba was the sacred temple of the entire Islamic world, pilgrims from all over witnessed the display of these textiles and read the inscriptions on them. As the Kaaba covering was symbolically and ritually significant, rulers from as far as India contributed coverings voluntarily.[8]

The pilgrimage season at Mecca was also the time for a great festival and fair. Pilgrims brought goods for trade. On the night of the new moon of the Month of Rajab, the streets of Mecca would be full of *hawdaj* (dome-shaped camel howdahs) on camels covered with silk drapings, or linen drapings for the least affluent people. Ladies sat in these howdahs for the festival. Some of them displayed their affluence and status by wearing long trains of silk draping dragging on the ground. Pilgrims commented on the howdahs and identified them with the names of influential

---

[8] An Indian ruler, Mahmud Ibn Sabuktagin, made a cover of yellow brocade for the Kaaba. It covered the Kaaba in the year 466 AH/AD 1073–74 (Serjeant 1972, 215), 43 years after Mahmud's death (AD 1030). It is hard to say whether there was a chronological mistake in the record, or there were so many donations for the Kaaba, that every piece had to wait for years before it got its turn to be used on the Kaaba.

families (Broadhurst 1952, 127–8). According to Ibn Jubayr, this festival started even before Islam came to Mecca (ibid., 127). But the display of silk textiles may have developed when the silk industry and trade brought enough silk textiles to Islamic countries. Religious practices actually drew a more substantial quantity of silk and other precious textiles made expressly for the sacred places into the core region of Islamic culture than did the markets located in the sites of the caliphate—Damascus or Baghdad.

Textile Revenue

Perhaps one of the reasons of establishing an extensive ṭirāz system was to channelize and regulate the textile revenue to the centre. In the early stage of the Islamic empire, textiles and clothing were major items given as tax, because this had been the prevailing custom before the spread of Islam, and because textiles were a major form of wealth in the late antiquity and early medieval world. The well-known Yemen striped textiles were given as tributes to the Sassanid. The textile was so sought after that it was used to enshroud the ancestors of the Prophet. When the Persian governor of Yemen converted to Islam in AD 628, this portion of the tax naturally went to Medina (Serjeant 1972, 123–4). Similarly, in the year AD 716/98 AH, the Djurdjan region tributed 1000 pieces of ibrīṣm silks to the Caliph (ibid., 80). From the Caspian region of Tabaristan, the local ruler, Ispahbad, sent the same textile tax to the Abbasid Caliph, Manṣūr (AD 754–75/136–58 AH), as to the Sassanid, namely 300 bales of green silk carpets and quilts, plus an amount of cotton, embroidered garments called Rūyānī and Lafūradj, and saffron (ibid., 74). As a token of recognizing his vassalage, Manṣūr sent a crown and a robe of honour, probably with a ṭirāz (ibid.). By the ninth century, various provinces in a paid much of their taxes in textiles and silk: 20 garments Gīlān; 300 pieces of attābī (half silk) of different colours Sīstān; 600 Tabaristān carpets; 200 garments, 500 tunics, 300 napkins from Ṭabaristān, Rūyān and Nihāvand; 1000 es of silk from Gurgān; and 27,000 pieces of textiles from rāsān (Ackerman 1981, 1995).

he Armenian Caspian region maintained close contacts with ntium, and sent garments of 'Rumi (Roman) brocade' as ites to the caliphate from the early eighth century (Serjeant

1972, 62–3, 67). Interestingly, the ṭirāz city, Merv in Khurasan, produced textiles that resembled those of the Tinnis-Damietta on the Delta of Egypt, with a silk ṭirāz border. The excellent textiles of this region became so famous that the province sent thousands of garments to Baghdad in tribute (ibid., 87–9).

The exact contribution of ṭirāz to the textile revenue is not clear. Both the ṭirāz and the textile revenue were institutions established under the caliphate, and both served the central power of the Islamic world. Ṭirāz was an invention of the Islamic polity, whereas textile revenue was an inheritance from older civilizations. This inheritance may have inspired the 'Commanders of the Faithful' to establish the ṭirāz system to control the production of textiles and secure revenue. However, both the ṭirāz system and tax collection in the form of textiles became less important after the power of the caliphate diminished. And after the establishment of Islamic coinage, taxes were collected more in cash than in textiles. In AD 1212–13/609 AH, in the trading city of Aleppo in Syria, the tax in cash was extracted from textiles. The tax on dyeing factories was 80,000 dirhams; on indigo (reading doubtful) 20,000 dirhams; and on silks, 80,000 dirhams (Serjeant 1972, 115). Silk ceased to function as a medium of currency in some Islamic countries at the time.

Ṭirāz, Silk, Status

Having established a big empire, having inherited a textile industry and a revenue system from old civilizations, and having built up the ṭirāz system to control industry and revenue, the Muslim rulers certainly wanted to enjoy and display their luxuries in court and impress their contemporary rulers. I have drawn attention to the political practice of using silk textiles as status regalia in both the Byzantine and Chinese courts, and the similar religious practices among Buddhists and Christians of using silk textiles as a symbol of devotion. It appears that Muslims also adopted these practices. However, as Islamic ideological and institutional systems—religious and political at the same time—differed from those of Byzantium and T'ang China fundamentally, the similar practices may have been based on a different rationale and thus had different results.

The wardrobe or warehouses of the Caliph in Baghdad were

probably as large and as full of beautiful textiles and garments
as those of contemporary Constantinople and Ch'ang-an. Muslim
rulers shared the same passion for luxurious textiles as did the
rulers of Byzantium and China. While Byzantine emperors always
tried to show their superiority by displaying their splendid silk
attires and decorations, the Muslim rulers tried to convince
Byzantine envoys that they were as civilized as the Romans. The
Abbasid Caliph, al-Muktadir, received a Byzantine ambassador
in AD 917/305 AH with:

The number of gold curtains of brocade (dībādj) with magnificent gold
embroideries (ṭirāz), with figures of cups, elephants, horses, camels, wild
beasts, and birds, and large Basinna, Armenian, Wasit, and Bahnasa
curtains, plain (sādhidj), or with drawings (? or coloured, mankūsh),
and Dabīkī with the ṭirāz which were suspended in the castles of the
Commander of the Faithful al-Muktadir bi'llāh, consisted of 38,000
curtains, of which the aforementioned gold curtains of brocade made
up the number of 12,000. The number of carpets (busuṭ), and strips
(ankhākh) of Djahram and Dārābdjird and Dawrak in the passages and
in the courts, on which the generals and envoys of the emperor of Rum
trod, from the New Public Gate to the presence of al-Muktadir bi'llāh,
not counting the Ṭabarī and Dabīkī carpets (anmāṭ) which were under
them, in the private rooms and in the assembly rooms, for display, and
not to be trodden upon, came to 22,000 pieces (Serjeant 1972, 22).

Local Muslim rulers also competed for the splendour of textile
display on ceremonial occasions. The Fatimids, who possessed
rich textile resources in Egypt, eagerly decorated their palaces and
even the city with all kinds of textiles on religious and other festive
occasions. The 'draping universe' of the palace, saddles and tents
impressed all visitors (Bierman 1980, 89). To achieve this visual
effect, state factories employed many weavers. A prince may have
had 10,000 workers engaged in making precious textiles and
garments for his wardrobe (Marzouk 1955, 57–8). However, all
the textiles and garments did not only serve these few rulers. Many
were honorary robes granted to officials and others who pleased
the Caliphs. This practice again is similar to the robe-granting
practices that prevailed at the time. But robe-granting had different aims and results in Islamic society than it had in Byzantium
and T'ang China. The word for the 'robe of honour', *khil'a*, often
appears in Arabic works. Manufacturing robes of honour was
budgeted for by the Caliphs (Serjeant, 1972, 21–2). The Abbasid

Caliphs granted to an appointed Sultan a robe of black satin with a golden ṭirāz border, in addition to a gold necklace, a pair of gold bracelets, a sword with a gold covered scabbard, a horse with a gold saddle and a black standard with the name of the Caliph written in white (ibid., 24). This set of insignia was parallel to the seven items that T'ang emperors granted to vassals. The black robe and black standard of the Abbasids were so famous that, in T'ang China, the Abbasid empire was known as the 'Black Robe Arabs' (Hei-i Ta-shih) or simply as the 'Black Robes' (CHL II, 125; CTS 198/5316; TFYK 971/18b–20b). It appears that the Abbasids gave all their vassals black robes. There were no variations in colour and design to mark the rank or status of the grantee, as in T'ang China or Byzantium. The gift was merely a symbol of mutual recognition between the suzerain and the vassals.

On special occasions, the Abbasids and other Muslim rulers granted robes of honour, often colourful gala robes, to victorious generals, learned scholars and even merchants who served the rulers well (Goitein 1967, 272). On these occasions, the ceremony of robe-granting was impressive, as is evident from Mas'ūdī's description of a celebration of triumph in AD 896/283 AH:

Mu'tadid returned to Baghdad. Pavilions were erected in the capital and the streets were hung with banners. The Caliph drew up his army in perfect battle array before the Shammasiya Gate and then crossed the town to the Hasani Palace. *To honour Husain ibn Hamdan, the Caliph gave him a splendid gala robe and clasped a gold chain about his neck. A number of knights of his entourage and important men of his family were also presented with robes of honour.* As a reward for their courage and prowess, they rode in triumph before all the people and, on the orders of the Caliph, Harun al-Shari was mounted on an elephant. *He was dressed in a sleeved robe of silk brocade and on his head was a tall headdress of raw silk.* His brother followed, mounted on a Bactrian camel. They came immediately after Husain ibn Hamdan and his escort. Mu'tadid followed them, wearing a black robe and a tall pointed headdress; he was riding an ash-grey horse . . . (emphases mine) (VIII, 168–75, Lunde & Stone 1989, 355).

During the entire celebration, the robes for the grantees and those of the grantor and other participants were the foci of attention and comments.

Under the rule of the Fatimid caliphate, robe-granting was expanded to cover a larger personnel. The Caliph granted

garments to all officials and their dependents twice a year (Marzouk 1955, 76). As enemies of the Abbasids, the robes of the Shi'a
Fatimids were purposely not black. This large-scale granting of
robes was necessary because these robes became rank-markers in
the court. Soon after they came to Egypt, in the mid-tenth century,
the Fatimids established a hierarchy of administration as well as
that of clothes. The robes of the prime minister (wazir), the chief
judge (qadi) and the head chamberlain were of silk with a golden
ṭirāz. The lesser officials received linen robes with a golden or silk
ṭirāz (Bierman 1980, 77–80). This practice reminds us that Egypt
was under Byzantium before it came under Islamic rule, and the
Fatimids maintained close contact with the Byzantines.

Even among the Fatimids, the luxury robes of honour were not
only for the ruling class. At his will, the ruler would grant robes
to an artist or to others who pleased him. The Fatimid Caliph,
al'Aziz, had been granting robes of honour to jurists residing in
the mosque of al-Azhar on the day of breaking their fast since the
year AD 988 (Lewis 1987, 4). High officials followed the example
of the Caliph to show their patronage of the arts and learning.
Yazuri, a minister in the court of the Fatimid Caliph, Mustansir
(AD 1035–1094), once bestowed robes of honour on two artists
who executed beautiful paintings (Arnold 1928, 22).

As discussed earlier, the thrust of Islamic sumptuary rules was
not to demarcate the ruling from the ruled, but to facilitate a
compromise between religious asceticism and hedonism in Arabian traditional culture. The mitigation of the gap between the
ideal of equality of all Muslims and the stark reality of social
stratification was a mechanism to consolidate Islamic society. So
was the robe-granting practice under most Islamic regimes. From
time to time there were discriminative laws against non-Muslims
which forbade them from wearing luxurious clothes (Goitein
1973, 77, note 23). Among the Muslims, the Sufis were the most
persistent group that opposed the luxury of wearing fine linen and
silks and expressed disagreement with the corrupt society by in-
sisting on wearing wool (Arberry 1964, 199).[9] Their mysticism,
to some extent, reflected the asceticism of early Islam. Otherwise
there were no strict rules about wearing silk for common Muslims.
In Fatimid Egypt, where silk was still limited, only the highest

[9] Arabic *suf* means wool; Sufi was 'the man of wool'.

officials received silk robes. But even so, there was no rule prohibiting the rich from buying silk robes for themselves. Commoners also ordered special garments, often of silk, during festivals or for ceremonial occasions (Golombek 1977, 89, Goitein 1973, 77, 141, 265). The letters of Jewish traders, as seen in the Geniza documents, show that the Jewish people under Islamic regimes wore gorgeous, colourful clothes of such good quality that they were fit for Muslim rulers (Goitein 1967, I, 72). In regions where silk was abundant, it often formed part of the salaries paid to servants, and Caliphs and great nobles often donned their servants with silk garments (Serjeant 1972, 22). A writer living around AD 860–936/246–325 AH described the attire worn by the 'elegant' of his time, including various silk textiles with or without ṭirāz, such as _khazz, ibrīsm,_ brocade, Armenian, Chinese or Kufan, etc. (ibid., 213–15). Under Islamic rule, silk production and trade flourished to such an extent that rich commoners could afford silk textiles from all parts of the Eurasian continent.

Chapter VII

Silk Trade under Islamic Rule

Merchants enjoyed a high status in Islamic society, and among them the most prestigious were the textile merchants. There are many quotations ascribed to the Prophet in praise of trade as the best livelihood, and traders as the best Muslims:

The honest, truthful Muslim merchant will stand with the martyrs on the Day of Judgment.

I commend the merchants to you, for they are couriers of the horizons and God's trusted servants on earth (Al-Muttaqī, Kanz al-'Ummāl, ii, pp. 193–203, 212–13, quoted in Lewis 1987, 126).

Since textiles played such a significant role in Middle Eastern life, the early Muslims specifically appreciated trade in cloth: 'If God permitted the inhabitants of paradise to trade, they would deal in cloth and perfume' (ibid., 127). The enterprising spirit displayed by merchants increased with the expansion of the Islamic empire and with the rise in demand for textiles and other goods. Muslim traders were active in T'ang China in the east, and in the west they reached as far as the western Mediterranean. Under the Islamic religious and administrative system, rulers and other affluent individuals constructed and maintained public facilities such as caravansaries and bridges, from a sense of obligation and charity (*waqf*) (Spuler 1970, 15). These were availed of by pilgrims, scholars, or more frequently, traders.

The spread of the ṭirāz system in Islamic countries and the fashion among the common Muslims of wearing silk or partially silk clothes indicated that silk production and trade increased substantially in a large area during the first five or six centuries of Islamic rule. When sericulture and silk weaving reached lands as far as North Africa and Spain, silk weavers from all the Islamic countries legitimately produced silk textiles for the people who could afford them. Silk was more valuable than other materials, and so traders invested in silk and carried it across continents. In the complex picture of transactions in various silk fibers and textiles, a market network based on the supply and demand emerged, which linked the many Islamic and non-Islamic ethnic groups and civilizations and helped to transfer ideas and fashions beyond the borders of the major religions and languages of the early medieval world.

Sericulture

When the Muslims took over the eastern territory of Byzantium in the seventh century AD, sericulture was either not known there or had just been established. It is difficult to discern how much sericulture they inherited from the Byzantines; they probably inherited more from the Sassanids than from the Byzantines. Whatever the truth, a few centuries later, Arabic literature referred to mulberry trees and sericulture frequently in these regions. While eastern Turkestan knew of sericulture since the sixth century, sericulture in places in western Turkestan, such as Khoresm, was mature at the latest by the time of Yakut (AD 1179–1229) (Serjeant 1972, 105). From the tenth century, there were many references to sericulture in the Armenian Caspian regions (ibid., 69, 71, 76). A twelfth century record referred to many mulberry trees in Yezd in Fars, Iraq (ibid., 55). A thirteenth century writer mentioned that in Manbidji in north Mesopotamia, most of the trees were mulberry trees, grown for the purpose of rearing silk worms (39). The many mulberry trees for sericulture in Granada, Spain, and Tripoli, North Africa (172a, 180b) were certainly grown after Islam spread to these regions.

More important, the technique of protecting the long filament of silk became widely known in Islamic society. In eastern Turkestan, when Hsüan-tsang visited Khotan, it was customary to wait for the silkworms to gnaw through the cocoons before starting to process the fibre. In this way silk yarn was spun out of broken cocoons (HT 1021–22). The Indians adopted a similar method to process 'wild silk' or kauśaya (see Chapter III). An Arabic document of the thirteenth or fourteenth century contains details of the filature of ibrīsm silk. The word ibrīsm, Persian in origin, appears in Islamic vocabulary much earlier than in this document, which is of more recent origin. The standard technology, as recorded in this document, differs only slightly from that of the Chinese. While in China the cocoons were baked or steamed in order to kill the worms, under Islamic law, they were dried under the sun (Serjeant 1972, 198b). This method provided long filaments to weavers to make fine and thin silk textiles. This and perhaps other technical differences in sericulture and filature, also resulted in differences in the texture and lustre of the fibre, and thus a style of textiles was created which was different from that of Chinese silks. Islamic countries imported silk material from China. Even in the Armenian Caspian regions, where sericulture was well established, ibrīsm silk was imported, (ibid., 73). 'Chinese silk' (ḥarīr sīnī) is frequently mentioned in Arabic literature (ibid., 217b). These countries imported Chinese silk yarn because their own sericulture was not sufficient to supply their looms, and because Chinese silk, yarn or fabric, was different from their indigenous products and thus more exotic.

Silk Textiles in the Islamic Empire

Textiles, along with paper and sugar, were major industries in the early phase of the Islamic economy. As mentioned earlier, due to the tent culture of the Arabs, textiles were not only used for clothing, but were also widely used as articles of furniture in the palaces of Caliphs and in the houses of commoners. Precious textiles, mostly silks, constituted major family investments (Goitein 1967, I, 101ff). As the vast empire inherited a variety of textile traditions, the textile industries in different regions continued to develop individually, although all of them were influenced by Islamic rules and values. First of all, the basic materials for textiles varied from region to region. Textile experts agreed that Lower Egypt produced mainly linen up to the twelfth century AD; India, Mesopotamia, Persia and Yemen produced cotton; Mesopotamia and Upper Egypt were famous for woolen textiles; while Persia, western Turkestan and part of Mesopotamia were known for their silk and half silk (mulham) (Gervers 1977, 83; Britton 1983, 23). However, when textile experts follow this guideline, based on archaeological finds, to trace the provenances of textile samples, there are discrepancies between archaeological evidence and literary references. Yemen was presumably famous for its cotton ground striped (ikat) cloth, which represented the most orthodox Islamic style and one of the earliest known Kaaba covers. Yet, literary sources refer to variegated silks made in Yemen, Kufa and Alexandria. Similarly, most of the Egyptian textiles were of linen. Specialists treated the few Abbasid silks found in Egypt as foreign products (Kühnel 1957, 370). But literary sources refer to silk brocade (dībāj) and other types of silk material in Egypt (Marzouk 1955, 54–5, 64). Considering that the Egyptians rarely buried their better clothes with the dead, one cannot exclude the possibility that they too wove large quantities of silk textiles.

The most famous textile that Egypt contributed to the Islamic world was *qabati*, the Egyptian textile made in the Coptic tradition. Under Islamic rule, Coptic weavers gradually changed the style of their weaving. Silk replaced wool for the tapestry of the ṭirāz or decorative border; lac-dye replaced kerms for the red colour (Britton 1983, 37–9). The use of lac-dye instead of kerms after the Arabs conquered Egypt was probably due to a lack of supply of kerms from Asia Minor and the borders of the Black Sea, and to a new trading relationship with India, which made lac-dye more readily available (ibid., 37). The replacing of wool with silk in tapestry cloth borders was more an administrative action to demonstrate the power of Islamic rule. The quantity of silk required may not have been large, but the use of silk actually revised the style of Coptic textiles and evolved it into the Arabic qabati.

In addition to the qabati, other textile traditions of Christian Byzantine persisted in the Islamic empire. Cities on the eastern Mediterranean coast, such as Gaza, which used to be silk weaving centres for Byzantium, continued to produce excellent silk textiles, presumably in the Roman style (Serjeant 1972, 119). In the big cities, such as Hira, Maison and Basra in Iraq, there were many Byzantine prisoners, and many of the weavers were Christians (ibid., 37–8).

Jews were another group involved in the textile industry in the Islamic world. They almost monopolized the craft of dying and were reluctant to reveal the professional secrets of their occupation (Goitein 1967, I, 51). Jewish dyers worked in Bethlehem, Jerusalem, near Damascus, in North Africa, and were famous in

Armenia (Serjeant 1972, 206–7). The Jews in Fez and Maghreb even dealt in textiles of purple hue (ibid., 187).[1]

Since different textile traditions persisted and various religious groups participated in silk and textile production under Islamic rule, a variety of weaving technologies and artistic styles flourished. The following terms for different types of silks are gleaned from *Islamic Textiles: Material for a History up to the Mongol Conquest* by R.B. Serjeant:

harīr	silk in general
buzyūn or rūmī	Byzantine brocade or silk brocade in Byzantine style (pp. 65, 220)
washi	variegated silk (p. 14)
ibrīṣm	silk yarn or textile made of unbroken cocoon
khazz	floss silk
mukhmal	velvet, pile
mulham	half silk textile, with silk warp and other materials as weft
dībāj	silk brocade
qabati, kubati	silk tapestry border on a linen ground made in Egypt or in the Coptic style
harīr sīnī	Chinese silk in general
kamkhā	a kind of figured Chinese silk and many kinds of Chinese silks

Both the half-silk mulham from the traditional silk land of Persia and the linen with silk borders from the traditional linen land of Egypt were popular with commoners who were of moderate means. Even whole silk garments were more readily available in Islamic countries than in Byzantium and Christian Europe. In fact, silk was so common in Islamic countries that a certain gentleman in Cordova, Spain, clothed his slave girl in brocade and ṭirāz silk (Serjeant 1972, 172b) and Jewish traders ordered silk garments for their religious festivals (Gervers 1983, 298–9). These instances not only testify to the increase in silk production in Islamic countries, but also show that silk as a luxurious

---

[1] This fact again shows that Byzantine monopoly was not the only reason that the purple colour did not gain in popularity in Islamic countries. It seems that purple did not catch the fancy of the Muslims, and they never treated it as the most prestigious colour.

commodity served a different purpose here than in the Byzantine empire and in T'ang China.

Silk Trade

Silk transactions in the Islamic empire also took the form of gift-exchanging, robe-granting and trade, as elsewhere in the contemporary world, but covered a much larger geographical area. Unlike the rulers of other big empires, the governments in Islamic countries did not monopolize or restrict trade in silk. In fact, they themselves indulged in the lavish consumption of silk and other luxuries. Sometimes the Caliphs and Sultans demanded the best silks for themselves from traders. The demand from the rulers was so great that whenever traders had difficulty in selling their stock they could always sell it to the government (Goitein 1967, I, 60). This kind of attitude encouraged silk trade in particular. Tu Huan, a Chinese military person who was taken prisoner in AD 751 by the Arabs in the battle of Talas and who returned to China in AD 762, described the commercial prosperity in Arabian cities:[2]

Inside the city walls, along the streets and lanes, everything produced from the land were available. Vehicles came from all directions. A great variety of goods were abundant in quantity and cheap in price. *Silks of featured weaving and that with embroidery* and jewels were full in the markets and stores (Chang I-ch'un 1963, 52. The translation and emphases are mine).

Under the Abbasids, the cosmopolitan nature of the capital city of Baghdad was reflected in the silk textiles available in the city. The stories of the *Arabian Nights* often refer to Syrian damask, Persian velvet, Indian brocade, Roman silks and Egyptian *gapati* (qabati). In the ninth century, it was found that 'so much commerce goes to it from Hind, Sind, China, Tibet, the Turks, Dailam, the Khazars, the Abyssinians, and other countries, that most articles of merchandise are to be found there than in the countries of origin themselves (Ya'ḳūbī, *Kitāb al-Boldān, Bibliotheca Geographorum*

---

[2] As Tu Huan stayed in the Arabian empire in the period between the time that the Abbasids gained power (AD 750) and the time Baghdad became the capital of the Abbasids (AD 762), the city he describes could be Kufa, the first residence of the Abbasid Caliph; however, it could also be one of the other flourishing cities in the Islamic empire.

Arabicorum, VIII, 234, 245, quoted in Serjeant 1972, 27). The precious silk textiles which flowed into the capital were distributed in the form of robes of honour. Baghdad was the market where pilgrims brought silks and precious robes from as far as Khurasan to be processed before being sent to Mecca. For instance, a ruler of Tabaristan (AD 1183—84/579 AH) donated silks to the poor in Mecca and Medina annually. Instead of sending the silks directly to the holy cities, he had the silks sold in Baghdad and with the money bought cotton, which he then distributed among the poor in Mecca (Serjeant 1972, 78–9). As silk was more valuable than other textiles, traders and pilgrims preferred carrying silk over long distances which fetched them higher profits.

The elegant ladies and gentlemen of Baghdad also wore silks from China and other distant countries. There were many important ports and routes that linked Baghdad and the core Islamic land to the world. Zabid on the Red Sea was the gateway to China and the seaport of Yemen (Serjeant 1972, 132b). Aden was a port that received goods from 'Sind, Hind, China, Zandj, Fars, Basra, Jidda, and Kulzum' (ibid., 127a). Baghdad was linked to Raisut by road and caravans transported textiles from Baghdad to other countries and brought back Indian products (ibid., 134a).

Egypt was another international trading centre in the Islamic world. Jewish merchants were the main agents of trade, and silk was the principle form of investment. Even before the reign of the Fatimids, the ṭirāz cloth of Alexandria was so famous that it was traded in remote countries, from Scotland to India (ibid., 147b–8a). Even Delhi imported robes made in Alexandria for honorary gifts (Marzouk 1955, 57). Egypt also imported silk textiles. The saddle cloth of the Fatimids was made of rūmī (Byzantine) brocade and of būkalamūn, the name indicating that it was from Bukhara. The Egyptians merely added an inscription bearing the name of the Sultan on the borders of the saddle cloth (Serjeant 1972, 162b).

Ships from Alexandria carried rare items made in Egypt, Yemen, India and China to other North African ports, such as Bidjaya (Bougie), where ships from the Byzantine empire also docked (ibid., 186a). The network of textile trade covered the entire Mediterranean region and extended through Central Asia to East Asia. The textiles of Merv in Central Asia were so famous that even Africa and Spain imported these textiles (ibid., 89).

Samarkand in Central Asia was the meeting place of merchants trading in goods from Transoxiana. From Samarkand, brocade and other silk textiles were transported to the nomadic Turks (ibid., 101). The Khazars of Central Asia, who did not produce any textiles, obtained their clothes from the Caspian countries and from Byzantium (ibid., 81).

Among the high quality silks traded in the Mediterranean, Byzantine brocade and Persian silk were probably most in demand. According to the Geniza letters, a Jewish bride who resided in the Muslim East required a Rūm kerchief for her wedding. The wealthier people even had a Rūm brocade bedcover or couch (Goitein 1967, i, 46). Even though imitation Tabaristan upholstery was available in Egypt and other Mediterranean countries, contracts of marriages often listed genuine Tabaristan upholstery (ibid., i, 50).

An interesting fact is that the relatively young silk producing countries of Spain and Sicily exported silk textiles to the eastern countries. In the tenth century, Spanish textiles were exported to Egypt, Khurasan and other Islamic countries (Shepherd 1978, 126). Under Almoravid (AD 1056–1148), the city of Almeria owned 800 ṭirāz factories which produced a great variety of silk textiles: precious mantles, brocades, siklāṭun, Iṣfahānī, Djurdiānī, curtains decorated with precious stones, cloth with circled patterns, small mats, 'attābī, veils and other silk items. These commodities attracted merchants, who sailed from Alexandria and Syria to Sicily for the purpose of trade (Serjeant 1972, 170a).

According to the documents of Caro Geniza, Spain became the leading country in silk production in the Mediterranean world from the late tenth century onwards (Goitein 1967, 102). After Spain came Sicily, whose sericulture supplied the whole silk industry of Fatimid Egypt (Bierman 1980, 107). In the eleventh century, ships laden with the most expensive as well as the cheapest silk filaments and fabrics sailed from Sicily to other countries (Goitein 1967, 102). The silk trade from Islamic Spain and Sicily to Christian Europe not only brought Islamic textiles with Arabic inscriptions into churches, but also exerted a profound economic impact on urban life in the north.

However, by the late middle ages, the silk industry and trade in Christian Europe gradually surpassed those of the Islamic world. One of the many causes of this development in the silk trade was the limitations on artistic designs imposed by Islamic religious institutions. This limitation reminds us of the inherent contradiction between the hedonism of traditional Arabian culture and the asceticism of religious theory and practice in Islam. This contradiction had an effect on the artistic and technological development of Islamic textiles from the beginning to the time that they began to lag behind in international competition in the textile industry.

Styles of Islamic Silks

When discussing the early Islamic sumptuary laws in the last chapter, I mentioned that there were rules restraining silk weaving and prohibiting human and animal figures on art works. With the development of sericulture and silk industry, silk and partially silk textiles became rather common materials that commoners could afford to wear. The dispute about whether a good Muslim should wear silk became obsolete. Though silk was still more precious than cotton, linen and wool, its value as a luxury depended more and more on its weaving and design. However, as Islamic society combined its state machinery with its religious institutions, practical art works such as architecture and textile had spiritual aims. The Arab conquerors were motivated to seize all the silk workshops that belonged to previous regimes and establish the ṭirāz system by the desire to build a new institution for the Islamic polity and religion. In this context, it is not surprising to see that Islamic innovation on silk textiles began with calligraphy and inscription.

Early ṭirāz inscriptions were executed in square, angular kufic letters with silk thread, on linen textiles in Egypt, and cotton and mulham textiles in Mesopotamia (Britton 1982, 30, Kuhnel 1952). The emphasis was on the content of the inscription. From the twelfth century, the Fatimids began to use more decorative, round *naskhi* letters (Kühnel 1952, 3). Gradually the inscription became illegible due to distortion for decorative purposes.

Meanwhile, as the Arabian empire inherited textile technology from older civilizations, the artistic traditions of these countries were inevitably manifested in Islamic textiles. In a simplistic way one may trace these traditions to the four ancient textile-producing lands by their names: Byzantine, Coptic, Persian and Chinese. In Arabic literature regarding textiles, there are many references to

Byzantine silks. Some of them refer to silks brought from Byzantium, while others refer to silks produced in the Byzantine style in the Islamic world. According to Ackerman (1981, 1998–99), the Byzantine silk patterned with eagles found in the tombs near Rayy in the western Iranian plateau, along with many other pieces, were not necessarily Persian in origin but in fact were in the Byzantine style. A silk textile from south Persia was also called rūmī (Serjeant 1972, 63), probably based on its Byzantine style. That Maisan in Iraq produced rūmī silks is understandable as the city was colonized by Roman prisoners (ibid., 33). Armenia kept close commercial ties with Byzantium and imported Byzantine silks. However, when the governor sent a hundred garments of rūmī brocade along with the annual tax to the caliphate (ibid., 62–3), probably part of the shipment, if not all, consisted of local products rather than imported silks from the Byzantine empire.

Muslim weavers followed the Byzantine design because it represented high fashion at the time. Another Christian tradition, the Coptic tradition, had deeper roots in Islamic Egypt because the weavers themselves were Copts or the descendants of Copts. A group of silk textiles with Abbasid inscriptions dated to the ninth century was found in Egypt. Kuhnel considers that these textiles were not made in Egypt because only linen was used as ground material for ṭirāz in that country (Kuhnel 1957, 369). As these silks have both a Persian and a Coptic flavour, he suggests that they were made in Baghdad where both Persian weavers and Lower Egyptian weavers were settled (ibid., 369–71). However, one cannot exclude the possibility that the silks were produced in Egypt merely on the basis that Egypt only made linen. During the reigns of the late Abbasids and the early Fatimids, there was a revival of Coptic themes on multi-coloured silk, instead of on traditional linen and wool, for the tapestry band. This combination of classical themes and new technological means created a new style of ṭirāz textiles in the late tenth and early eleventh centuries. In the words of Lise Golombec and Veronika Gervers: 'The group with large medallions imitate a new fashion in aristocratic ṭirāz fabrics, featuring bands of animals in cartouches à la copte' (Gervers 1977, 88). Similarly, a group of textiles from Faiyum in Upper Egypt, characterized by figurative designs and illegible inscriptions, also represented a revival of Coptic traditions in the tenth to the eleventh centuries (ibid.).

Muslim weavers in Persia did not need to change the material they were accustomed to working on. Persian art tradition was even more pronounced on Islamic silks than the Coptic tradition. From the time of the Umayyad caliphate (AD 661–750), fine silks from Khuzistan were favoured by the gentlemen of the court (Ackerman 1981, 1995). The more extravagant Abbasid court followed the pattern of the Persian kings (Britton 1983, 26). The commercial network of the Islamic empire spread Sassanian art styles, as well as the Persian language, over an increasingly larger area than that of the old Persian empires. In 1969, the Hermitage Museum obtained a caftan (robe with sleeves) of patterned silk from the site of Mochtchevaya Balka in Northern Caucasus (Riboud 1976). This silk caftan found in a tomb dated to the eighth or ninth century probably belonged to a local chieftain (ibid., 24). The pattern is typical Sassanian simurgh in pearl roundels, though a scholar argues that it was made in a Byzantine workshop (Starensier 1982, 121–31). The dating of this piece to more than a hundred years after the end of the Sassanian regime (AD 651) means that the Sassanian textile tradition persisted, whether in Persia or else-where, and this kind of textiles was widely dispersed.

Though Chinese influence on Islamic silk is rarely discussed by textile experts, it certainly did exist. China introduced silk weaving, and its technology and art style permeated all silk weaving regions. Meanwhile, styles in China changed greatly and varied markedly with geographical diversity during the course of the few thousand years of its silk weaving. It is difficult to tell which features on Islamic textiles were typically Chinese. As mentioned above, there were quite a few words denoting different silk textiles made in China or in the Chinese style. A golden woven type (*kamkhā* or *kīmkhā*) was a well known Chinese silk in Islamic communities and was copied by Muslims. Persian weavers made kamkhā at Tabriz and Heerat (Ackerman 1981, pp. 1998, 2006). Thin, monochrome silks dated to the eleventh century have been found in the graves of Rayy in Central Persia, which are Chinese in style (ibid., 2008). Here again the problem arises of distinguishing local products with Chinese patterns from imported Chinese silks. Tu Huan even gave the names of a few Chinese artisans who worked in Islamic cities, including painters and weavers whom he encountered or heard of during his stay in the mid-eighth century as a war prisoner (Chang I-ch'un 1963, 55).

Whether Byzantine, Coptic, Persian or Chinese, all the artistic traditions inherited by the Islamic countries lay emphasis on animal and human figures. We do not know how persistent these features that appeared on Islamic textiles were, but there was certainly a lingering continuity, as in the case of the Coptic tradition in Egypt. With the passage of time, some characteristic Islamic figurative designs appeared. One of the best examples was the 'Bishop Gurb silk' from a thirteenth century Spanish tomb and related silks. Probably derived from Sassanian royal motifs of feasting and hunting, the figures in roundels on these silks represented Islamic eschatological views. The inscription 'there is no god but God' on the Bishop Gurb silk provided the religious context of the design, which demonstrated to the faithful that the life they could enjoy in heaven was similar to the royal life on earth (D.G. Shepherd, 187). However, as the development of visual arts was limited by the aniconic principle of Islamic religion, especially in the homeland of Islam, fancy designs on textiles were exceptional rather than usual.

The Aniconic Principle and Islamic Textiles

If iconoclasm was an episode, no matter how important, in the history of the Christian church, aniconic rules were among the basic rules in Islamic history. Whether this principle was followed in all forms of Islamic arts is debatable, but on mosques and other sacred architecture human and animal figures were totally absent.

However, even in Islam, the aniconic principle was not a strict rule from the very beginning. Early Islamic leaders were not that particular about excluding images of creatures. It is said that the Prophet tolerated the figures on woven textiles in his house in Medina (Arnold 1928, 7). He even protected a painting on a pillar in the Kaaba which depicted the Virgin Mary with Jesus on her lap (ibid.). His early followers accepted tributes from many countries—textiles and utensils with decorative figures—without dispute (ibid., 7–8). The aniconic trends developed in later Hadīth traditions, including those of both the Sunnites and Shiites (ibid., 11). The general argument was that the artists who created images actually imitated God by this act, and were therefore doomed for their offense (ibid., 5–6).

Aniconism in Islam was probably inspired by Judaism, as

synagogues forbade images since the fifth and sixth centuries AD (Vasiliev 1955–56, 25). The aniconic principle in Islam soon surpassed that of Judaism because Islam became a more influential religion. The Umayyad Caliph, Yazid II, launched an iconoclast drive in AD 721 which spread to Christian churches under Islamic rule. Greek, Syriac and Arabic sources blamed a Jewish magician who persuaded Yazid II to have all mosaic and altar cloth pieces with human figures destroyed (ibid., 28 ff). The Byzantine Emperor, Leo III, issued an iconoclast edict in AD 726 (ibid., 26). In subsequent years, Muslims and Christians accused each other of being idolaters. However, the iconoclastic drive launched by Yazid was not based on established Islamic regulations and was revoked soon after his death in AD 724 by his successor, Hisham (Creswell 1946, 163). Whether the Jewish magician was legendary or real, the iconoclastic action of Yazid II and probably also the Hadīth traditions against images stemmed from competition and conflicts among the three major monotheist religions, especially from the antagonism between Islam and Christianity (the Christian churches used rich imagery decorations). The edict of Leo III and the following iconoclastic movements in Byzantium were more or less defensive reactions to accusations from the followers of Islam. On this matter, the Jews and Muslims followed the same line of thought. Creswell attributes the evolution of an anti-image tradition in Islam to Jewish converts in Islamic society. Some of the converts gained high esteem and became authorities on the Hadīth traditions (Creswell 1946, 165). The movement that banished images from religious and secular life probably began in the late eighth century AD (ibid., 162).

Despite the rigorous actions taken and strict rules imposed against images, Islamic paintings and other forms of visual arts flourished, especially in the peripheral regions. Arnold has pointed out the divergence between creed and practice that existed in other aspects of Islam too, such as drinking, making luxurious tombs, etc. (1928, 15, 16). Islam developed and changed in response to internal and external challenges. Even though the Koran set a fixed code, the pronouncements of God and the Prophet had to be interpreted in new ways to cope with emerging problems. The contradictions inherent in the religion could be exploited to suit current needs. I have mentioned the heroism as well as the hedonism in pre-Islamic Arabic poetry which became a vital part of

Islamic culture. As animals were critical to both nomadic life and caravan commerce, the pre-Islamic Arabs loved and cared for their camels, horses and sheep. Descriptions of animals were the most evocative in Arabic poetry. Once the concept of one god was accepted, the Arabs did not have to conceal their affection for animals and Islamic folk art outside mosques constantly went back to decorative animal motifs.

As mentioned earlier, it was said that the Prophet Muhammad tolerated the image of Mary and Jesus in the temple of Kaaba. The Koran recognizes Jesus as a prophet and Mary as his mother. The followers of the prophet, however, had to create a definite demarcation in religious practices to distinguish Islam from other religions when dealing with a much larger and complex population. The caliphate which established the ṭirāz system as a state apparatus intentionally excluded Christian motifs from textiles during the reigns of both the Umayyads and Abbasids, at least in the core region of the empire. Once Islamic dominance was firmly established in the conquered regions, the rules against images relaxed. Perhaps most of the Copts had already converted to Islam by the time the animal figures in neo-Coptic style became popular in Fatimid Egypt in the eleventh century.[3]

Post-Imperial Islamic Society and Silk Trade

After the disintegration of the Abbasid Caliphate in the ninth century, adjustments in Islamic institutions and the reorganization of the state and society affected long distance trade in general and silk trade in particular. The Islamic empire separated into two major linguistic domains. While Arabic continued to be the official language of the western sphere, Persian became the lingua franca of the region much larger than the former Persian empires, including Central and South Asia. The empire divided into regional states. While the Ghaznavids and Saljuqs still sought legitimacy from the caliphate in Baghdad, Shi'ite regimes, such as the Buwayhids, Hamdanids, Qarmatians and Fatimids threatened

---

3 According to some conservative estimates, the Coptic urban population remained in vigour by the tenth century (Bulliet 1979, 102). The conversion process in Egypt passed the half way point around 900, and was almost completed by 1010, though a portion of the Christian population did not change its religion (96, 102).

the dominance of Sunni orthodoxy. The Buwayhids even claimed glory by establishing a link with ancient Iranian kings (Lapidus 1088, 147).

At the core of the political power of the caliphate, a military elite composed of slaves emerged and disturbed the whole state and social structure. Slaves in Islamic communities enjoyed more social mobility than in any other civilization. Most Caliphs were born of slave mothers. The second Abbasid Caliph, Mansūr (AD 754–75), was born of a Berber slave girl (Lunde & Stone 1989, 21). The mothers of Caliphs could be Greek, Slavic, Central Asian, Afghan or black African. From the ninth century, Turkish slaves swarmed into Baghdad. Since the policy of territorial expansion had ended, the Arabs gave up their military careers under the command of the Caliph, and joined other ethnic groups to pursue administrative, commercial, scholarly and religious careers. Also, the Arabs who established themselves as local rulers often defied and even rebelled against the authority of the Caliph. Hence, the Caliphs had to buy Turkish slaves whom they then trained and equipped as mercenaries. In course of time a few of the freed slaves rose to key posts in the caliphate and began to manipulate the succession to the throne and to dabble in politics. Badz, a powerful figure under Caliph Multadid (AD 892–907), was a freed Turkish slave (ibid., 329). The presence of these powerful Turkish mercenaries in Baghdad caused violence and bloodshed during the waning period of the caliphate. Meanwhile, the Central Asian nomadic people, the Turks being the most important among them, embraced Islam. Their military valour drew the attention of various local Caliphs and helped to elevate them to positions of political importance. The presence of this slave-nomadic military elite in important positions led to disturbances, shattered any remaining administrative or social hierarchy, and hastened changes in the social status of individuals.

While the state machinery of the Abbasid Caliphate was falling apart, religious institutions took up the task of reorganizing society. In such chaotic times, Buddhists, Christians, Jews and followers of other religions in the Islamic domain converted in large numbers in order to seek security in the religious communal fold. The ulemas of the Shi'ite sect, Sunnite schools of law and theology and Sufi brotherhoods provided the leadership for reorganizing the social and business structure. Islam was no longer an urban-based institution. The glory of the caliphate was now so dim that it could not reach the diverse communities with their different religious practices under the canopy of Islam. These communities developed new foci of worship in addition to Mecca, often around saints and tombs. From the ninth century AD, the Sufis, Shias and Sunnites began to worship saints and their tombs. Perhaps the Sufi saints initiated this movement. Even for orthodox Sunnites, this was a legitimate alternative religious practice to pilgrimages to Mecca (Lapidus 1988, 223, 225). In the next two or three centuries, hundreds of sanctuaries were established throughout the Islamic world and they became the destinations of pilgrims and provided lodgings to travellers. Their architecture, guides and manuals regarding miracles and rituals were testimony to the dominance of Islam.

This practice reminds us of the saint and relic worship among both the Christians and Buddhists. Though Islam had been influenced by converts from these religions, it had taken time to realize the importance of the world to come and thus the importance of saints who had passed to another world. We may recall that the pre-Islamic Arabs were very much people of 'this world'. Islam not only presented the reality of God and the absolute necessity to obey God, but also a vision of the world after death. The warning of the final judgment by God and the rewards gained in the afterlife were important messages contained in the religion. Nevertheless, the glory of military victories and economic and cultural success often made the rulers and wealthy people forget these warnings and disregard the rewards.

In the new social order the difference between the Arabs and non-Arab Muslims lost all meaning. On the contrary, the Persian Muslims were proud of their rich culture, the Turkish Muslims were proud of their fighting ability and even the black Muslims claimed equality with their co-religious fellows (Lewis 1987, 207–212). In spite of the disintegration of a central government, most of the people in the vast conquered land accepted Islam as their religion. An Islamic scholar like al Biruni (AD 973–1050) could travel in the Islamic world and obtain knowledge which ranged from Greek philosophy and the sciences to the caste system of India. Mosques, sanctuaries, tombs and caravanserais lodged travellers and traders. These advantages helped develop economic ties within the Islamic world as well as with the world outside the Islamic domain.

The Arabian empire established diplomatic contact with T'ang China from as early as the mid-seventh century when, in AD 651, Caliph Uthmān sent an envoy to T'ang China (Chang Kuang-ta 1987, 748). However, conflicting interests between the Arabian empire and T'ang China in Central Asia soured this relationship. China provided asylum to the defeated Sassanian prince, Firuz, and became an ally of the Central Asian forces that were resisting conquest by Arabia. After defeating the Chinese forces at Talas, the Arabs halted their march further east. The Arabs took as prisoners many artisans who transferred the technology of paper-making and silk-processing to the Islamic world. Diplomatic relations with China were renewed later. Fortunately, military and political tensions did not deter traders from going to China.

Before the Islamic empire extended over the vast area of Central Asia, the Turkish people who occupied this area often acted as hosts for travellers. The tomb stele of Turkish rulers often bore both Turkish and Chinese inscriptions which testifies to the frequent contact with China. An eighth century monument of Kul Tigin of Goktur Khanate, located in the Orhun valley, Mongolia, shows the hospitality of Turkish rulers: 'If you remain in Otuken and send caravans and trains, all your troubles will be at an end. If you live in Otuken, you will have a homeland for eternity' (Diyarbekirli 1992, 172). After the Turks embraced Islam, the hospitable customs became systemized and institutionalized. Saljuq rulers ensured the security of the caravan trade by paying compensations out of state treasuries for losses incurred by traders due to robbery (ibid., 174). Turkish states built fortified caravanserais every 30 to 40 kms along the routes based on an average day's journey and provided free lodgings and services for three days (ibid., 175).

On the western section of the route, Ṣuhār on the south Arabian Peninsular functioned as a gate to China. According to Mas'ūdī, sailors from Oman (Ṣuhār) and Siraf sailed all the way to China, Sind, Zanguebar, Yemen, d'al-Qul-zum and Abyssinia (Pellat, 1962, I, 305, p. 115 [I, 281–2]). Silks from China went to Islamic countries by sea and land. Ib Khordādzbeh wrote in the mid-ninth century that China exported silk textiles such as white silk (ḥarīr), varicoloured silk (firanb) and golden brocade (kīmkhaw) (*Kitāb al-rusul wa'l mulūk*, Ferrand 1914, 51, Chinese trans. 47). Many of the Muslim traders went and resided in the T'ang commercial cities of Yang-chou and Canton.

Probably most of the Muslims who went to T'ang China spoke Persian. The Chinese did not differentiate between the Persians and the Arabs, and often referred to all of them as Persian traders. Indeed, even the classical Chinese word for Arabia, *Ta-shih*, originated from the Persian name for an Arabian tribe, *Tacik* (Chang Kuang-ta 1987, 748). Some Arab-Muslims settled and married in China, and a few even passed the imperial examinations and became T'ang officials (ibid., 755). A man from Basra, Ibn Wahab, went to China in AD 870, and sought and received an audience with the T'ang emperor, Hsi-tsung. With the help of an interpreter he informed the emperor about Islam and the Prophet. The emperor showed him icons of various religions kept in the imperial palace. Ibn Wahab saw portraits of Muhammad, of Noah and his Ark, of Moses, Jesus and his apostles, and of many sages and deities of India and China. All these paintings were captioned with Chinese characters (Pellat 1962, I, 342–54, p. 128–31; Broomhall 1966, 40–5). Ibn Wahab left China 'honoured with many presents' (ibid.).

The development of a silk industry in Islamic lands and the aesthetical values and variety of Islamic silks enabled Persian-Arabian merchants to export silks to China. The famous zandanījī, woven in the Bukhara region, found its way to Tunhuang as wrappings of Buddhist texts (Shepherd & Henning 1959, 22). One of the silk pieces excavated from Turfan, patterned with confronting rams and birds around trees, bears a close analogy with zandanījī (Sinkiang Uighur Autonomous Region, Museum of, 1975, pl. 79). Its theme and style indicate that it was made either in Islamic Central Asia or was dictated by Islamic fashion.

Islamic Silks in the Christian World

Islamic silks were available in the medieval Christian world, both in Byzantium and west Europe. When discussing the monopoly that Byzantium had in the silk market, I had mentioned that there was a guild in Constantinople that dealt exclusively with Syrian silks, i.e. the silks from the Arabian world. However, the Christians of west Europe had to pay a duty to the Byzantines to get Islamic

silks through this market. Only with the Latin occupation of
Antioch (AD 1098–1268) and the kingdoms of Acre and Jerusalem
(AD 1098–1187), were Italian merchants able to import Syrian
textiles in quantity (Starensier 1982, 294). Similarly, the Norman
occupation of Sicily, the base of sericulture for the Fatimids, made
Fatimid silks more readily available in European countries (Bierman 1980, 113).

Spain was another point of contact between the Muslims and
Christians. In addition to regular trade, regional politics encouraged the exchange of gifts among Islamic rulers and Christian
princes. In AD 997/387 AH, after a military victory, the Muslim
minister, Manṣūr, rewarded Christian princes and the Muslims
who supported him with 2285 pieces of various kinds of ṭirāz silk,
21 pieces of sea wool (ṣūf al-baḥr), 2 robes perfumed with ambergris, 11 pieces of scarlet cloth (siklātūn), 15 of striped stuff, 7
carpets of brocade, 2 garments of Roman (Rūmī) brocade and 2
marten furs (Serjeant 1972, 169a). These items remind us of the
Islamic silks found in Christian Spain, like the figured silk with
Arabic inscriptions found in the tomb of Bishop Gurb of Barcelona
and the Islamic silks used for Christian liturgy (Shepherd 1978).

Christian churches in Europe also preserved silk samples from
a more remote country, Bukhara in Central Asia. In Chapter VI,
I mentioned that most of the zandanījī silks produced near Bukhara were preserved in European churches and that the Bukhara
region continued to produce zandanījī after it came under the
influence of Islam. Since Shepherd and Henning published their
discovery of zandanījī silks, Soviet archaeologists have found many
more similar silk samples in north Caucasus. These finds further
prove that zandanījī silks were produced near Bukhara, the ancient
land of Sogdiana, because north Caucasus was the route linking
Central Asia to Byzantium avoiding Persia (Shepherd 1981, 108).
Shepherd has classified the 102 pieces of zandanījī into three major
categories according to their technological differences and variations in design. Based on the original deciphering of the inscription on a sample of the first category, zandanījī I, Shepherd has
dated this category to the seventh century, and the other two
categories to the eighth century, though some archaeological finds
and literature refer to a later date (ibid., 117–18). By the tenth
century, zandanījī silk was 'better known than these garments in
all the provinces', and merchants took them to Syria, Egypt and

Byzantium (Serjeant 1972, 99). It appears that most of the zandanījī silks found in western Europe came through Byzantium.

Due to the frequent contact between Islamic countries and Byzantium, the Christian practice of presenting religious themes on silk textiles crept into the design of zandanījī. A sample of zandanījī II found in Moshchevaya Balka, north Caucasus, represents the sacrifice of Abraham[4] (Shepherd 1981, 109). The unique find has led Shepherd to conclude that some of the so-called Coptic silks found in Egypt were actually zandanījī made in Central Asia (ibid., 110). Another famous Islamic piece preserved in a western church was the elephant silk associated with St Josse, preserved in the Louvre. The inscription, 'Glory and prosperity to the Qā'id Abū Manṣūr Bukhtakin, may God prolong his existence', helped to date the silk to the mid-tenth century in the Khurasan and Transoxiana region (Ackerman 1981, 2002). This typical Persian textile has the 'effect of very heavy jewellery, with a barbaric boldness and ostentation that are of the heart of Asia', combined with some features of the Far East (ibid., 2003). This is again an example of cultural interactions linking the entire Eurasian continent.

Though Islamic silks entered the Byzantine market, and many of the pieces even found their way to western Europe, they were not usually associated with Byzantine churches and reliquaries. Eunuchs in Constantinople may have worn mulḥam garments, the half-silk textile product made in West Asia, during festivals (Gervers 1977, 83). But the Byzantine silk industry was mature enough to meet its peoples' needs for sacred objects. Nevertheless, competition between the Islamic empire and the Christian empire led to some fundamental Islamic influence on Byzantine textiles. In the ninth century, Greek inscriptions appeared on the borders of clothes in the court of Constantinople. The textile was assigned to the factory of a certain prince (Bierman 1980, 31–2). A silk patterned with lions recorded in the *Gesta pontificum Autiossodorensium* carried the following inscription: 'During the reign

[4] All the three major monotheist religions traced their spiritual ancestors to Abraham, as exemplified by the common theme 'sacrifice of Abraham' shared by all the three religions. The son who was to be sacrificed but who was saved was Isaac, the ancestor of the Hebrews. Muslims traced their ancestor to another son of Abraham, Ishmeal, by a slave girl Hagar.

of Leo, the devout ruler'. This was probably Leo VI (AD 886–912) (Muthesius 1982, I, 22). Another lion-patterned silk from the shrine of St. Anno at St. Servatius, bears this inscription: 'During the reign of Romanos and Christophoros, the devout rulers'. Romanos and Christophoros were co-emperors from AD 921 to 931 (ibid., 16).

If the imitation of ṭirāz inscriptions on silk was a fashion, a beautiful sample of Byzantine silk from the ninth or tenth century was a minute copy of the Persian style. The elephant, simurgh, and flying horse inside pearl roundels were such characteristic Sassanian motifs that only the typical Byzantine colour combinations and details made it possible for experts to classify the silk as Byzantine (Ackerman 1981, 2002, pl. 983a). It appears that both the classical Persian style imitated by Islamic weavers and the Islamic invention of the ṭirāz style were representative of high culture in the eyes of the Byzantines.

Chapter VIII

Concluding Comments

This last chapter attempts to tie up some of the loose ends in the story of silk, summarize the patterns of silk transactions and religious activities which have emerged from the discussions, and speculate on some of the questions raised. The roles of several minor religious sects which were active in the manufacture and trade of silk have not been analyzed because information on these sects is even more sporadic and less conclusive than is information on the major religions, and to trace details of their activities and ascertain their functions are beyond the scope of this book. However, their presence in the silk transactions cannot be ignored as this would make many phenomena unexplainable. To fill the gaps in the picture that emerges when pursuing the thread that silk textile became a real commodity by the end of the period under study, I will first analyze the roles of various lesser religious groups in the silk trade and their contributions towards building a Eurasian silk market, before trying to outline the patterns of Eurasian silk trade. The activities of the smaller religious groups could be divided between activities on the land routes through Central Asia and those on the sea routes from the ports of southeast China to the Mediterranean.

The Central Asian Scene

On the eve of Islamic expansion into Central Asia, many people were trading along the silk routes from China to Europe. Earlier, in the Later Han Period, i.e. in the first two centuries AD, some final silk products, whether patterned Han silk brocade and damask or the finest gauze, reached the Mediterranean through Central Asia, western Asia and Kushan India. When silk weaving developed in the Byzantine empire, western demand from China tended to be silk material or plain silk textile, the weaving of which could be undone and which could then be rewoven into special textiles.[1] Sassanid Persia was a major silk producer and a silk broker to the west which meant that it needed Chinese silk material and plain silk textiles. Persians founded Zoroastrian temples which were also used as centres of trading diaspora in China long before the T'ang Dynasty. Soon after consolidating its power, the T'ang empire set up a special office to deal with Persian-Zoroastrian affairs in AD 621 (Tu Yu, 1103/40).[2] Zoroastrianism was not a proselytizing religion in China. As temples were also trading centres for Persian traders, their temples were located near market places in cities and along trade routes. During the reign of the T'ang Dynasty, there were Zoroastrian temples not only in the two capitals, Ch'ang-an and the supplementary capital Lo-yang, but also in Liang-chou along the silk route (Chang Chuo, 64–5). The temple in Ch'ang-an became the asylum for Zoroastrian refugees after the Islamic conquest of Sassanid Persia. However, many of the merchant-Zoroastrians were actually Sogdians whose ancestors had traded in China for centuries and left their names in Chinese historical records with the title of *sa-pao*, i.e. head of a caravan (Matsuda 1936, 10/134).

In competition with the Persians were the Turks. As a nomadic people, they did not produce silks but benefited from trade by selling cotton, iron and horses to the Chinese and silks to the West. One may recall that in early T'ang China the pilgrim Hsüan-tsang brought yards of silk for Yabgu Khan of the Western Turks (Chapter III). Turkish rulers also made alliances with Sogdian traders. The envoy sent by a Chinese emperor to the

---

[1] A literary record of the fourth or fifth century mentioned that Romans really wanted Chinese silk yarn, *ssu*, to make their patterned silk (*ling*, similar to damask); they thus had to trade with Persians. But the author also assumed that there already was sericulture in that country (*San-kuo Chih*, 860/30. Here the author quoted from a lost book *Wei-lüeh* [A history of the Wei]). This record obviously combined the presumption that Romans should have had sericulture as a civilized people and the fact that they had to buy Chinese yarn to make textiles in their own style. The T'ang scholar, Tu Yu, while repeating much of the former literature about the Romans, said that the Romans wanted plain silk textiles which they then unravelled to make ling and patterned silk of a dark red colour (Tu Yu, 5265/193).

[2] The name for the office was *sa-pao*. According to Matsuda (1936, 10/134), this word was probably from the Sanskrit word, sārthavāha, the head of a caravan. Zoroastrian religious activities were inseparable from the caravan trade.

Turks in AD 545 was probably a Sogdian (Matsuda 1936, 9/133). In about the same period, a Turkish ruler sent an envoy to the court of Justin II (AD 565–74) in Constantinople to make an alliance against the Persians in order to guarantee the security of west-bound silks. This envoy was also a Sogdian (Lieu 1985, 185). Though rivals of the Sassanid Persians, the Turkish groups engaged in the silk trade in the early seventh century were probably also Zoroastrians, as Hsüan-tsang noticed when he was a guest of Yagbu Khan of the Western Turks in AD 628 (Hui-li & Yen-tsung 28).

Another religious group that reached T'ang China through Central Asia was the Nestorians. Though the Nestorian church was considered heretical by the Christians, it nevertheless provided links between China and the Christian world. According to the inscriptions on the Monument Commemorating the Propagation of the Ta-ch'in Luminous Religion in the Middle Kingdom, a Nestorian missionary, A-lo-pen, reached Ch'ang-an in the year 635 and established a monastery in 638 which was authorized by the T'ang government (Saeki 1951, 57). In AD 742, when the Nestorian monastery was flourishing, it once received a grant of 100 bolts of plain silk (Saeki 1951, 60; CHL vol. I, 115). One of the outstanding Nestorian priests even reached the status of a 'Monk (who) Received a Purple Robe' (Saeki 1951, 63; CHL vol. I, 116). The Nestorians were not the only Christian sect which tried to build a church in T'ang China. Among the many missions from Byzantium to China in the T'ang period, at least two of them, one in AD 719 and the other in AD 742, were *ta-te-seng*, normally translated as 'archbishop' (CTS 5315/198; TFYK 11411/971). It is not clear which denominations they represented, but surely they were not Nestorians because they were missions from Byzantium where Nestorianism was considered a heresy. Whichever school they belonged to, they did not leave much trace in China. The story that Nestorian monks stole some silkworm eggs for Justinian may only be a legend, but the Nestorian church probably maintained contact with the church in Constantinople. They may have been the only group to be aware and conscious of the parallel institutions of the clothing code and the high status of purple silk in both Byzantium and China. The Nestorians established many churches in China in their heyday under the T'ang. However, during the religious persecution in AD 845, the

Nestorian church disappeared from the interior of China and appeared again only after the Mongols conquered China.

Manichaeism was the most enterprising religious body that came to China in the T'ang Dynasty. Emerging from a Christian background, manichaeism was almost treated as a Christian heresy by the Christians (Lieu 1985, 6–7). But in Central Asia where the religion flourished more than anywhere else, Manichaeism adopted many Buddhist ritual forms and iconography, and thus was often confused with Buddhism. This annoyed the T'ang emperor Hsüan-tsung, who issued an edict in AD 732 which said: 'Manichaeism was originally a heretic religion. As it claims Buddhism to confuse people, it should be banned. However, because it is the home religion of the western barbarians, they are allowed to follow it among themselves without punishment' (Tu Yu 1103/40). They left many monastic remains in Central Asia, but scholars have to distinguish them from Buddhist remains carefully. In a recent archaeological survey near Turfan, Ch'ao Hua-shan distinguished more than seventy Manichaean caves which comprised over one third of all the monastic caves in this region (Kuang-ming Daily, 1 Feb. 1993, p. 1). The Manichaean monasteries in this region existed from the seventh to the tenth centuries, and some of them were quite grandiose (ibid.).

The achievements of Manichaeism in Central Asia had to be attributed to its Sogdian and Uighur converts. The Sogdians who traded along the routes in the Tarim Basin, not those in their homeland, were followers of Manichaeism by this time.[3] An important event helped to convert the powerful Uighur empire to Manichaeism. After helping the T'ang government to suppress the rebellions of the military commanders, An Lu-shan and Shih Ssuming, in the mid-eighth century, the Uighurs received many luxurious items from the T'ang court as rewards and made large-scale horse and silk trade arrangements with the T'ang empire.

[3] Sogdian merchants seemed to be willing to adopt any religion. They were known as propagators of Buddhism in China from the second to the fourth centuries AD; they were Zoroastrians like the Persians; by the eighth century, they were known as Manichaeans. Yet according to the archaeological works of B.I. Marshak and Valentin I. Raspopova, in the Sogdian homeland of Panjikent, murals of the home of a granary owner shows a hierarchy of family patron deities, where the Buddha only occupies a small corner (1990, 153). The paintings in the whole room show the universal religious view of the Sogdian people (ibid., 173).

According to T'ang official history, the T'ang government traded more than one million bolts of plain silk for 100,000 horses annually (CTS 1346/51). Considering that in the mid-eighth century, the most prosperous days of the T'ang Dynasty, the government collected 7,400,000 bolts of plain silk in tax annually, the figure of silk for horses made a dent in the T'ang government's revenue. The Uighurs continued to come to China for trade at the price of 40 bolts of silk for a horse and brought with them thousands of horses (CTS 5207/195). These silks could not all have been used by the Uighurs themselves. One scholar has argued that the Uighurs who depended on the Sogdians to make a profit on silks by selling them to the West adopted the religion of the Sogdians, which in this case was Manichaeism (Lin Wu-shu 1987, 90–2). Uighur started a Manichaean monastery in 768 in China and established more monasteries in the prefectures of Ching, Yue, Hung, along the Yang-tze and Huai rivers in 771, and even more in 807 in the Tai-yüan and Honan prefectures (ibid., 94–5). Lin Wu-shu points out that the locations and the time sequence of building the monasteries corresponded with commercial interests. In other words, the Manichaean institution did not expand from a base to a larger area contiguously, but to several distant regions from its base at different times because the community's commercial interests determined where and when a monastery should be built. Manichaean temples were not only religious centres for the Uighurs and Sogdians but also storage houses for commodities (ibid., 94). Relations between the Manichaean-Uighurs and the T'ang government were most cordial in the early ninth century when the Uighur ruler married a T'ang princess (ibid., 97). However, tensions mounted when the Uighurs became arrogant enough to assume the role of protectors of the T'ang regime. Defeated by the Kirghiz in AD 840, and having suffered a famine, the Uighurs demanded payment for their horses and started to harass Chinese towns along the T'ang border. The T'ang government felt that the payment for the horses was a financial burden and the transgressions of the Uighurs on the borders were annoying. When a war between the T'ang and the Uighurs finally broke out and the T'ang princess returned home, the property of the Manichaean monasteries was confiscated in AD 843, followed two years later by a general persecution of all foreign religions (Beckwith 1993; CTS 594/18a). Even the

Manichaean caves in Chinese Central Asia were transformed into Buddhist shrines.

After the persecution of religions in the T'ang empire, the Uighur state disintegrated. But the horse–silk trade between the Uighurs and the Chinese continued till the reign of the Northern Sung Dynasty (AD 960–1127). In the process of migrating and in the dynamics of Central Asian politics, the Uighurs gave up Manichaeism and converted to Buddhism. After the Islamic Saljuq empire extended into Central Asia, the Turkish people, including some Uighurs, converted to Islam in the tenth and eleventh centuries. However, by this time, traders coming through Islamic Central Asia did not deal directly with the Chinese but with the Tanguts, the Khitans and the Jerchins who received their silks from the Sung government as war compensation or purchased silk as a commodity. The quantity was substantial but was much less than in the T'ang period.

The Sea Routes

The role of sea routes in linking the East and the West gained significance during the T'ang age, and gradually superseded the land route through Central Asia after the mid-ninth century religious persecution in China. The Muslims, Jews, Zoroastrians, Sogdians, Nestorians and Christians were the conveyors of silk on the sea routes.

After the first direct military contact between the Arabic empire and T'ang China at the battle of Talas in 751 where the Arabs defeated the T'ang army, the more friendly commercial contacts between the two empires were mostly by sea. Ships from the Arab world arrived at the ports of Canton, Yang-chou and Ch'üan-chou. Muslim traders, Persians among them, were portrayed as a fabulously rich people in Chinese literature since the mid-T'ang period. They came to China to trade, not to proselytize. Though there are numerous records of envoys from the Abbasid empire in T'ang historical records, there are no indications of Islamic religious communities around the capitals. The early Arab traveller, Ibn Wahab, who visited the T'ang court in the mid-ninth century did not mention any Islamic religious community or activities in the capital region (Broomhall 1966, 46). But in Canton the Muslim community enjoyed certain extra-territorial privileges and had their own judges to decide on affairs within the community (ibid., 47–8). Thanks to Muslim traders Chinese coloured silk textiles (firanb) and golden brocade (kīmkhaw) reached the Islamic world (Chang, Kuang-ta 1987, 751, Ibn Khordādhbeh, 73). Fine Chinese textiles appeared in the markets of Baghdad and were recorded in the stories of the *Arabian Nights*. But plain silks or silk materials, probably the largest in quantity among the traded goods, may also have entered into Mediterranean markets by the sea routes. This was the case with another kind of Chinese silk which was glossy but quite cheap compared to other silk materials in the Mediterranean market. It was called zaytūnī, meaning from the Chinese port Zaytūn, Ch'üan-chou (Goitein 1967, note. 53, p. 455).

The most important trade community which linked ports in south and southeast China to the Mediterranean ports was probably the Jewish traders. Ibn Khordādhbeh (c. AD 820–912) mentioned that Rādhāniyyah (Latin) Jews went to China and India by sea routes (ibid., 164). But, like Muslim traders, Jewish traders did not proselytize and thus left few records in China. Their activities in the Mediterranean, however, have been well-recorded in the Geniza documents. The Mediterranean market was a haven for traders of various communities since the mid-tenth century, particularly for the Jewish traders. The government exercised little power, and traders followed the laws of their respective religious communities (Goitein 1967, 29). Jews, Christians and Muslims traded with each other peacefully as their business ethics were basically the same (Goitein 1973, 8). There were not many travel barriers even when the different regimes were at war (Goitein 1967, 59, 70). On the northern coast of the sea, Venice and other Italian republics held naval superiority and traded under the flags of their patron saints. Silks were transported to Pavia in Lombardy and then to various parts of Europe. The Scandinavians also joined Italian cities in seeking silks, either Chinese or Byzantine (bisanzio) (Luigi De Rosa 1992, 197). The Norman occupation of Sicily in the mid-eleventh century also brought silks to Europe. In the southern Mediterranean, Jewish communities engaged in silk production and traded under an Islamic regime, the Fatimid caliphate. The silk dyers of the entire Islamic world were mostly Jews (Serjeant 1972, 64–6, 206ff). In the mid-twelfth century, the Rabbi, Benjamin Tudela, noticed that in Greece, Jews were the best silk artificers and dyers (Adler 1907, 10). In Solonica, in Greece, the Jewish community comprising 500 families lived on silk weaving (ibid., 11). As mentioned in Chapter VIII, the Jews of Fez in northwestern Africa dealt with various textiles and dyes, including the purple dye (Serjeant 1972, 187). With commercial and communal networks across the Mediterranean, Jewish dyers in Islamic countries could have mastered the resources and technology of purple dying as had their co-religionists in Byzantium. However, since the Muslims did not crave for purple clothes as their contemporary Christians did, the purple dye and textiles were probably aimed at the European market. One may recall that Charlemagne received gifts of purple dye from envoys of African countries (Thorpe 1969, 147).

According to the Geniza papers, among the commodities traded by Jewish traders in the Mediterranean, silk was a kind of standard cash, along with gold and silver (Goitein 1967, 230, 245). The standard silk was ḥarīr, at a price of 20 to 30 dinars for 10 pounds of silk (note 53, pp. 222, 454). There were various other silks, superior and inferior in quality or in price, including ibrīsm from Iran and zaytūnī from China (ibid.). The different types of silks were probably silk yarn because they were measured by weight and not by size. With the development of sericulture and filature under Islamic regimes, many silk materials were produced in Mediterranean countries. In the eleventh century, Spanish silk was exported to Egypt (Goitein 1967, 302). Silk was so abundant that Jewish traders carried it to India as standard payment in lieu of cash (Goitein 1973, 25, 193, 195; 1967, 222). These 'cash-silks' were probably raw materials. But Ibn Khordadhbeh also referred to silk brocade (dibaj) carried by Jewish traders to India (ibid., 164).[4] In short, Jewish traders in the Mediterranean traded silk, both materials and fabrics, as real commodities and carried silk to wherever they could make a profit, with no boundaries and no taboos.

[4] India's status as a silk importer, whether from China or from the West, changed soon after the invasion of the Islamic Turks in the eleventh century. Muslims brought in not only silk but also sericulture of mulberry silk, and filature of long filaments. By the time of Ibn Battuta (mid-fourteenth century), silk robes produced in the workshops of the Delhi Sultan were famous in the Islamic world.

A Summary: Three Circles and Two Monopolies

During the period from late antiquity to the early Middle Ages, the circulation of silk textiles followed certain routes. Among the large quantity of silks flowing out of China, the elaborate silk textiles which required special weaving technology and thus acquired an artistic value rarely reached Europe. Most of them were carried to India while some were traded along Central Asian routes. When fancy silk textiles such as brocade and damask were supposedly under the monopoly of the T'ang government, and many other varieties were forbidden to be taken across the border by law, Buddhist pilgrims and missionaries actually facilitated the transaction of silks of various qualities to India. At a deeper level, as Buddhism shaped the eschatology of the Chinese people, from the rulers down to the people on the lowest rung in society— peasants, slaves, artisans, etc., their concern for a better afterlife, either for their loved ones or for themselves, made them donate their wealth, in the form of the finest silk textiles and clothing, to Buddhist institutions and priests. The worship of Buddha's relics and the translation of relics from India to China best exemplifies how the T'ang Chinese made every effort to save themselves from damnation through material means, and how silks flowed into religious institutions, including those outside China, in spite of prohibitions imposed by a powerful government. The overlap of this circle of silk transactions with the Buddhist domain was not a fortuitous coincidence.

Similarly, the exportation of exquisite silk textiles woven in the Byzantine empire also followed certain routes, guided by religious activities. While Byzantine emperors decorated their churches and donned Christian priests with various kinds of fancy silks, silks flowed into Europe with pilgrims, missionaries and relics of saints. While Christian eschatology shaped the mind of the European people, the final judgment, and hell and heaven, loomed large in the process of decision making of kings, nobles, popes, archbishops, merchants, artisans or peasants. Their concern for the afterlife made Christians accumulate wealth in churches, use church grounds as graveyards, decorate their cathedrals with silks, and cover the tombs, icons and relics of their saints with silks. In order to be close to the saints who would help the devout go to heaven, or even to identify themselves as saints, western European rulers not only had themselves buried in churches but also had their tombs covered with fancy silks similar to those of saints. Rulers like Charlemagne who did not care for luxurious clothes when alive were enshrouded with the best quality silk textiles. Almost 200 years after Charlemagne's death, Otto III added another cover on his remains in the cathedral of Aachen with the famous silk textiles containing elephant designs (Volbach 1969, 133). By this time, the Carolingian emperor was probably treated as a saint.

Between the two seemingly separate religious domains, there were striking similarities in the functions of silk textiles as status and religious symbols. The foremost similarity lay in the two major centres of silk production or the two monopolies of high style silk textiles—the Byzantine empire and T'ang China. The similarity ran through the secular and religious institutions of both empires, in content and in form. Both the Byzantine empire and T'ang China had a bureaucratic hierarchy and a set of clothing code to mark the different levels of officials. While in Byzantium the clothing code emerged in the process of erasing all traces of republican traditions and consolidating monarchical rule, the one in T'ang China was established after the triumph of the bureaucratic elite over the aristocracy. In Byzantium, purple was considered the highest and the most sacred colour; and purple was almost the highest status symbol in T'ang China, as even the daily clothes of the emperor were purple in colour, save the yellow colour which was used for the ritual robe of the emperor (CTS 1941/45). Both Byzantine T'ang emperors granted honorary silk clothes and textiles to religious institutions and priests. While Byzantine emperors only patronized Christianity and tried to assume the leadership of the Christian world, the T'ang emperors granted purple robes to prestigious religious figures of different religions.

If we look into the details of silk textiles used in the courts and religious institutions of both countries, the similarity is even more interesting. The costumes of T'ang officials were not only of different colours, but also carried different patterns. In the year 694, the empress Wu Tse-t'ien issued a kind of vest for officials. The textile designs on the vests included confronting lions, confronting kylins (Chinese unicorn), confronting tigers, leopards, eagles, confronting falcons and confronting *chih*, a kind of footless animal. The clothes for princes carried the pattern of dragons and deer; the pattern on the clothes of prime ministers was a phoenix with water (*feng-ch'ih*) or confronting ducks (CTS 1953/45). In the Byzantine court, the *Book of Ceremonies* recorded the motifs on the textiles of officials during a ceremonial occasion: 'Green and rose eagles, oxen, eagles in circles, the same of marine creatures, the same of white lions' (Starensier 1982, 215–16). Silk samples from both Byzantium and T'ang China show motifs of confronting or single animals such as ducks, lions, peacocks, deer, etc. with or without a pearl roundel. The colours and artistic styles of the designs may differ greatly, but the basic motifs are the same. It would have been spectacular had someone drawn a picture of the two courts with the officials donned in their patterned silk costumes. The essence of the similar practices in using silk textiles was that both empires established a set of clothing code and a monopoly on the most exquisite silks, and a set of sumptuary laws to implement the code and protect the monopoly. Both empires succeeded to a certain extent in controlling the production and transactions of high quality silk textiles in a couple of hundred years. It is even more true that in both empires the government monopoly was never comprehensive and started to crumble soon after its implementation. The sumptuary laws were violated continually by both the rulers and the ruled, leading to a total collapse.

Surely the rulers did not willingly give up their control of the precious goods, and were never happy to see people of low status wearing the kind of clothing they wore. As discussed in Chapter III, the implementation of sumptuary laws in T'ang China could be very strict, and the punishment for transgressors could be quite severe, as in the case of the officer, Hou Si-chih, who was beaten to death in the court (Chang Chuo, 32). However, the rulers themselves often violated regulations for political reasons, and more often, for religious purposes, by granting silk textiles and special robes to lesser persons and priests. As early as in the mid-eighth century, there were complaints about an Indian monk who received so many precious items from a series of rulers of the T'ang Dynasty that most of the treasures in the royal storage were shifted to his home. By the early ninth century, the emperors had granted so many purple robes that the people no longer regarded official robes as prestigious and Emperor Hsien-tsung ordered an official, Cheng Yü-ch'ing, to compile all the rules about clothing issued by former T'ang emperors and reissued them for enforcement (CTS 4165/158).

Though T'ang rulers violated their own regulations for short-term gains, they did not hesitate to punish the beneficiaries who became too aggressive. The persecution of Buddhists and other religious groups in AD 843–45 was mostly due to economic reasons. To return 260,000 monks and nuns to secular life and to release slaves from the bondage of monasteries certainly increased the number of tax payers for the T'ang government; to confiscate millions of acres of monastery lands was of great economic gain (CTS 606/18a). But the arrogance of the Buddhists surely provoked the T'ang rulers to act as they did. Buddhist institutions had accumulated too much wealth and controlled too many labourers to be submissive and humble. Early in the eighth century, the scholar-official, Chang Chuo, complained that all treasures in the state treasuries went to a monastery through the patronage of a princess (ibid., 70). In his edict condemning the Buddhists, the emperor Wu-tsung not only accused the numerous monks and nuns of waiting for farmers to feed them and to raise silk cocoons to clothe them, but also showed his resentment for their splendid monasteries which imitated the architectures of the royal palaces in violation of the imperial law (CTS 605/18a).

However, Buddhism was so deeply rooted in China that even as hostile an emperor as Wu-tsung could not annihilate the religion the way he did Nestorianism, Manichaeism and Zoroastrianism. Soon after the edict announcing the persecution, some ministers petitioned that one Buddhist monastery should be saved in a big prefecture and ten monasteries should be saved on each of the two major streets in the two capitals of Ch'ang-an and Loyang.[5] They argued that according to the T'ang statutes, officials had to burn incense in a Buddhist monastery on state memorial days, i.e. on the anniversaries of former emperors (CTS 604–05/18a). Though the emperor insisted that Taoist temples could provide the same services on the anniversaries, he conceded that one monastery in good condition should be saved for a big

---

[5] Loyang was the supplementary capital to the major capital Ch'ang-an during the Sui and T'ang Dynasties. In addition to a royal residence, certain government offices and institutions attached to the government, such as the official monasteries, were situated there.

prefecture, and two monasteries should be saved for each of the two main streets of the two capitals (ibid.). To convert the monks and nuns who waited for others to raise silk cocoons to clothe them into tax payers was certainly beneficial for the state treasuries, but the religious-social functions of the monasteries could not be neglected totally. Four months after the declaration of the ban on monasteries, the emperor issued another edict moderating his prohibition orders. The edict acknowledged that since monks and nuns had returned to secular life, no one was in charge of the welfare of the dead and sick. Therefore, some land was allotted to existing monasteries for this purpose (CTS 607/18a). Soon after the death of Wu-tsung, the T'ang government started to patronize Buddhism with more enthusiasm. Exquisite silks again flowed into monasteries and the transgressions of Buddhist monks were again tolerated.

The loosening of control on luxury silks, especially when they were used for religious purposes, did not mean that the Chinese rulers were unwilling to maintain their monopoly on special silks and were willing to abandon sumptuary laws. Even after the Sung Dynasty was established in 960, the government made some effort to control the silks made in Sichuan, where the best brocades were produced in that period. An office was set up to collect all the better silks and to forbid their market transactions. This action actually caused a large-scale rebellion in this region. The rebellion was suppressed, but the matter of government monopoly on silks was dropped (Ho Chu-ch'i 1976, 23ff). In short, the various factors that worked against the government's control brought about the collapse of the monopoly and sumptuary laws. Before discussing these factors in detail, let us look at the decay of the system in the Byzantine empire.

The monopoly of the Byzantine empire on its special silk textiles lasted longer than that of T'ang China, partly because the Byzantine state lasted longer than the T'ang Dynasty, and the power of the central government continued for much longer. Chapter IV outlines the strict laws in the *Book of the Eparch* regarding the handling and selling of purple silk textiles and dye (Freshfield 1938, 25–6). Leo VI gave the ordinances to the Eparch of Constantinople around AD 895, when the T'ang Dynasty was close to its demise (AD 907). In the mid-tenth century, Byzantine custom officers did not allow Luitprand, an

envoy of Otto I, to carry some pallia of a forbidden colour or
size, not even for a church, out of Byzantium (Lopez 1945, 41).
In the words of Lopez, even in the twelfth century the emperor
defended every inch of forbidden cloth with the same doggedness
that he displayed in defending every inch of Byzantine soil
(Lopez 40). The fact that the manufacture of purple silk stopped
only after Constantinople finally fell to the Turks also proved
that the Byzantine government never loosened its grip on its
special silk textiles. Purple was never established as a colour of
status in Islamic culture, though it used to be regarded as such
in some of the near eastern territories of the Islamic empire, such
as Assyria and Persia (Reinhold 1970, 15 ff). It is interesting to
note that Christians outside Byzantium never learned the technology of making purple so that Pope Paul II had to decree that
the scarlet dye should replace the unavailable purple colour for
clerical robes and hats (ibid., 70).

In spite of the efforts made by Byzantine emperors to project
purple silk textiles as a prestigious symbol, their monopoly on the
supply of silk textiles to western Europe and the high esteem
commanded by their silk ended long before the fall of Constantinople in the early fifteenth century. Here again, factors outside
their control were working against their will, leading to a breakdown of the barriers of silk trade.

The parallels between the silk cultures of Byzantium and T'ang
China could not be purely coincidental. It is clear that the trend
of establishing a monopoly and a sumptuary code, the decline of
the institution, the similar details in colour and design, were not
totally coincidental. Certain historical conditions in the two countries shaped the development of their silk cultures in the same
direction. The changing international environment not only affected matters inside the two countries but also resulted in their
influencing each other.

It was the same internal need to establish a bureaucratic hierarchy in Byzantium and T'ang China that set the stage for the similar
silk cultures. The difference lays in historical conditions. The silk
industry and the institution of sumptuary laws were historical in
China. The rulers of the Sui and T'ang Dynasties only needed to
perfect the system and to promote the purple colour as the highest
in the clothing hierarchy. In contrast, it took the efforts of a few
generations of emperors to build the Byzantine silk industry, first

by fighting for imported silk materials and then by building up a domestic sericulture. Silk became a tool of diplomacy because both empires had to deal with less developed peoples along their borders, barbaric or nomadic, who harassed their frontiers. While China started to bribe the nomads to keep the peace as early as the second century BC, Byzantium started this practice only after it established its own silk industry. The greater forces that broke down the rulers' control over the production of silk were religious activities inside and outside their territories. In later antiquity, all major religions in Eurasia provided a clear eschatology for their followers. Buddhism and Christianity not only promised bliss or threatened terrible tortures in the world after death, but also functioned as institutions to help people cope with problems in this world and depart to the other world peacefully. The similar hopes and fears of all the people, from the elite to the lowest, helped to occasionally break down barriers between the different social strata.

The similarities in the silk culture of both Byzantium and T'ang China implies mutual influences and exchanges. However, between the Buddhist domain that encircled East Asia and South Asia in the same fold, and the Christian domain including the whole of Europe and parts of Asia, evidence of direct exchanges between the two trade circles and religious domains is too meagre to explain the striking similarities. The Islamic empire rose as another centre of silk culture and served as both a block and a link between the two domains.

The Islamic circle of silk trade brought in a new pattern of transaction between the two major centres of silk culture. Though it inherited a silk industry from both the former Byzantine and Sassanian territories, the Islamic empire did not inherit their clothing codes and sumptuary rules. While the caliphs ruled under the title of 'commander of the faithful', the Kaaba remained the highest religious symbol of the Arabic and Islamic world, and received respect and worship from all parts of the empire. One of the main ways to show piety and political patronage towards the religious symbol was to cover the Kaaba with a fine silk covering, inscribed with the names of Muslim rulers. The covering of the Kaaba was a means to display the balance of power in the Islamic world. Muslim rulers, caliphs or sultans, were not interested in using prestigious silk to distinguish themselves from their subjects, who were also the faithful followers of Allah. Instead, the Islamic empire made the silk industry a part of its state machinery. Trade brought silks and other precious textiles from Central Asia to Spain or vice versa, and ṭirāz inscriptions which were tapestried or embroidered with silk threads on the margins of textiles carried the message of the Islamic religion and the authority of the caliphs to all corners of the Islamic world. During the later period of the caliphate, the Islamic empire was both a large silk market and a big producer of silk textiles. Fancy patterned silks, cheaper half silks and cotton or linen textiles with silk ṭirāz borders were produced in large quantities. Whereas silk textiles from China, Central Asia and the Byzantine empire appeared in the eighth to the ninth century in Damascus and Baghdad, Islamic silks with their sacred and secular messages in Arabic and Persian entered Christian European markets. Though the Islamic silk textiles were not necessarily purple coloured, or brocaded and embroidered with golden threads, as the forbidden Byzantine and T'ang silk textiles were, they certainly provided another choice for countries who had not yet learnt to produce silks. More important, the development of sericulture in a large area from Central Asia to the Mediterranean not only made the materials for silk weaving more available in these regions and even throughout Eurasia, but also changed the people's attitudes towards the exquisite silk textiles under the monopoly of Byzantium and T'ang China. Even without high-level weaving technology, fine embroidery could change a piece of plain silk cloth into a work of art as exquisite as woven patterned silks. An increase in production and easy access to silk materials made silk textiles a common commodity, whether expensive or more reasonably priced. This development certainly served to decrease the demand for controlled silks.

The Islamic empire embraced many different ethnic and religious groups and Islamic silk culture was not dominated only by Muslims. Although the Islamic empire was contiguous to both the Christian world and the Buddhist cultural domain and although Muslims transacted business with heathens, Islam as a religion did not really act as an intermedia between the two. Strong religious beliefs could act as barriers to cultural communications. Religious groups of the time had little understanding of and sympathy for the religious feelings of other groups, even for the different religious communities which lived in the same country and managed to get along to a certain extent. The famous Caliph, Harun al-Rashid (AD 785–809), had several churches in Basrah and Uballah destroyed because he heard that the Christians worshipped the bones of the dead. He had the churches rebuilt after he was convinced that the information was incorrect (Vine 1980). We now have evidence that the Christians did worship the bones of their saints. The Christians probably found it too difficult to explain their religious practices and feelings to a Muslim ruler, no matter how liberal. For them, the best way to gain back their churches was perhaps to convince the ruler that they did not indulge in the practices that seemed so offensive to the Muslims. Therefore, it is not surprising that the knowledge about the Christians and Byzantines that reached China via the Arabic empire was vague. As a captive at Talas, Tu Huan came back to China by sea to Canton. He not only gave a description of the Arab world, but also an account of Byzantium. He was aware that Byzantium (Fu-Lin) was also called the Roman empire (Ta-ch'in). He noticed that the skin colour of the Romans were reddish-white, whereas former accounts of the Romans in Chinese official histories had described them as being similar in appearance to the Chinese. He mentioned that in the Byzantine empire the men wore plain clothes while the women were adorned with jewellery and brocade; they loved wine and bread; they were skilled in various handicrafts and their glass products were acclaimed in the world (Tu Huan, 12–15). Although Tu Huan improved knowledge of Byzantium in China by staying in the Arab world, he brought back little information about their political, social and religious institutions, and no details of the clothing code. Since the Islamic domain cannot be credited with the cultural communications that took place between the two religious domains of Christianity and Buddhism, individual ethnic and religious groups, some of whom lived in the territories of the Islamic states and who were active in the silk trade, may have provided links between the major religious domains and trade circles.

   Our story of silk, from its rise as a status symbol, controlled by the government, to its becoming a common commodity, and the participation of various religious communities in the process, ends here. However, there are surely many gaps to be filled, many exciting anecdotes to be told and many mysterious phenomena to be explored. However, this brief history of silk and religions may serve as an outline or background for scholars who happen to face some exciting archaeological discoveries or literary records which suggest cultural links between distant countries. Readers may get inspiration from this work if they happen to gaze at the purple silks with golden embroidery along with the glassware of Byzantium in the Buddhist cell containing relics in the Fa-men monastery near the site of the T'ang capital; or notice that some silk bindings of gospels in the West and Byzantium since the ninth century used materials similar to the book wrappings of Buddhist texts in the Chinese section of Central Asia; or read that in the ţirāz workshops of Sicily weavers produced silk textiles patterned in roundels, probably in imitation of the designs of roundels on the silks of Sassanid Persia, T'ang China and Byzantium. One may realize that at a time when religious piety was considered the most noble and virtuous emotion, silk was the kind of good carried to distant places not only for commercial profit, but also for meeting the other basic concerns of human society.

References

ACKERMAN, Phyllis, 1981, 'Textiles Through the Sassanian Period', in *A Survey of Persian Art*, ed. Arthur Upan Pope, first ed. 1938, repr. 1981, vol. II, pp. 681–714.

ADLER, Marcus Nathan, trans. & ed., 1907, *The Itinerary of Benjamin of Tudela* (New York: Philipp Feldheim, Inc.).

AGRAWALA, Vasudeva, 1969, *The Deeds of Harsha* (Varanasi: Prithivi Prakashan).

AIYANGAR, K.A., trans., 1928, *Maṇimegalai*, London.

ALEXANDER, Paul, 1977, 'Religious Persecution and Resistance in the Byzantine Empire of the Eighth and Ninth Centuries: Methods and Justifications', *Speculum*, vol. LII, no. 2, pp. 238–64.

APPADURAI, Arjun, ed., 1988, *The Social Life of Things*, Cambridge University Press.

ARBERRY, A.J., 1957, *The Seven Odes: The First Chapter in Arabic Literature*, London.

—— 1964, *Aspects of Islamic Civilization, as Depicted in the Original Texts*, paperback, University Michigan Press, 1967.

ARIES, Philippe, 1985, *Image of Man and Death*, trans. Janet Lloyd, Harvard University Press.

ARNOLD, Thomas, 1928, *Painting in Islam* (Oxford: 1928).

BANA, *Harshacharita*, ed. P.V. Kane, Bombay, 1918; English translation E.B. Cowell & F.W. Thomas (Delhi: Motilal Banarsidass, 1961).

BANERJEA, J.N., 1987, 'Some Early Literary and Archaeological Date About Tantricism', *Essays in Indian Art, Religion and Society*, K.M. Shrimali (ed.) (Delhi: Munshiram Manoharlal Publishers).

BARFIELD, Thomas, 1981, 'The Hsiung-nu Imperial Confederacy: Organization and Foreign Policy', *The Journal of Asian Studies*, vol. XLI, no. 1, pp. 45–62.

BASHAM, A.L., 1984, *A Cultural History of India* (Delhi: Oxford University Press).

BATTISCOMBE, C.F. et al., 1956, *The Relics of St. Cuthbert*, Oxford University Press.

BAYLY, C.A., 1986, 'The Origins of Swadeshi (Home Industry): Cloth and Indian Society, 1700–1930', in *The Social Life of Things*, ed. A. Appadurai, Cambridge University Press, pp. 285–321.

BAYNES, N.H., 1949, 'The Supernatural Defenders of Constantinople', *Analecta Bollandiana*, vol. 67, pp. 165–78.

BECKWITH, Christopher, 1991, 'The Impact of the Horse and Silk Trade on the Economics of T'ang China and the Uighur Empire', *Journal of the Economic and Social History of the Orient*, part II, vol. XXXIV.

BEDE, 1990, *Ecclesiastical History of the English People*, trans. Leo Sherley-Price, ed. & intro. R.E. Latham (London: Penguin Books).

BENTLEY, James, 1985, *Restless Bones: the Story of Relics* (London: Constable).

BHATTACHARYYA, Benoytosh, ed. & intro., 1931, *Guhya Samāja Tantra* or *Tathāgata guhyaka* (Baroda: Oriental Institute).

BIERMAN, Irene A., 1980, *From Politics to Art: the Fatimid Uses of Tiraz Fabrics*, Ph.D. Dissertation for University of Chicago, micro-film.

BIRCH, Cyril, 1965, *Anthology of Chinese Literature* (New York: Grove Press Inc.).

BRITTON, Nancy Pearce, 1983, *A Study of Some Early Islamic Textiles in the Museum of Fine Arts*, Boston.

BROADHURST, R.J.C., trans., 1952, *The Travels of Ibn Jubayr* (London: Jonathan Cape).

BROOMHALL, M., 1966, *Islam in China: A Neglected Problem* (New York: Paragon Book Reprint Shop).

BROWN, Peter, 1981, *The Cult of the Saints. Its Rise and Function in Latin Christianity*, University of Chicago Press.

BULLIET, Richard, 1975, *The Camel and the Wheel* (New York: Columbia University Press).

—— 1979, *Conversion to Islam in the Medieval Period* (Cambridge, MA: Harvard University Press).

BURROW, Thomas, 1940, *A Translation of Kharoshthi Documents from Chinese Turkestan* (London: The Royal Asiatic Society, 1940).

BURY, John B., 1889, *A History of the Later Roman Empire* (London: Macmillan and Company).

The Cambridge History of Iran (Cambridge University Press, 1983).

CHANG, Chuo (T'ang Dynasty), *Ch'ao-ye-ch'ien-tsa* (Anecdotes in and outside the court), ed. Chao Shou-yen (Beijing: Chung-hua Shu-chü, 1979).

CHANG, Hsing-lang, 1977–79, *Chung-hsi Chiao-t'ung Shih-liao Huipien* (Historical sources of communications between the West and China), first ed. 1930 (Beijing: Chung-hua Shu-chü).

CHANG, I-ch'un, ed., 1963, *Tu Huan: Ching-hsing-chi* (Records of travels by Tu Huan) (Beijing: Chung-hua Shu-chü).

CHANG, Kuang-ta, 1987, 'Hai-po Lai T'ien-fang, Ssu-lu T'ung Ta'shih' (Ships come from Arabia, the silk route leads to Arabia), in *Chung Wai Wen-hua Chiao-liu Shih* (Ho-nan: People's Publisher), pp. 743–802.

CHANG, Yen-yüan, *Li-tai Ming-shu-chi* (Famous writings in history), vols 3, 135, v. 500–01 in the series *Ts'ung-shu Chi-ch'eng Chien-pien*, 1965.

CHAO, Ch'ien, *Ta T'ang Ku-ta-te-tseng-ssu-k'ung-ta-pien-cheng-kuang-chih Pu-k'ung-san-tsang Hsing-chuang* (Biography of Pu-k'ung), Tripitaka, vols 50, 292–4.

CHAO, Shou-yen, ed., 1979, *Ch'ao-ye-ch'ien-tsai*, compiled by Chang, Chuo (T'ang Dynasty) (Beijing: Chung-hua Shu-chü).

CH'EN Liang-wen, 1987, 'T'u-lu-fan Wen-shu chung Suo-chien-te Kao-ch'ang T'ang Hsi-chou te Ts'an-sang ssu-chih-ye' (Sericulture and silk weaving in the Kao-ch'ang region under the T'ang rule according to the documents from Turfan), *Tun-huang hsüeh Chi-k'an*, 1987, vol. 1, pp. 118–25.

Chiu T'ang-shu (Old history of the T'ang), compiled by Liu Hsü et al. (Later Chin Dynasty) (Beijing: Chung-hua Shu-chü, 1975).

CHOU, I-liang, ed., 1987, *Chung-wai Wen-hua Chiao-liu-shih* (History of cultural exchanges between China and foreign countries) (Honan: People's Publisher).

Chou-shu (History of the Chou), compiled by Ling-hu Te-fen (583–666) (Beijing: Chung-hua Shu-chü, 1971).

CHOU Ta-fu, 1957, 'Kai-cheng Fa-kuo Han-hsüeh-chia Sha-wan tui Yin-tu ch'u-t'u Han-wen-pei te Wu-shih' (A criticism on the interpretation by the French sinologist Chavannes about the Chinese inscriptions excavated in India), *Li-shih Yen-chiou*, 1957, no. 6.

CHOU, Yi-liang, 1945, 'Tantrism in China', *Harvard Journal of Asiatic Studies*, vol. 8, nos 3–4, pp. 241–332.

Ch'üan T'ang Wen (A collection of all articles written in the T'ang) (Beijing: Chung-hua-shu-chü, 1983).

CORMACK, Robin, 1985, *Writing in Gold, Byzantine Society and its Icons* (New York: Oxford University Press).

Corpus Inscriptionum Indicarum, vol. III, 3rd rev. ed. (Varanasi: Indological Book House, 1970).

CRESWELL, K.A.C., 1946, 'The Lawfulness of Painting in Early Islam', *Ars Islamica*, vols XI, XII, 159.

CRONE, Patricia, 1987, *Meccan Trade and the Rise of Islam*, Princeton University Press.

CUNNINGHAM, Alexander, 1892, *Mahabodhi* (London: H.W. Allen).

DALTON, O.M., 1911, *Byzantine Art and Archaeology* (New York: Dover Publications Inc., repr. 1961).

DANIÉLOU, Alain, 1965, *Shilappadikaram, the Lady of the Anklet* (New York: New Direction Publishing Corporation).

DAY, Florence, 1937, 'Dated Tiraz in the Collection of the University of Michigan', *Ars Islamica*, vol. IV, pp. 420–47.

—— 1950, 'Silk of the Near East', *Metropolitan Museum of Art Bulletin*, pp. 857–66.

DIMAND, Maurice, 1930, 'Special Exhibition of Coptic and Egypto-Arabic Textiles', *Metropolitan Museum of Art, Bulletin*, New York, vol. 25, no. 5, pp. 126–31.

DIYARBEKIRLI, Nejat, 1992, 'Turkish Contributions to Cultural and Commercial Life along the Silk Road', eds Umesao and Sugimura, *Significance of Silk Roads in the History of Human Civilization* (Osaka: 1992).

DODWELL, C.R., 1982, *Anglo-Saxon Art, A New Perspective* (Manchester: Manchester University Press).

DUBY, Georges, 1968, 'The Diffusion of Cultural Patterns in Feudal Society', *Past and Present*, vol. 39, pp. 3–10.

—— 1974, *The Early Growth of the European Economy* (New York: Cornell University Press).

DURT, Hubert, 1987, 'The Meaning of Archaeology in Ancient Buddhism—Notes on the Stupas of Asoka and the Worship of the "Buddhas of the Past" According to Three Stories in the Samguk Yusa', in *Buddhism and Science* (Commemorative volume for the 80th anniversary of the founding of Tongguk University) (Seoul: Tongguk University), pp. 1223–41.

EBERSOLT, Jean, 1923, *Les Arts Somptuaires de Byzance* (Paris: Editions Ernest Leroux).

Encyclopaedia of Islam (Leiden: 1974).

Encyclopaedia of World Art (New York: McGraw-Hill Book Company Inc., 1960).

Exposition des tapisseries et tissus du Musée arabe du Caire (du VIIe au XViie siécle) (Paris: Musée de Gobelina).

Fa-hsien Chuan Chiao-chu (Edited biography of Fa-hsien), ed. Chang Hsun (Shanghai: Ku-chi Ch'u-pan-she, 1985).

Fa-men-ssu K'ao-ku-tui (Archaeological team at Fa-men Monastery), 1988, 'Fu-feng Fa-men-ssu T'ang-tai ti-kung Fa-chüeh Chienpao' (A short report on the excavations of the underground cell of Fa-men Monastery in Fu-feng), *Relics and Museology*, no. 2 of 1988.

FALKE, Otto von, 1922, *Decorative Silks* (New York: William Helburn Inc.).

FAN Ch'eng-ta, *Chi-ye Hsi-yü Hsing-ch'eng* (Travels of Chi-ye to the western land), Tripitaka, vol. 51, pp. 981c–982c.

Fa-yüan Chu-lin (Jewels of the Dharma), compiled by Shih Tao-shih, Tripitaka, vol. 53.

FERRAND, Gabriel, 1914, *Relations de Voyages et Texts Géographiques Arabes, Persans et Turcs Relatifs à L'Extrême-Orient, Du VIIIe au XVIIIe siécles* (Paris: Ernest Leroux, Chinese trans. Keng, Sheng and Mu, Ken-lai, Beijing: Chung-hua Shu-chü, 1989).

FICHTENAU, Heinrich, 1984, English trans. Patrick Geary, *Living in the Tenth Century, Mentalities and Social Orders* (Chicago and London: University of Chicago Press).

FRANK, Andre Gunder, 1992, *The Centrality of Central Asia* (Amsterdam: VU University Press).

FRESHFIELD, E., 1938, *Roman Law in the Later Roman Empire: Book of the Eparch*, Cambridge.

FRYE, Richard, 1972, 'Byzantine and Sassanian Trade Relations with Northeastern Russia', *Dumbarton Oaks Paper*, no. 26, pp. 263–7.

GE, Ch'eng-yung, 1988, 'T'ang-tai Fu-chuang yü Ch'ang-an Ch'i-hsiang (Clothes and fashion of Ch'ang-an city in the T'ang Dynasty), *Wen-po*, vol. 25, no. 4, pp. 49–54.

GEARY, Patrick, J., 1978, *Furta Sacra, Thefts of Relics in the Central Middle Ages*, Princeton University Press.

—— 1988, *Before France and Germany* (New York: Oxford University Press).

GEIJER, Agnes, 1951, *Oriental Textiles in Sweden*, Copenhagen.

—— 1979, *A History of Textile Art* (London: Pasold Research Fund).

—— 1983, 'The Textile Finds from Birka', in *Cloth and Clothing in Medieval Europe*, eds N.B. Harte and K.G. Ponting (London: Heinemann Educational Books Ltd.), pp. 80–99.

GERVERS, Veronika, 1983, 'Medieval Garments in the Mediterranean World, in *Cloth and Clothing in Medieval Europe*, eds N.B. Harte & K.G. Ponting (London: Heinemann Educational Books Ltd.).

GHOSH, A., ed., 1989, *An Encyclopaedia of Indian Archaeology* (Delhi: Munshiram Manoharlal Publishers).

GIBB, Hamilton, 1964, 'The Relation Between Byzantium and the Arabs, Report on the Dumbarton Oaks Symposium of 1963', *Dumbarton Oaks Paper*, no. 18, pp. 363–5.

GIBBON, Edward, 1776, *The Decline and Fall of the Roman Empire*, reprint, The Encyclopaedia Britannica, Inc., 1952. ·

GOITEIN, S.D., 1967, 1971, 1978, *A Mediterranean Society, the Jewish Communities of the Arab World as Portrayed in the Documents of the Cairo Geniza*, I, II, III, University of California Press.

—— 1973, *Letters of Medieval Jewish Traders*, Princeton University Press.

GOLOMBEK, Lisa & Veronika Gervers, 1977, 'Tiraz Fabrics in the Royal Ontario Museum', *Studies in Textile History*, ed. V. Gervers, Toronto.

GOYAL, S.R., 1984, *A Religious History of Ancient India* (Meerut: Kusumanjali Prakash).

GRABAR, Oleg, 1975, 'The Visual Arts', *Cambridge History of Iran*, vol. 4, ed. R.N. Frye.

GRIERSON, P., 1959, 'Commerce in the Dark Ages', *Transactions of the Royal Historical Society*, series 5, pp. 123–40.

GRIMME, Ernst Günther, 1972, *Goldschmiedekunst im Mittelalter; Form und Bedeudung des Reliquiars von 800 bis 1500*, M. Dumont Schaubers.

HAN, Kuo-p'an, 1979, *Sui T'ang Wu-tai Shih-kang* (An outline of the history of the Sui, the T'ang and the Five Dynasties) (Beijing: People Publisher).

Han-shu (History of the Former Han), compiled by Pan Ku (AD 32–92) (Beijing: Chung-hua Shu-chü, 1964).

HARTE, N.B. and K.G. PONTING, eds, 1983, *Cloth and Clothing in Medieval Europe* (London: Heinemann Educational Books Ltd.).

HERMANN-MASCARD, Nicole, 1975, *Les Reliques des Saints, Formation coutumiere d'un droit* (Paris: Éditions Klincksieck).

HO, Chu-ch'i, ed., 1976, *Liang-Sung Nung-min-chan-cheng Shih-liao Hui-pien* (A collection of historical materials on peasant rebellions during the Northern and Southern Sung Dynasties) (Beijing: Chung-hua Shu-chü).

HOLT, P.M. et al., eds, 1970, *The Cambridge History of Islam*, Cambridge University Press.

HOU-HAN Shu (The history of the Later Han), compiled by Fan Yeh (AD 398–445) (Beijing: Chung-hua Shu-chü, 1965).

HOU, Jo-ping, 1989, 'Fa-men-ssu Ti-kung Fa-hsien-te Chih-t'i chih T'a Ming' (Inscription on the chaitya stupa found in the cell of Fa-men Monastery), *Wen-po*, vol. 33, no. 6, pp. 88–9.

Hsi-ho Chi (Record of Hsi-ho region), compiled by Yü, Kuei, later Chin Dynasty (AD 317–420), ed. Chang Shu, *Ts'ung-shu Chi-ch'eng Ch'u-pien*, vol. 3181 (Shanghai: Commercial Press, 1936).

HSIA, Nai, 1963, 'New Finds of Ancient Silk Fabrics in Sinkiang', *Kao-ku Hsüeh-pao*, vol. 31, pp. 45–76.

HSIANG, Ta, 1957, *T'ang-tai Ch'ang-an yü Hsi-yü Wen-ming* (Ch'angan city and the civilization in Central Asia during the T'ang Dynasty), San-lien-shu-tien.

Hsin T'ang-shu (New history of the T'ang), compiled by Ou-yang Hsiu et al. (Beijing: Chung-hua-shu-chü, 1975).

Hsü Kao-seng-chuan (Supplement to the biographies of outstanding monks), compiled by Tao-hsüan, Tripitaka, vol. 50, pp. 425–707.

HSÜAN-TSANG, *Ta-T'ang Hsi-yü-chi Chiao-chu* (Travels of Hsüan-tsang), eds Chi, Hsien-lin et al. (Beijing: Chung-hua-shu-chü, 1985).

HUANG, Neng-fu, 1985, *Yin-ran-chih-hsiu* (Printing, dyeing, weaving and embroidering), *Chung-kuo Mei-shu Ch'üan-chi* (A comprehensive collection of Chinest art works), vol. 6 (Beijing: Wen-wu Ch'u-pan-she).

HUDSON, Geoffrey, 1970, 'Medieval Trade of China', *Islamic and the Trade of Asia*, ed. D.S. Richard, Bruno Cassirer Oxford and University of Pennsylvania Press.

HUI-CH'AO (Korean), *Wang-Wu-T'ien-chu-kuo Chuan* (Travels in the five parts of India), Tripitaka, vol. 51, 975a–979b.

HUI-LI & YEN-TSUNG, *Ta-ts'u-en-ssu San-tsang-fa-shih Chuan* (Biography of Hsüan-tsang), eds Sun Yü-t'ang & Hsieh Fang (Beijing: Chung-hua-shu-chü, 1983).

HUSSEY, J.M., ed., 1966, 'The Byzantine Empire', *The Cambridge Medieval History*, vol. IV, Cambridge University Press.

IBN Khordādhbeh, *Kitāb Al-Masālik Wa'l-Mamālik*, E.J. Brill, 1889, Chinese trans. *Tao-li Bang-kuo Chih* by Sung Xien (Beijing: Chunghua Shu-chü, 1991).

I-CHING, *Nan-hai Chi-kui-ne Fa-chuan* (A Description of the Monastic Discipline from the South Sea Back to China), Tripitaka, vol. 54, pp. 204c–34c.

The Institute of Archaeology, CASS, 1984, *Archaeological Excavation and Researches* (Beijing: Cultural Relics Publishing House).

JAIN, Jagdishchandra, 1984, *Life in Ancient India as Depicted in the Jain Canon and Commentaries* (Delhi: Munshiram Manoharlal).

KANE, P.V., 1918, *The Harshacharita of Bāṇabhaṭṭa, Sanskrit text*, Bombay.

KĀNGLE, R.P., ed. & trans., 1969–73, *The Kauṭiliya Arthaśāstra*, University of Bombay.

Kao-seng-chuan (Biographies of outstanding monks), compiled by Hui-chiao, Tripitaka, vol. 50, pp. 322–423.

Kuang Hung-ming-chi, Tripitaka, vol. 52.

KÜHNEL, Earnst, 1952, *Catalogue of Dated Tiraz Fabrics* (Washington D.C.: Textile Museum).

KÜHNEL, Earnst, 1957, 'Abbasid Silks of the Ninth Century', Ars Orientalis, vol. 2, pp. 367–71.

KUWAYAMA, Seichi, 1990, Kāpishī Gandāra shi Kenkyu (History of Kapisa and Gandhara) (Kyoto: Kyoto University).

KYBALOVA, Ludmila, 1967, Coptic Textiles (London: Paul Hamlyn).

KYRIAKOS, J., 1974, 'Byzantine Burial Customs: Care of the Diseased from Death to the Prothesis', The Greek Theological Review, vol. XIX, no. 1, pp. 37–72.

LAFONTAINE-DOSOGNE, Jacqueline, 1981, Textiles islamiques l'Iran et Asie centrale (Bruxelles: Muse'es royaux d'art et d'histoire).

LAPIDUS, Ira M., 1988, A History of Islamic Societies, Cambridge University Press.

LEGGETT, William, 1944, Ancient and Medieval Dyes (Brooklyn, N.Y.: Chemical Publishing Co. Inc.).

—— 1949, The Story of Silk (New York: Lifetime Editions).

LEI, Hsüeh-hua, 'Lüeh-shu T'ang-ch'ao tui Hsi-yü te Shang-ye Mao-i Kuan-li' (A summary of T'ang administration on the trade with the Western Region) in Tun-huang Hsüeh Chi-k'an, no. 4, pp. 117–21.

LETHABY, W.R., 1913–14, 'Byzantine Silks in London Museums', Burlington Magazine, London, 1913–14, vol. 24, no. 129.

LEVY, Reuben, 1965, The Social Structure of Islam, Cambridge University Press.

LEWIS, Bernad, ed. & trans., 1987, Islam, from the Prophet Muhammad to the Capture of Constantinople, vol. II, Religion & Society (New York: Oxford University Press).

LIEU, Samuel, 1985, Manichaeism, in the Later Roman Empire and Medieval China, a Historical Survey, Manchester University Press.

LIN, Wu-shu, 1987, Mo-ni-chiao chi-ch'i dung-chien (Manichaeism and its spread to China) (Beijing: Chung-hua Shu-chü).

LINDSAY, Jack, 1952, Byzantium into Europe (London: The Bodley Head).

LIU, Man-ch'un, 1982, 'Han T'ang chien Ssu-ch'ou-chih-lu shang-te Ssu-ch'ou Mao-i' (Silk trade along the silk route from the Han to T'ang), in Ssu-lu-fang-ku (Visiting the past on the silk route) (Lanchou: People's Publisher).

LIU, Xinru, 1988, Ancient India and Ancient China, Trade and Religious Exchanges AD 1–600 (New Delhi: Oxford University Press).

LO, Ch'ang-an, 1987, 'A Great Number of Rare Relics Were Unearthed in Famen Temple', Wen-po, vol. 19, no. 4, pp. 3–4.

LOPEZ, R.S., 1943, 'Mohammed and Charlemagne: A Revision', Speculum, vol. XVIII, pp. 14–38.

LOPEZ, R.S., 1945, 'Silk Industry in the Byzantine Empire', *Speculum*, vol. xx, pp. 1–43.

—— 1959, 'The Role of Trade in the Economic Readjustment of Byzantium in the Seventh Century', *Dumbarton Oaks Papers*, no. 13, pp. 67–86.

LUDDEN, David, 1994, 'History Outside Civilization and the Mobility of South Asia', paper to be published in *South Asia*.

MA, Yung, 1986, 'T'u-lu-fan Ch'u-t'u Kao-ch'ang-chün Shih-chi Wen-shu Kai-shu', *Wenwu*, no. 4, pp. 29–33.

McNEILL, William, 1982, *The Pursuit of Power, Technology, Armed Force, and Society Since AD 1000*, University of Chicago Press.

MAECHEN-HELFEN, 1943, 'From China to Palmyra', *Art Bulletin*, no. 25, pp. 358–62.

MAGUIRE, Eunice Dauterman, Henry P. Maguire & Maggie J. Duncan-Flowers, 1989, *Art and Holy Powers in the Early Christian House* (Urbana & Chicago: University of Illinois Press).

Mahāvastu, trans. J.J. Jones (London: Luzac & Company Ltd., 1949).

MAITY, S.K., 1957, *Economic Life of Northern India* (Calcutta: The World Press Private Ltd.).

MAJUMDAR, R.C., ed., 1964, 'The Age of Imperial Kanauj', *History and Culture of the Indian People*, vol. 4 (Bombay: Bharatiya Vidya Bhavan).

MALIK ibn Anas, *Al Muwatta*, trans. Aisha Abdurrahman Bewley (London & New York: Kegan Paul International).

MANGO, Cyril, 1972, *The Art of the Byzantine Empire, 312–1453, Sources and Documents* (Englewood Cliffs, New Jersey: Prentice-Hall Inc.).

MANNING, Patrick, 1993, 'World History, Modern and Ancient: The Literature We Inherit', Northeastern University, unpublished paper.

MARSHAK, B.I. & Valentina I. Raspopova, 1990, 'Wall Paintings from a House with a Granary, Panjikent, 1st Quarter of the Eighth Century AD', *Silk Road Art and Archaeology, Journal of the Institute of Silk Road Studies*, Kamakura, pp. 123–76.

MARZOUK, Mohammad Abdil Aziz, 1943, 'The Evolution of Inscriptions on Fatimid Textiles', *Ars Islamica*, vol. x.

—— 1955, *History of Textile Industry in Alexanderia, 331 BC–1517 AD*, Alexanderia University Press.

MA'SŪDĪ, *The Meadows of Gold, the Abbasids*, trans. into English by Paul Lunde & Caroline Stone (London & New York: Kegan Paul International, 1989); *Les Prairies D'or*, trans. by Barbier de Meynard and Pavet de Courteille, revised by Charles Pellat, Paris, 1962.

MATSUDA, Toshio, 1936, 'Kenma bōeki oboegaki' (Documents on silk and horse trade), *Rekishigaku Kenkyū*, vol. 6.2, 2–13.

—— 1959, 'Kenma boeki ni Kansuru shiryo' (Historical materials on the silk and horse trade), *Yuboku shakai shi tankyu*, vol. I, pp. 1–14.

MEISTER, Michael, 1970, 'The Pearl Roundel in Chinese Textile Design', *Ars Orientalis*, vol. VIII, pp. 255–67.

MEYENDORFF, John, 1968, 'Justinian, the Empire and the Church', *Dumbarton Oaks Papers*, no. 22, pp. 43–60.

MUTHESIUS, Anna Maria, 1982, *Eastern Silks in Western Shrines and Treasuries Before 1200*, Ph.D. thesis for Caurtauld Institute of Art, University of London.

—— 1984, 'A Practical Approach to the History of Byzantine Silk Weaving', *Jahrbuch der Osterreichischen Byzantinistik*, vol. XXXIV, pp. 235–54.

—— 1990, 'The Impact of the Mediterranean Silk Trade on Western Europe Before 1200 AD', in *Textiles in Trade, Proceedings of the Textile Society of America Biennial Symposium*, Washington D.C., 1990.

ODA, Yoshihisa, 1976, 'Torufan Shutsudo no zuiso Ibutsuso ni tsuite' (Notes on the list of clothes and other objects found at Turfan), *Ryukokudaigaku Ronshu*, Kyoto, no. 408, pp. 78–104.

OIKOMONIDES, Nicolas, 1986, 'Silk Trade and Production in Byzantium from the Sixth to the Ninth Century: The Seals of Kommerkiarioi', *Dumbarton Oaks Papers*, vol. XI, pp. 33–53.

OWEN-CROCKER, Galer, 1986, *Dress in Anglo-Saxon England* (Manchester: Manchester University Press).

P'ANG, Chin, 1989, 'T'ang Ch'ing-shan-ssu She-li-t'a Pei-wen Chiao-chu-ch'üan-i' (A complete translation of the edited inscription on the relic stupa in Ch'ing-shan monastery dated to the T'ang Dynasty), *Wen-po*, vol. 23, no. 2, pp. 19, 35–40.

PANOFSKY, Erwin, ed. & trans., 1979, *Abbot Suger, on the Abbey Church of St. Denis and its Art Treasures*, 2nd ed., Princeton University Press.

Periplus Maris Erythraei, trans. & annot. W.H. Schoff (New York: Longmans, Green and Co., 1912).

PFISTER, R., 1934–40, *Textiles de Palmyre*, Paris.

—— 1948, 'Le role de l'Iran dans les textiles d'Antinoe par R. Pfister', *Ars Islamica*, vols 13–14, pp. 46–74.

PLACHER, William, 1983, *A History of Christian Theology* (Philadelphia: The Westminster Press).

PLINY, *Natural History*, trans. H. Rackham (Cambridge, Mass.: Harvard University Press, 1956–62).

POSTAN, M.M. & Edward MILLER, eds, 1987, *The Cambridge Economic History of Europe*, 2nd ed.

PREBISH, Charles S., 1975, *Buddhist Monastic Discipline*, Pennsylvania State University Press.

PRITCHARD, Frances, A., 1984, 'Late Saxon Textiles from the City of London', *Medieval Archaeology*, vol. XXVIII, pp. 46–76.

Procopius, trans. H.B. Dewing (Cambridge, Mass.: Harvard University Press, 1935).

The Qur'an, trans. E.H. Palmer, 1880, Clarendon Press, vols VI & IX of *The Sacred Books of the East*, repr. by Motilal Banarsidass, 1977.

REINHOLD, Meyer, 1969, 'On Status Symbols in the Ancient World', *Classical Journal*, vol. 64, pp. 300–4.

—— 1970, *The History of Purple as a Status Symbol in Antiquity*, Bruxelles: Latomus.

RIBOUD, Krishna, 1976, 'A Newly Excavated Caftan from the Northern Caucasus', *Textile Museum Journal*, Washington D.C., vol. IV, no. 3, 1976, pp. 21–42.

—— 1977, 'Some Remarks on the Face-covers (fumien) Discovered in the Tombs of Astana', *Oriental Art*, vol. XXIII, pp. 38–54.

RICHARD, D.S., ed., 1970, *Islam and the Trade of Asia*, University of Pennsylvania and Oxford University Press.

RICHÉ, Pierrie, 1973, *Daily life in the World of Charlemagne*, English trans. Ann McNamara (Philadelphia: University of Pennsylvania Press, 1978).

ROGERS, Clive, ed., 1983, *Early Islamic Textiles* (Brighton: Rogers & Podmore).

ROSA, Luigi De, 1992, 'Silk and the European Economy', in *Significance of Silk Roads in History*, eds Umesao, Tadao & Toh Sugimura, pp. 193–205.

SABBE, E., 1935, 'L'importation des tissus orientaux en Europe occidentale au haut moyen age', *Revue belge de phil. et d'hist.*, vol. XIV, pp. 811–48, 1261–68.

Saddharmapuṇḍarika, trans. H. Kern, Oxford University Press, 1884.

Saeki, P.Y. & O.B.E.D. Litt, 1951, *The Nestorian Documents and Relics in China* (Tokyo: The Maruzen Company Ltd.).

San-kuo-chih (History of the Three Kingdoms), Ch'en Shou (AD 233–97); commentary by P'ei Sung-chih (AD 372–451) (Beijing: Chung-hua Shu-chü, 1959).

SCHOFF, Wilfred H., 1974, *The Periplus of the Erythraean Sea*, 2nd ed. (New Delhi: Oriental Books Reprint Corporation).

SCHAFER, Edward, 1963, *The Golden Peaches of Samarkand*, California.

SCHOPEN, Gregory, 1989, 'The Stupa Cult and the Extant Pāli Vinaya', *Journal of the Pāli Text Society*, vol. XIII, pp. 83–100.

—— 1990, 'The Buddha as an Owner of Property and Permanent Resident in Medieval Indian Monasteries', *Journal of Indian Philosophy*, vol. 18, pp. 181–217.

—— 1991, 'Monks and the Relic Cult in the Mahāparinibānasutta: An Old Misunderstanding in Regard to Monastic Buddhism', from Benares to Beijing: In Honour of Professor Jan Yün-hua, Oakville, Ontario.

SEMAAN, Khalil I., 1980, *Islam and the Medieval West* (Suny: State University of New York Press).

SERJEANT, Robert Bertram, 1972, *Islamic Textiles* (Berut: Librairie du Liban).

SHAHID, Irfan, 1979, 'Byzantium in South Arabia', *Dumbarton Oaks Papers*, no. 33, pp. 23–94.

SHARMA, R.S., 1987, 'Material Milieu of Tantrism', *Feudal Social Formation in Early India*, ed. D.N. Jha (Delhi: Chanakya Publications), pp. 348–75.

SHEPHERD, D.C. & W.B. Henning, 1959, 'Zandanījī Identified?', *Aus der Welt de Islamischen Kunst*, Festschrift Ernst Kühnel, Berlin, pp. 15–40.

SHEPHERD, D.C., 1978, 'A Treasure from a Thirteenth Century Tomb', *Bulletin*, Cleveland Museum of Art, vol. 65, no. 4, pp. 111–29.

—— 1981, 'Zandanījī Revisited', *Documenta Textilia*, eds M. Fleury-Lemberg & Karen Stollers, Munich.

SHEPHERD, Massey H. Jr., 1967, 'Liturgical Expressions of the Constantinian Triumph', *Dumbarton Oaks Papers*, no. 21, pp. 57–78.

SHERRARD, Philip, 1982, *Athos, the Holy Mountain* (Woodstock, New York: The Overlook Press).

SIMMONS, Pauline, 1956, 'Some Recent Developments in Chinese Textile Studies', *Museum of Far Eastern Antiquities Bulletin*, Stockholm, no. 28, pp. 19–44.

Sinkiang Uighur Autonomous Region, Museum of, 1972, *Ssu-ch'ou chih Lu (Han T'ang chih-wu)* (The silk road, textiles of Han and T'ang times) (Beijing: Editions Wenwu).

—— 1975, *Cultural Relics Unearthed in Sinkiang* (Beijing: Editions Wenwu).

SPULER, Bertold, 1970, 'Trade in the Eastern Islamic Countries in the Early Centuries', *Islam and the Trade of Asia*, ed. D.S. Richard.

STARENSIER, Adele La Barre, 1982, *An Art Historical Study of the Byzantine Silk Industry*, Ph.D. dissertation, Columbia University.

Su, Er, *Tu-yang Tsa-pien* (Anecdots of Tuyang), vol. 16 of *Hsüeh-chin T'ao-yüan*, ed. Ch'in-ch'uan Chang-shih.

Sui-shu (History of the Sui), compiled by Wei, Cheng et al. (Beijing: Chung-hua-shu-chü, 1973).

Sukhāvatīvyūha, trans. Max Muller, in vol. 49 of the *Sacred Books of the East*, Oxford University Press, 1894.

Sung, Hsien, 1987, 'T'ang-tai Yang-chou te Ta-shih Shang-jen' (Arabian traders in Yang-chou during the T'ang times), *Chung-hua Wen-shih Lun-ts'ung* (Essays on Chinese literature and history), vol. 41, no. 1 (Shanghai: Ku-chi Ch'u-pan-she).

Sung, Hsien, trans. & ed. in Chinese, 1991, 'Tao-li-pang-kuo-chih', from the *Kitāb al-Masālik Wa'l-Mamālik* by Ibn Khordādhbeh, E.J. Brill, 1889.

Sung Kao-seng-chuan (Biographies of outstanding monks compiled during the Sung Dynasty), compiled by Tsan-ning, Tripitaka, vol. 50, pp. 900–7.

Ta-pan-nieh-chin huo-fen (Supplement to the sutra of the great nirvana), translated into Chinese by Hui-ning and Ch'iu-na po-to-lo, Tripitaka, vol. 12, pp. 900–6.

T'ang Hui-yao (Important events in the T'ang), compiled by Wang, P'u (Beijing: Chung-hua-shu-chü, 1957).

T'ang Lü shu-i (A commentary and connotation of T'ang law), compiled by Chang-sun Wu-chi et al. (T'ang Dynasty), ed. Liu, Chün-wen (Beijing: Chung-hua Shu-chü, 1983).

T'ang-ta-chao-ling-chi (Major edicts issued in the T'ang), compiled by Sung, Min-ch'iu (Beijing: Commercial Press, 1959).

Thapar, Romila, 1992, 'Black Gold: South Asia and the Roman Maritime Trade', *South Asia*, Australia, New Series, vol. xv, no. 2, pp. 1–27.

Thorpe, Lewis, trans., 1969, *Einhard and Notker the Stammerer, Two Lives of Charlemagne* (London: Penguin Books).

—— trans., 1974, *Gregory of Tours, A History of the Franks* (London: Penguin Books).

Ts'e-fu-Yüan-kuei, compiled by Wang, Ch'in-jo (Beijing: Chung-hua-shu-chü, 1960).

Tu, Huan, *Ching-hsing Chi* (Records of travels), ed. Chang I-ch'un (Beijing: Chung-hua Shu-chü, 1963).

T'u-lu-fan Ch'u-t'u-wen-shu (Documents excavated from Turfan) (Beijing: Wen-wu Ch'u-pan-she, 1981).

Tu, Yü (AD 735–812), *T'ung-tien* (A history of institutions), eds Wang, Wen-chin et al. (Beijing: Chung-hua Shu-chü, 1988).

TUAN, Ch'eng-shih, *Yu-yang Tsa-tsu* (Miscellaneous information), ed. Fang Nan-sheng (Beijing: Chung-hua Shu-chü, 1981).

UDOVITCH, Abraham, 1970, 'Commercial Techniques in Early Medieval Islamic Trade', *Islam and the Trade of Asia*, ed. D.S. Richard.

UMESAO, Tadao & Toh Sugimura, eds, 1992, 'Significance of Silk Roads in the History of Human Civilization', *Senri Ethnological Studies*, no. 32 (Osaka: National Museum of Ethnology).

VASILIEV, A.A., 1955–56, 'The Iconoclastic Edict of the Caliph Yazid II, AD 721', *Dumbarton Oaks Paper*, no. 10, pp. 23–47.

VINE, Aubrey R., 1980, *The Nestorian Churches* (London: Independent Press Ltd.).

VOLBACH, W. Fritz, 1969, *Early Decorative Textiles* (Middlesex: Hamlyn Publishing Group Limited).

WALKER, Williston, Richard A. Norris, David W. Lotz, Robert T. Haudy, 1983, *A History of the Christian Church* (New York: Charles Scribner Sons).

WANG Chung-lo, 1979, *Wei-chin Nan-pei-ch'ao Shih* (History of the Wei, Chin and Northern and Southern Dynasties) (Shanghai: People's Publisher).

WANG Pang-wei, ed., *Ta-T'ang Hsi-yü-ch'iu-fa-kao-seng-chuan* (Outstanding monks who went to the west land to learn Dharma during the great T'ang), compiled by I-ching (Beijing: Chung-hua-shu-chü, 1988).

WANG Ren-po, 1988, 'Cultural Flourish and the Open Policy of the T'ang Dynasty', *Wen-po*, vol. 25, no. 4, pp. 38, 43–8.

—— 1993, 'An Explanatory Note in the Itinerary of Ji Yie's Travel to the "Western Regions"', *South Asian Studies*, Beijing, no. 2, pp. 36–40.

WANG Ts'ang-hsi, 1989, 'Fa-men-ssu Kung-wu-chang Shih-i' (Interpretation of the problems in the inscription of the inventory of donations in the Fa-men Monastery), *Wen-po*, vol. 33, no. 4, pp. 30–3.

WARMINGTON, E.H., 1974, *The Commerce Between the Roman Empire and India*, 2nd ed. (London: Curzon Press Ltd.).

WEBB, J.F. & D.H. Farmer, trans., eds, intro., 1988, *The Age of Bede* (London: Penguin Books).

WEINSTEN, Stanley, 1987, *Buddhism under the T'ang*, Cambridge University Press.

WHEELER, Mortimer, 1954, *Rome Beyond the Imperial Frontiers* (London: G. Bell and Sons Ltd., repr. by Greenwood, Westport, Connecticut, 1971).

WILSON, Stephen, ed., 1983, *Saints and their Cults*, Cambridge University Press.

WINTERNITZE, M., 1933, *A History of Indian Literature*, trans. from German by S. Kerkar & H. Kohn (New York: Russell & Russell).

WRIGHT, F.A., 1930, *The Works of Liudprand of Cremona* (London: George Routledge & Sons Ltd.).

YANG Hsüan-chih, *Loyang Ch'ieh-lan Chi* (Memories of holy places in Loyang) (Shanghai: Ku-chi Ch'u-pan She, 1978).

YUAN-CHAO, *Wu-k'ung Ju-chu-chi* (Travels of Wu-k'ung in India), Tripitaka, vol. 51, pp. 979b–982c.

ZURCHER, E., 1972, *The Buddhist Conquest of China* (Leiden: E.J. Brill).

Chronological Table

AD	China	South Asia	Western and Central Asia	Byzantium and Europe
481–511				Clovis united the Franks
499–640	The Kao-ch'ang state in Turfan ruled by the Ch'ü family			
c. 500–751				Merovingian rule of the Franks
518–527				Justin, Emperor of Byzantium
527–565				Justinian I, Emperor of Byzantium
c. 539–594				Gregory of Tours

AD	China	South Asia	Western and Central Asia	Byzantium and Europe
565–575				Justin II, Emperor of Byzantium
568				Lombards invaded Italy
c. 570–632			Muhammad the Prophet	
581–618	The Sui Dynasty			
582	The Sui emperor, Wen-ti, distributed the relics of the Buddha all over China			
590–604				Pope Gregory the Great
600–630		Mahendra Varman I, who established Pallava power		
606–647		Harsa Vardhana, the king of Kanauj		
608–642		Palakeshin II, who established Chalukya power		
618–907	The T'ang Dynasty			
621	The T'ang government set up the office of Sa-pao			

AD	China	South Asia	Western and Central Asia	Byzantium and Europe
622			Hijra	
627–649	Rule of Emperor T'ai-tsung			
630–644		Hsüan-tsang visited India		
632–661			Rashidun Caliphs	
634–687				St. Cuthbert
635			Arab conquest of Syria and Mesopotamia	
641			Arab conquest of Egypt	
642–651			Arab conquest of Sassanid Persia	
643–711			Arab conquest of North Africa	
643	Wang Hsüan-ts'e visited India as an envoy of the T'ang			
647				
657–661				
656–661			First civil war of the Muslims	
660				Arabs failed to capture Constantinople

AD	China	South Asia	Western and Central Asia	Byzantium and Europe
661–750			Umayyad Caliphate	
668				Arabs failed to capture Constantinople
673–695		I-ching visited India		
673–735				Bede
c. 680–755				St. Boniface
684–705	Rule of Empress Wu Tse-t'ien			
711–759				Arab conquest of Spain
712		Arab conquest of Sind		
712–713			Arabs captured Bukhara and Samarkand	
712–756	Rule of Emperor Hsüan-tsung			
717–718				Arabs failed to capture Constantinople
714–741				Charles Martel ruled Franks

AD	China	South Asia	Western and Central Asia	Byzantium and Europe
721			Yazid II started the Aniconic movement	
726				Leo III started iconoclasm in Byzantium
749–974			Abbasid Caliphate to the disintegration of the empire	
751	T'ang army was defeated at Talas by the Arabs. Tu Huan was captured as a war prisoner			
751–762			Tu Huan stayed in Islamic countries	
751–987				Carolingian Frankish dynasty
754–775			Caliph Mansur	
755–763	Rebellions of An-Lu-shan and Shih-Ssu-ming			
762			Baghdad became the capital of the Islamic empire	

AD	China	South Asia	Western and Central Asia	Byzantium and Europe
768	Uighurs started a Manichaean monastery in T'ang China			
768–814				Charlemagne, king of the Franks
785–809			Caliph Harun-al-Rashid	
800				Charlemagne revived Roman empire
c. 820–912			Ibn Khordādhbeh	
827				Arab conquest of Sicily
841–846	Rule of Emperor Wu-tsung			
843				Treaty of Verdun divided Carolingian empire
845	Emperor Wu-tsung persecuted Buddhism and other foreign religions			
871–899				Alfred established Anglo-Saxon kingdom in England

AD	China	South Asia	Western and Central Asia	Byzantium and Europe
874–888	Rule of Emperor Hsi-tsung			
c. 896–957			Mas'ūdī	
c. 907		Parantaka I established Chola power in South India		
916–1125	Liao Dynasty in North China			
936–973				Otto I, king of Germany
945–c.1220			Post-Caliphate states	
960–1279	The Sung Dynasty			
964		Chinese monk, Chi-ye, went to India		
973–1050			Al-Biruni	
997–1030		Raids of Mahmud of Ghazni in Northwest India		
1016				Normans arrived in Italy

AD	China	South Asia	Western and Central Asia	Byzantium and Europe
1066				Norman conquest of England
1030		Al-Biruni in India		
1077–1133				Norman rule of Sicily
1099				First Crusade
1115–1234	Chin Dynasty in North China			
1147				Second Crusade
1189				Third Crusade
1202–1204				Fourth Crusade, sack of Constantinople
c. 1220–1260			Mongol invasions	
1234	Mongols conquered China			
1288, 1293		Marco Polo's visits to India		

Index

Constantinople 77, 78, 81, 116,
175, 181, 192
as capital 80
city of Virgin 87
conversion
to Christianity in Europe 101,
102
to Islam 172, 173
Copt(ic), silks 177
tradition 167
weavers 144, 145, 161
cosmology, Buddhist 38
cotton(s) 54, 149, 160
Indian 22, 51, 53
robes for Buddhist monks 51
cremation custom 24
cultural exchanges 2
cultural influence 83, 92

Damascus 152
ṭirāz factories in 146
damask 67, 179, 187
Dar al-Ṭirāz 142
death and afterlife, concept 99,
100–2
Delta region, Caliph's control of
textile production in 145
Deusdona 110
dharma literature, on ceremonial
clothing 53
'Dharma relics' 43
Dhu-Nuwas, king 75
dībāj, silks 150, 186
in Egypt 161
donations
of silks to Buddhist institutions
67, 68
to Christian saints and churches
114, 119
to religious institutions and
priests 188
'dragon horse' status 10

dragon motifs on silks in China
81, 189
dress code, see clothes
dukūla silk 5

Eadbald, King 96
eagle, silks patterned with 167
Easter 117, 119
ecclesiastic purpose, silks for 121
ecclesiastical
independence, of Venice 128
institutions 93, 94, 95, 104
economic and cultural interaction 1
Edwin, King of Northumbria 100
Edwin, King 120
Egbert, English King 104
Egypt 22, 77
burial practice under Islamic
rule in 114
coverings for Kaaba from 150,
151
import of textiles during
Fatimid 146
Islamic state in 2, 145
limitations on silk in 156
linen and silk brocades in 161
silk production in 167
as silk trading centre 164
ṭirāz textiles in 143–4
Egyptian silks 77
elephant designs, on silks 188
elephant silk, and St. Josse 177
embroidery, on silks 120–2, 141
Ethiopian war 75
Eurasia
cultural pattern in 1
silk trade 75, 179
Europe
Christianization of 92
Islamic silks in 175, 177
silk markets in 124–9

linen cloth 149, 160, 162
lion-patterned silk 178
liturgy 107

magic invocation, in Buddhism 30
Mahabodhi monastery, Bodh
  Gaya 34, 35, 69, 72
Mahacīna, silk producing centre
  55
mahādhana silk 52
Mahakasyapa 72
mahanirvāṇa 46
Mahayana Buddhism 12, 25, 28
  Madhyamika school of 29
  and taxation 28–9
  Yogacarin school of 29
Mahayana texts 37
Maitreya 43, 72, 89
Mandasor silk weaving guild 20
Manichaen monasteries/temples
  183
Manichaean travellers, as silk
  carriers 24
Manichaeism 26, 40, 182, 183
Manning, Patrick 5
Marco Polo 52
Martel, Charles 95
martyria 97
Mary Magdalene, relics of 111
mass, for dead in Christianity
  101–2
Mas'udī 52
matriarchal practice 29
mawālīs, of Greek and Persian
  origin 133, 134
McNeill, William 3
Mecca 149
  pilgrimage to 151, 173
  trade in 130*n*
Median 152
Mediterranean region 7
  commercial community in 129

silk markets in 125, 126, 127,
  185, 186
silk weaving in 146
Meister, Michael 125
merchants, status of, in Islamic
  society 158
Merovingian period, Christianity
  during 93, 94
Merv, Central Asia, textiles from
  164
Mesopotamia, Islam in 1
Michael VIII, Emperor 91
monasteries
  as centres of religion and
    culture 96
  for pilgrims 35
  relics bringing wealth to 109
Mongols, conquering China 182
monochrome silks 168
mosaic(s) 116–17
  of Justinian and Theodora 116
  at St. Sophia 116, 117
mulberry
  silk worms/cocoons 15, 50
  trees 159
mulham 137, 140, 160, 162
Muslim(s) 78*n*
  rulers, displaying textiles on
    ceremonial occasion 154
  traders 77
Muthesius, Anna Maria 8, 126

Nagarahara 69
  bones of Buddha in 33
Nagarjuna 28, 29
Nalanda University 28
Nestorian churches, and China
  181–2
Nestorianism 181
Nestorian travellers, and silk 24
Netra silk 52
Nicaea, Council of 86

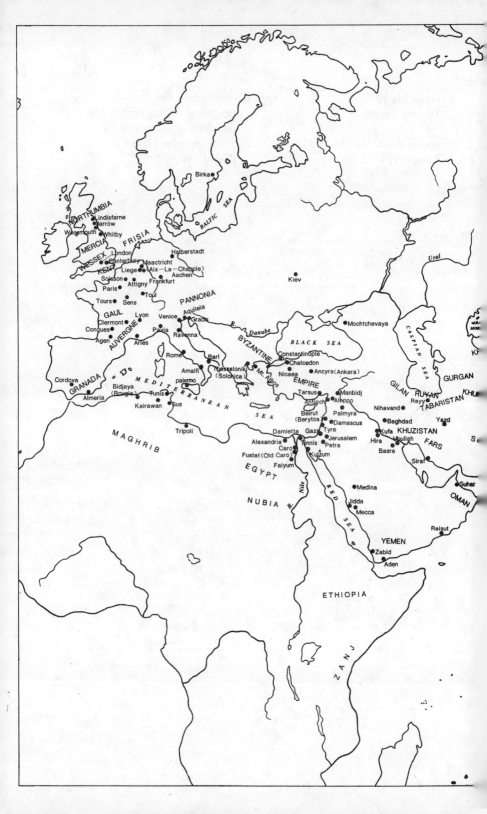